Lotus® 1-2-3™ SmartStart

Linda Ericksen
Umpqua Community College

Rick Winter

Lotus® 1-2-3™ SmartStart.

Copyright © 1993 by Que® Corporation.

All rights reserved. Printed in the United States of America. No part of this book may be used or reproduced in any form or by any means, or stored in a database or retrieval system, without prior written permission of the publisher except in the case of brief quotations embodied in critical articles and reviews. Making copies of any part of this book for any purpose other than your own personal use is a violation of United States copyright laws. For information, address Que Corporation, 201 W. 103rd St., Indianapolis, IN 46290.

Library of Congress Catalog No.: 93-83861

ISBN: 1-56529-245-6

This book is sold *as is*, without warranty of any kind, either express or implied, respecting the contents of this book, including but not limited to implied warranties for the book's quality, performance, merchantability, or fitness for any particular purpose. Neither Que Corporation nor its dealers or distributors shall be liable to the purchaser or any other person or entity with respect to any liability, loss, or damage caused or alleged to be caused directly or indirectly by this book.

96 95 94   4

Interpretation of the printing code: the rightmost double-digit number is the year of the book's printing; the rightmost single-digit number, the number of the book's printing. For example, a printing code of 94-3 shows that the third printing of the book occurred in 1994.

Screens reproduced in this book were created using Collage Plus from Inner Media, Inc., Hollis, NH.

Lotus 1-2-3 SmartStart is based on Lotus 1-2-3 Releases 2.4 and earlier.

Publisher: David P. Ewing

Associate Publisher: Rick Ranucci

Product Development Manager: Thomas A. Bennett

Operations Manager: Sheila Cunningham

Book Designer: Scott Cook

Production Team: Claudia Bell, Paula Carroll, Laurie Casey, Brad Chinn, Brook Farling, Carla Hall, Caroline Roop, Linda Seifert, Tina Trettin, Donna Winter, Michelle Worthington

About the Authors

Linda Ericksen is associate professor of computer information systems at Umpqua Community College in Roseburg, Oregon. She teaches computer courses ranging from using and programming Lotus 1-2-3 to data communications and networking, technical writing, advanced DBMS programming, AutoCAD, systems analysis, desktop publishing, and basic programming. She does specialized trainings for businesses and government agencies. She has a Master of Science degree in computer science/education and a Master of Arts degree in English literature.

Rick Winter is a senior partner at PRW Computer Services. He has trained more than 1,500 adults on personal computers. Rick is a revision script writer for Video Professor Lotus 1-2-3 Releases 2.2 and 3.0, Levels I and II, and a script writer for Video Professor Lotus 1-2-3 Releases 2.2 and 3.0, Level III.

Title Manager
Carol Crowell

Senior Editor
Jeannine Freudenberger

Production Editor
Jo Anna Wittman Arnott

Editorial Assistant
Elizabeth D. Brown

Formatter
Jill Stanley

Trademarks

All terms mentioned in this book that are known to be trademarks or service marks have been appropriately capitalized. Que cannot attest to the accuracy of this information. Use of a term in this book should not be regarded as affecting the validity of any trademark or service mark.

1-2-3 and Lotus are registered trademarks of Lotus Development Corporation. HP and LaserJet are registered trademarks of Hewlett-Packard Company. IBM is a registered trademark of International Business Machines Corporation. Rolodex is a registered trademark of Rolodex Corporation.

Composed in Garamond and MCPdigital by Que Corporation

Give Your Computer Students a SmartStart on the Latest Computer Applications

Que's SmartStart series from Prentice Hall Computer Publishing combines the experience of the Number 1 computer book publisher in the industry with the pedagogy you've come to expect in a textbook.

SmartStarts cover just the basics in a format filled with plenty of step-by-step instructions and screen shots.

Each SmartStart chapter ends with a "Testing Your Knowledge" section that includes true/false, multiple choice, and fill-in-the-blank questions; two or three short projects, and two long projects. The long projects are continued through the book to help students build on skills learned in preceding chapters.

Each SmartStart comes with an instructor's manual featuring additional test questions, troubleshooting tips, and additional exercises. This manual will be available both on disk and bound.

Look for the following additional SmartStarts:

Word for Windows SmartStart	1-56529-204-9
Windows 3.1 SmartStart	1-56529-203-0
Excel 4 for Windows SmartStart	1-56529-202-2
MS-DOS SmartStart	1-56529-249-9
WordPerfect 5.1 SmartStart	1-56529-246-4
dBASE IV SmartStart	1-56529-251-0

For more information call:
1-800-428-5331
or contact your local Prentice Hall College Representative

Contents at a Glance

Introduction 1

1 An Overview of 1-2-3 7

2 Getting Started 21

3 Introducing Worksheet Basics 49

4 Modifying the Spreadsheet or a Range 77

5 Modifying a Worksheet 107

6 Using Functions 125

7 Printing Reports 151

8 Printing with Wysiwyg 175

9 Creating and Printing Graphs 201

10 Managing Data 229

11 Understanding Macros 249

A Enhancing and Printing Graphs
   in Wysiwyg in Releases 2.3 and 2.4 271

Index 279

Table of Contents

Introduction 1
    What Is New in 1-2-3 Release 2.4? 1
    Understanding the Differences between Releases 3

1   An Overview of 1-2-3 7
    Objectives 7
    Objective 1: To Become Familiar with Manual
        and Electronic Spreadsheets 9
    Objective 2: To Learn 1-2-3's Spreadsheet Capabilities 11
    Objective 3: To Understand 1-2-3's Graphics Features 14
    Objective 4: To Become Familiar with 1-2-3's
        Database Management 15
    Objective 5: To Overview 1-2-3's Other Features 15
    Summary 16
    Testing Your Knowledge 17

2   Getting Started 21
    Objectives 21
    Objective 1: To Start Lotus 1-2-3 23
    Objective 2: To Exit Lotus 1-2-3 25
    Objective 3: To Use the Keyboard 26
    Objective 4: To Use a Mouse in 1-2-3 33
    Objective 5: To Understand the 1-2-3 Screen 36
    Objective 6: To Learn the Icons in Release 2.4 39
    Objective 7: To Understand 1-2-3's Menu System 41
    Objective 8: To Use the 1-2-3 Help System
        and On-Line Tutorial 45
    Summary 46
    Testing Your Knowledge 46

3   Introducing Worksheet Basics 49
    Objectives 49
    Objective 1: To Enter and Edit Data 50

Objective 2: To Enter Formulas and Functions 57
Objective 3: To Use the Undo Feature
  in Releases 2.2, 2.3, and 2.4 65
Objective 4: To Name, Save, Print, and Retrieve Files 67
Summary 73
Testing Your Knowledge 74

4   Modifying the Spreadsheet or a Range 77

Objectives 77
Objective 1: To Understand the Range Concept in 1-2-3 79
Objective 2: To Understand the Worksheet Commands 84
Objective 3: To Format the Worksheet 85
Objective 4: To Insert and Delete Columns and Rows 99
Objective 5: To Recalculate the Worksheet 101
Summary 103
Testing Your Knowledge 104

5   Modifying a Worksheet 107

Objectives 107
Objective 1: To Move Data or Formulas in the Spreadsheet 108
Objective 2: To Copy Cells in the Spreadsheet 111
Summary 122
Testing Your Knowledge 122

6   Using Functions 125

Objectives 125
Entering a 1-2-3 Function 126
Objective 1: To Learn To Use Statistical Functions 126
Objective 2: To Learn To Use Financial Functions 133
Objective 3: To Learn To Use Date and Time Functions 137
Objective 4: To Learn To Use Logical Functions 140
Objective 5: To Learn To Use Special Functions 143
Summary 147
Testing Your Knowledge 148

7   Printing Reports 151

Objectives: 151
Objective 1: To Print Simple Spreadsheets 152

Objective 2: To Print Multiple Page Reports 157
Objective 3: To Print Excluding Segments of the Spreadsheet 160
Objective 4: To Learn about Other Print Options 162
Summary 172
Testing Your Knowledge 172

8 Printing with Wysiwyg 175

Objectives 175
Objective 1: To Become Familiar with Wysiwyg 176
Objective 2: To Change Fonts 181
Objective 3: To Enhance Cells with Shading,
 Lines, Bold, and Grid Lines 185
Objective 4: To Manage Formats 193
Objective 5: To Print in Wysiwyg 195
Summary 198
Testing Your Knowledge 198

9 Creating and Printing Graphs 201

Objectives 201
Objective 1: To Create a Simple Graph 203
Objective 2: To Become Familiar with Graph Types 207
Objective 3: To Specify Data Ranges 211
Objective 4: To Enhance the Appearance of a Graph 213
Objective 5: To Save a Graph 218
Objective 6: To Print a Graph 220
Summary 225
Testing Your Knowledge 226

10 Managing Data 229

Objectives 229
Objective 1: To Become Familiar with Databases 230
Objective 2: To Become Familiar with the /Data Menu 231
Objective 3: To Plan and Build a Database 233
Objective 4: To Sort Database Records 235
Objective 5: To Search for Records 239
Summary 245
Testing Your Knowledge 245

11 Understanding Macros 249
Objectives 249
Objective 1: To Become Familiar with Macros 250
Objective 2: To Become Familiar with the Learn Feature 260
Objective 3: To Execute Macros 261
Objective 4: To Debug and Edit Macros 262
Objective 5: To Add Macros to SmartIcons 264
Objective 6: To Use the Macro Library Manager Add-In 268
Summary 268
Testing Your Knowledge 268

A Enhancing and Printing Graphs in Wysiwyg in Releases 2.3 and 2.4 271
Adding Graphs to the Worksheet 271
Making Changes to the Added Graph 273
Using the Graphics Editor 275

Index 279

Introduction

There are no prerequisites for using this book or for using 1-2-3. The assumption is, of course, that you have the software, the hardware, and a desire to learn to use the program.

The following hardware is required to run 1-2-3 Release 2.4:

- An IBM PC or compatible computer
- A hard disk with at least 8M available disk space
- DOS Version 2.1 or later
- At least 384K of RAM. To run the Wysiwyg add-in, 512K is required. To run additional add-ins, 640K is required.
- A monitor that supports VGA, EGA, CGA, or the Hercules Graphics Adapter
- A printer (optional)

What Is New in 1-2-3 Release 2.4?

This version of 1-2-3 has been enhanced with such additional features as the following:

- *SmartIcons*, which are graphical representations of commands. You can quickly choose a SmartIcon to sum a range, move around the worksheet, format and highlight ranges, delete and insert rows and columns, and perform many other commands. SmartIcons speed up many common procedures. You can also customize your own SmartIcon palette and attach macros to a palette.

- *The capability to print in Landscape mode* with both laser and dot-matrix printers

With the exception of other changes, Release 2.4 also incorporates the following features that were added to the previous version, Release 2.3:

- *Wysiwyg*, a what-you-see-is-what-you-get spreadsheet publishing add-in, which lets you use different fonts, underlining, outlining, and shading on selected ranges. You can combine text and graphics on printed output. After you are in Wysiwyg, you can make changes to a worksheet or graph and see how the final printed output will look.
- *Mouse support*, with and without Wysiwyg. You can quickly select commands and highlight ranges with a mouse.
- *Dialog boxes*, which enable you to keep track of available choices. Dialog boxes show current settings for options and enable you to change the options by using the keyboard or the mouse. You can also change options by using the regular command menu displayed above the box. 1-2-3 automatically displays dialog boxes when you use print, graph, database, and some worksheet commands.
- *Three new add-ins* in addition to Wysiwyg. The *Auditor* helps you find errors in your worksheet formulas. The *Tutor* teaches you how to use 1-2-3. The *Viewer* enables you to look at files before you retrieve them to help locate the right file to retrieve.
- *Two tutorials, 1-2-3-Go!* and *Wysiwyg-Go!*, which teach you how to use 1-2-3 and Wysiwyg
- *Background printing*, which lets you continue working on a worksheet while it is printing
- *Encoded printing*, which enables you to print your output to a disk. The file on disk will have specific instructions for the printer, including all enhancements. You do not need to be in 1-2-3 to print the encoded file.
- *Two new graph types—mixed* (a combination of bar and line) and *HLCO* (high-low-close-open, for stock and other analyses)
- *Additional graph features* that enable you to change the orientation of the graph, show stacked lines, change the border around the graph, create 3-D effects, and turn a line graph into an area graph

Introduction

Release 2.4 also incorporates the following features that were added to Release 2.2:

- *An Undo feature*, which enables you to reverse the last command or action taken. Not only can you undo a mistake, but you can also try unfamiliar commands freely, knowing that you can undo many unsatisfactory results.
- *File linking*, which lets you use formulas to link the cell(s) of one worksheet to the cells in other worksheets. When a linked worksheet is retrieved, it is automatically updated.
- *Minimal recalculation*, which requires no special action on your part; only relevant formulas are recalculated when you make changes to the worksheet. This feature results in faster, more responsive worksheets.
- *Search and replace*, which enables you to search for the occurrence of a string in a selected range and gives you the option of replacing some or all instances with a different string
- *Group options* in **/W**orksheet and **/G**raph commands that simplify multiple column-width changes and graph-range definitions
- *Enhanced graph images* that make line, bar, and stacked-bar graphs easier to read. Grid lines appear behind bars.
- *Macro names* can be descriptive names up to 15 characters long, which increases readability and tracking.

Understanding the Differences between Releases

Release 2.01 has been available since 1986. You make choices only through the menu and function keys. You cannot show a graph and worksheet on the same screen. Release 2.2's screen looks identical to the Release 2.01 screen, with the exception of the added Undo feature.

With Release 2.2, Lotus added settings sheets that enable you to see, but not edit, choices relating to the same menu item. You continue to make the same menu choices as were available Release 2.01, but the settings sheets show the choices selected.

Choosing **/P**rint **P**rinter brings up the Print Settings sheet in Release 2.2.

Lotus 1-2-3 SmartStart

Another addition to Release 2.2 was the desktop publishing add-in Allways. Allways enables you to add and enhance graphics to your spreadsheet as well as enhance data with boldface, italics, lines, and shading. However, you cannot work in both the worksheet and Allways at one time. A separate Allways menu appears when you choose the forward slash (/). The normal way to select a range in Release 2.01 is to select the commands and then identify a range. Release 2.2 Allways enables you to select the range first and then apply one or more highlighting commands to that range.

Release 2.3 replaced Allways with the publishing add-in Wysiwyg, short for "what you see is what you get." In contrast to the back-and-forth nature of procedures necessary to work with the spreadsheet and the Allways publishing add-in, Wysiwyg enables you to work in a spreadsheet and publisher at the same time. After you load Wysiwyg, you access Wysiwyg's publishing menu with a colon (:) and still access the normal 1-2-3 menu with the forward slash (/). You can preselect a range with Wysiwyg as you can with Allways in Release 2.2.

Release 2.3 also added mouse support that is available whether or not Wysiwyg is attached. If you have a mouse driver loaded, you will see mouse icons on the right portion of the screen.

Release 2.3 contained another major addition: the settings sheets in Release 2.2 were changed to dialog boxes. Like the settings sheets, the dialog boxes display a summary of settings that relate to a command. Unlike the settings sheets, however, the dialog boxes also enable you to change settings within the dialog box by using the mouse or the F2 key. As with previous versions, Release 2.3 also lets you make changes by choosing options from the 1-2-3 menus.

Release 2.4 does maintain the changes made to 2.3—including Wysiwyg and dialog boxes—but Release 2.4 adds a new dimension. SmartIcons now appear on the right side of the screen (provided that you choose to load the icons). You can select a SmartIcon to perform an action instantly instead of wading through a battery of menus and dialog boxes. The icons perform both worksheet and Wysiwyg commands.

Although the screens may appear slightly different in different versions, the majority of forward slash (/) commands and functions remain the same in Releases 2.01, 2.2, 2.3, and 2.4. You can use this book if you have any of those versions.

Introduction

Conventions Used in This Book

A number of conventions are used in *Lotus 1-2-3 SmartStart* to help you learn the program. This section provides examples of these conventions to help you distinguish among the different elements in 1-2-3.

References to keys are as they appear on the keyboard of the IBM Personal Computer and most compatibles. The function keys, F1 through F10, are used for special situations in 1-2-3. In the text, the function key name and the corresponding function key number are usually listed together, such as Graph (F10).

Direct quotations of words that appear on the screen are spelled as they appear on-screen and are printed in a `special typeface`. Information you are to type is printed in **boldfaced blue type** in numbered steps and in **boldfaced type** elsewhere. The slash and the first letter in each command from the 1-2-3 menu system also appear in boldfaced blue or boldfaced type: **/R**ange **F**ormat **C**urrency and **/R**ange **F**ormat **C**urrency. Also, the colon and the first command letter of Wysiwyg commands appear in boldface: **:T**ext **E**dit and boldfaced blue in numbered steps: **:T**ext **E**dit.

Elements printed in uppercase include range names (SALES), functions (@PMT), modes (READY), and cell references (A1..G5). You do not need to type range names, functions, and cell references in uppercase letters; 1-2-3 accepts them in either upper- or lowercase letters.

If you use a mouse, this book assumes that it is a standard two- or three-button mouse and that it is configured normally for right-handed people. The left mouse button acts as the Enter key. The right mouse button, in most cases, is the equivalent of pressing the Esc key.

Several SmartIcon palettes are loaded with Wysiwyg in Release 2.4. Without Wysiwyg, there are up to 10 palettes. You can customize the first palette to include different icons. In most cases, figures include the first palette with the original icons, unless the focus is on the icons themselves. Tables show how the icons look with and without Wysiwyg.

Macros enable you to automate frequently performed tasks by storing a series of keystrokes and commands to a single range name. The following special conventions pertain to macros:

> Single-character macro names (Alt-character combinations) appear with the backslash (\ ) and single-character name in lowercase: \a. In this example, the \ indicates that you press the Alt key and hold it down while you also press the A key.

Lotus 1-2-3 SmartStart

- 1-2-3 menu keystrokes in a macro line appear in lowercase: /rnc.
- Range names within macros appear in uppercase: /rncTEST.
- In macros, representations of direction keys such as {DOWN}, function keys such as {CALC}, and editing keys such as {DEL} appear in uppercase letters and are enclosed by braces.
- The Enter key is represented by the tilde (~).

When two keys appear together, for example Ctrl+Break, you press and hold down the first key as you press the second key. When two keys appear together without the plus sign, such as End, Home, the first key is pressed and released before the second key is pressed. In numbered steps, the keys are in blue key cap characters: Ctrl + Break.

Note: Most screens in this book were captured in Release 2.4 with the Wysiwyg add-in active. Most screens also display a worksheet grid (added with the Wysiwyg command :Display Options Grid Yes).

An Overview of 1-2-3

Before starting Lotus 1-2-3, you need to know the range of capabilities of this software package. This chapter provides an overview of Lotus 1-2-3. Later chapters discuss the details of each of these features.

Objectives

1. To Become Familiar with Manual and Electronic Spreadsheets
2. To Learn 1-2-3's Spreadsheet Capabilities
3. To Understand 1-2-3's Graphics Features
4. To Become Familiar with 1-2-3's Database Management
5. To Overview 1-2-3's Other Features

1

Key Terms in This Chapter

Electronic spreadsheet	The electronic replacement for the accountant's pad.
Worksheet	The 1-2-3 spreadsheet.
Wysiwyg	An acronym for "what-you-see-is-what-you-get"—the name of the spreadsheet publishing add-in provided with Releases 2.3 and 2.4.
Direction keys	The keys that allow movement within the 1-2-3 worksheet—including PgUp, PgDn, Home, End, Tab, and the arrow keys.
Cell	The intersection of a row and a column in the 1-2-3 worksheet.
Cell pointer	The highlighted bar that enables you to enter data into the worksheet area and identifies the current cell.
Formula	An action performed on a specified cell or group of cells. The formula +A1+B1, for example, sums the contents of cells A1 and B1.
Function	A shorthand method of using formulas. Instead of typing the formula +A1+B1+C1+D1+E1, for example, you can use the @SUM function @SUM(A1..E1).
Command	A menu selection used to carry out an operation within the worksheet.
Mouse	A device that attaches to your computer and enables you to choose cells and commands quickly by simply clicking a button.
SmartIcon	A graphical representation of a 1-2-3 procedure. The SmartIcons are an add-in provided with Release 2.4.
SmartIcon Palette	A column of SmartIcons that appears to the right of the worksheet.
Add-in	An additional program that enhances Lotus 1-2-3; this program is either provided with 1-2-3 when you buy the program or can be purchased separately.

Objective 1: To Become Familiar with Manual and Electronic Spreadsheets

Sometimes known as a *ledger sheet* or *accountant's pad*, a *spreadsheet* is a specialized piece of paper on which information is recorded in columns and rows. Spreadsheets usually contain a mix of descriptive text and accompanying numbers and calculations. Typical business applications include balance sheets, income statements, inventory sheets, and sales reports.

Although you may be unfamiliar with business applications for spreadsheets, you already use a rudimentary spreadsheet if you keep a checkbook. Similar to an accountant's pad, a checkbook register is a paper grid divided by lines into rows and columns. Within this grid, you record the check number, the date, a transaction description, the check amount, any deposits, and a running balance (see fig. 1.1).

NUMBER	DATE	DESCRIPTION OF TRANSACTION	PAYMENT/DEBT (−)	✓	FEE IF ANY (−)	DEPOSIT/CREDIT (+)	BALANCE
							1000 00
1001	9/3/89	Department Store Credit	51 03				948 97
1002	9/13/89	Electric	95 12				853 85
1003	9/14/89	Grocery	74 25				779 60
1004	9/15/89	Class Supplies	354 57				425 03
	9/16/89	Deposit				250 00	675 03
1005	9/21/89	Telephone	49 43				625 60

Fig. 1.1
A manual checkbook register.

What happens when you make an invalid entry in your checkbook register, or you have to void an entry? Such procedures are messy because you have to erase or cross out entries, rewrite them, and recalculate the totals. The limitations of manual spreadsheets are apparent even with this simple example of a checkbook register.

For complex business applications, the dynamic quality of an electronic spreadsheet, such as 1-2-3, is indispensable. You can change one number and recalculate the entire spreadsheet in an instant. Entering new values is nearly effortless. Performing calculations on a column or row of numbers is accomplished with formulas—usually the same type of formulas that calculators use.

Compare the manual checkbook register to the electronic register shown in figure 1.2. Notice that the electronic checkbook register is set up with columns and rows. Columns are marked by letters across the top of the spreadsheet; rows are numbered along the side. Each transaction is recorded in a row—the same way you record data in a manual checkbook.

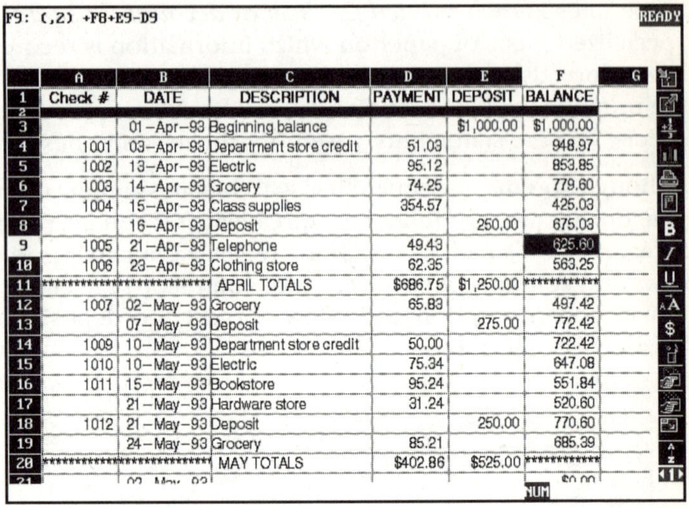

	A	B	C	D	E	F	G
1	Check #	DATE	DESCRIPTION	PAYMENT	DEPOSIT	BALANCE	
2							
3		01-Apr-93	Beginning balance		$1,000.00	$1,000.00	
4	1001	03-Apr-93	Department store credit	51.03		948.97	
5	1002	13-Apr-93	Electric	95.12		853.85	
6	1003	14-Apr-93	Grocery	74.25		779.60	
7	1004	15-Apr-93	Class supplies	354.57		425.03	
8		16-Apr-93	Deposit		250.00	675.03	
9	1005	21-Apr-93	Telephone	49.43		625.60	
10	1006	23-Apr-93	Clothing store	62.35		563.25	
11	************	************	APRIL TOTALS	$686.75	$1,250.00	************	
12	1007	02-May-93	Grocery	65.83		497.42	
13		07-May-93	Deposit		275.00	772.42	
14	1009	10-May-93	Department store credit	50.00		722.42	
15	1010	10-May-93	Electric	75.34		647.08	
16	1011	15-May-93	Bookstore	95.24		551.84	
17		21-May-93	Hardware store	31.24		520.60	
18	1012	21-May-93	Deposit		250.00	770.60	
19		24-May-93	Grocery	85.21		685.39	
20	************	************	MAY TOTALS	$402.86	$525.00	************	

Fig. 1.2
An electronic checkbook register.

Assigning column letters and row numbers lends itself well to creating *formulas.* Note the following formula in the upper left corner of the electronic checkbook:

```
+F8+E9-D9
```

These instructions to 1-2-3 translate to the following calculation:

Previous BALANCE plus DEPOSIT minus PAYMENT

As you can see from this simple example, formulas enable you to establish mathematical relationships between values stored in certain places on your spreadsheet. With formulas, you easily can make changes to a spreadsheet, and you can quickly see the results. In the electronic checkbook, if you delete an entire transaction (row), the spreadsheet automatically recalculates itself. You also can change an amount and not worry about recalculating your figures because the electronic spreadsheet updates all balances.

If you forget to record a check or deposit, 1-2-3 lets you insert a new row at the location of the omitted transaction and enter the information. Subsequent entries are moved down one row, and the new balance is calculated automatically. Inserting new columns is just as easy. Indicate where you want the new column to go, and 1-2-3 inserts a blank column at that point, moving existing information to the right of that column.

What if you want to know how much you have spent at the local department store since the beginning of the year? With a manual checkbook, you have to look for each check written to the store and total the amounts. Not only does this task take considerable time, but you may overlook some of the checks. An electronic checkbook can sort your checks by description so that all similar transactions are together. You then can create a formula that totals all the checks written to the department store.

Objective 2: To Learn 1-2-3's Spreadsheet Capabilities

1-2-3 has many capabilities, but the foundation of the program is the electronic spreadsheet. The framework of this spreadsheet contains the graphics and data management elements of the program. You use spreadsheet commands to create graphics. Data management occurs in the standard row-and-column spreadsheet layout.

The importance of the spreadsheet as the basis for 1-2-3 cannot be overemphasized. You enter data into the cells of the column and row format of the spreadsheet. Lotus 1-2-3 commands act on the entire spreadsheet or on a group of cells in the spreadsheet. To create a graph, you use the data in the spreadsheet. When you work with database commands, the database is composed of records that are actual rows of cell entries in a spreadsheet.

The Size of 1-2-3's Worksheet

With 256 columns and 8,192 rows, the 1-2-3 worksheet contains more than 2 million cells. The columns are lettered from A to Z, AA to AZ, BA to BZ, and so on, ending with IV. The rows are sequentially numbered from 1 to 8192.

A good way to visualize the spreadsheet (or *worksheet*) is as a giant sheet of grid paper that is about 21 feet wide and 171 feet long (see fig. 1.3).

An Overview of 1-2-3

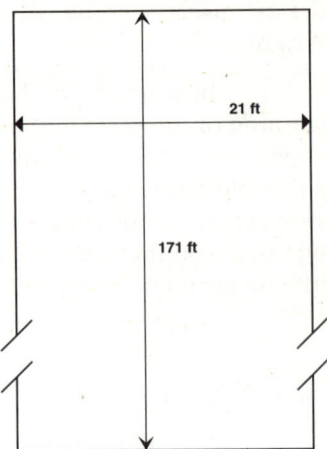

Fig. 1.3
It helps to visualize the spreadsheet as a giant piece of grid paper.

Although the 1-2-3 worksheet contains so many columns and rows, there are some limitations to using the entire sheet. If you imagine storing just one character in each of the 2,097,152 available cells, you end up with a worksheet that is far larger than the old standard of 640K random-access memory (RAM) of an IBM PC. If you are using the newer Releases 2.2, 2.3, and 2.4, they require at least 384K of RAM. In addition, features such as the Wysiwyg add-in (provided with 1-2-3 Release 2.3 and 2.4), require a hard disk on your computer and at least 512K of RAM.

Understanding the Worksheet Window

Because the 1-2-3 grid is so large, you cannot view the entire worksheet onscreen at one time. The screen thus serves as a *window* onto a small section of the worksheet. To illustrate the window concept, imagine cutting a one-inch square hole in a piece of cardboard. If you place the cardboard over this page, you will be able to see only a one-inch square piece of text. The rest of the text is still on the page; the data is simply hidden from view. When you move the cardboard around the page (the same way that the window moves when the direction keys are used), different parts of the page become visible.

The default 1-2-3 worksheet displays 8 columns (each 9 characters wide) and 20 rows (see fig. 1.4).

You can change the default number of columns that appear by narrowing or widening one or more of the columns. Wysiwyg also enables you to change the height of individual rows and the width of individual columns.

To Learn 1-2-3's Spreadsheet Capabilities

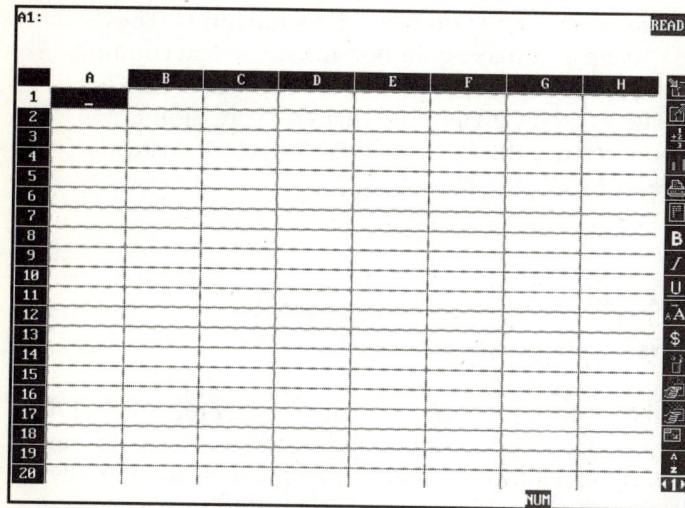

Fig. 1.4
The default 1-2-3 worksheet.

Cells

Each column in a 1-2-3 worksheet is assigned a letter, and each row is assigned a number. The intersections of the columns and rows are called *cells*. Cells are identified by their column and row coordinates. The cell located at the intersection of column A and row 15, for example, is called A15. The cell located at the intersection of column X and row 55 is named X55. Cells can be filled with two types of information: labels, which are text entries; or values, which consist of numbers, formulas, or both.

A *cell pointer* enables you to enter information into the current cell. In 1-2-3, as in most spreadsheets, the cell pointer looks like a highlighted rectangle on-screen. The cell pointer typically is one row high and one column wide.

To move the cell pointer on-screen, you can use the direction keys on your keyboard. If you have a mouse, you also can use the mouse to move the pointer.

Formulas and Functions

You can create simple *formulas*, involving only a few cells, when you refer to the cell addresses and use the appropriate operators (+, –, /, and *). Each formula is stored in memory and only its value appears in the cell.

13

An Overview of 1-2-3

You can create complex formulas when you use 1-2-3's functions. These *functions* are shortcuts to help you make common mathematical computations with a minimum of typing. Functions are like abbreviations for long cumbersome formulas. The @ sign signals 1-2-3 that an expression is a function. For instance, you can use the function @SUM(A1..E1) instead of typing the formula +A1+B1+C1+D1+E1.

Objective 3: To Understand 1-2-3's Graphics Features

The worksheet alone makes 1-2-3 a powerful program, which includes all the functions many users need. The addition of graphics features, which accompany the worksheet, makes 1-2-3 a tool you can use to present data visually and to conduct graphic what-if analyses. You can quickly design and alter graphs as worksheet data changes. This means that you can change graphs almost as fast as 1-2-3 recalculates data.

The pie graph shows only one data series, in which the parts total 100 percent of a specific numeric category (see fig. 1.5). Note in this example that the parts total 199.9 percent, due to rounding.

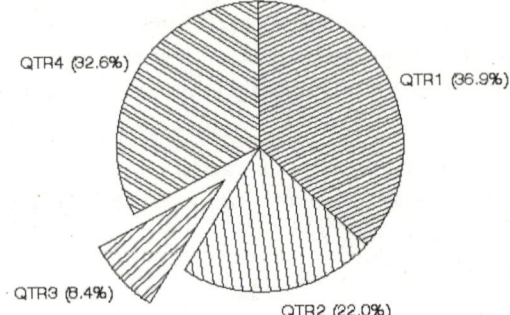

Fig. 1.5
A pie graph.

Objective 4: To Become Familiar with 1-2-3's Database Management

The row-and-column structure used to store data in a spreadsheet program is similar to the structure of a relational database. When you use 1-2-3's true database management commands and functions, you can sort, query, extract, and perform statistical analyses on data in up to 8,191 records (with up to 256 fields of information).

A row in 1-2-3 is equal to a record in a conventional database. In that record, you might store a deductible expense amount and explanation of the expense on one line.

Using 1-2-3, you enter each record across a single row. Each database field is located in a separate column of the worksheet (see fig. 1.6).

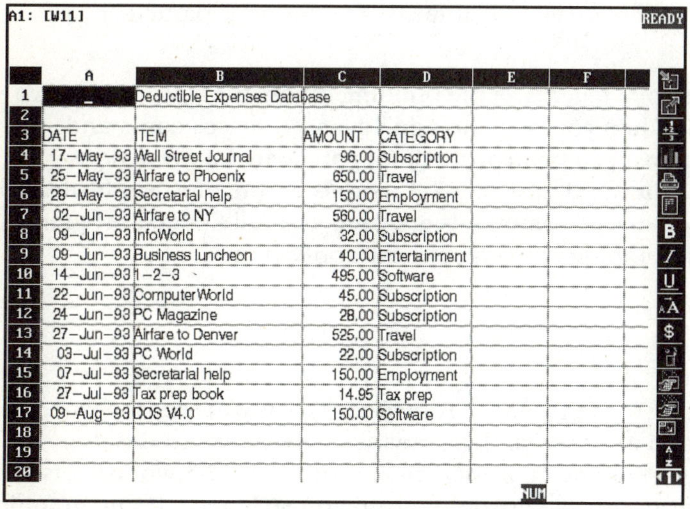

A1: [W11] READY

	A	B	C	D	E	F
1		Deductible Expenses Database				
2						
3	DATE	ITEM	AMOUNT	CATEGORY		
4	17-May-93	Wall Street Journal	96.00	Subscription		
5	25-May-93	Airfare to Phoenix	650.00	Travel		
6	28-May-93	Secretarial help	150.00	Employment		
7	02-Jun-93	Airfare to NY	560.00	Travel		
8	09-Jun-93	InfoWorld	32.00	Subscription		
9	09-Jun-93	Business luncheon	40.00	Entertainment		
10	14-Jun-93	1-2-3	495.00	Software		
11	22-Jun-93	ComputerWorld	45.00	Subscription		
12	24-Jun-93	PC Magazine	28.00	Subscription		
13	27-Jun-93	Airfare to Denver	525.00	Travel		
14	03-Jul-93	PC World	22.00	Subscription		
15	07-Jul-93	Secretarial help	150.00	Employment		
16	27-Jul-93	Tax prep book	14.95	Tax prep		
17	09-Aug-93	DOS V4.0	150.00	Software		
18						
19						
20						

NUM

Fig. 1.6
A sample database.

Objective 5: To Overview 1-2-3's Other Features

1-2-3 has other capabilities that make it such a popular spreadsheet program. Some of these capabilities include printing data and graphs, and even automating some common tasks.

An Overview of 1-2-3

Printed Reports and Graphs

By using 1-2-3's printing commands, you can print worksheet data and graphs for either draft review or formal presentations. You can send data and graphs directly from 1-2-3 to the printer or save worksheet data in a text file so that the data can be incorporated into another program, such as a word processing program.

Macros and the Advanced Macro Commands

Two other features, macros and advanced macro commands, help to make 1-2-3 the most powerful and popular integrated spreadsheet, graphics, and database program. A macro is a stored list of two or more commands. When you retrieve, or play back, a macro, it executes the commands and accomplishes the assigned task. When you use 1-2-3's macros and advanced macro commands, you can automate and customize 1-2-3 for your particular applications.

Think of simple keystroke macros as the building blocks for advanced macro command programs. When you begin to add advanced macro commands to simple keystroke macros, you control and automate many of the actions required to build, modify, and update 1-2-3 models. At the most sophisticated level, 1-2-3's advanced macro commands are used as a full-fledged programming language for developing custom business applications.

Wysiwyg

Release 2.3 introduced Wysiwyg—an acronym for "what-you-see-is-what-you-get." Wysiwyg is an add-in program that provides state-of-the art desktop publishing features for enhancing on-screen and printed 1-2-3 worksheets and graphics. With Wysiwyg, you can create presentation-style reports and graphics in minutes.

Summary

In this chapter, you learned how one of the simplest examples of a spreadsheet—a checkbook register—becomes easier to use in electronic form. You were introduced to the features of 1-2-3's spreadsheet, such as its size, window, and cells. You were given an overview of the spreadsheet, the graphics, and the database features.

Testing Your Knowledge

True/False Questions

1. The electronic spreadsheet is a replacement for the accountant's pad.
2. The columns of the electronic spreadsheet are lettered from A to Z, AA to AZ, BA to BZ, all the way to column IV.
3. The Lotus 1-2-3 worksheet has over 5 million available cells.
4. Cells in the worksheet are identified by their column and row coordinates.
5. You can draw any kind of drawing using the Lotus 1-2-3 Graphics features.

Multiple Choice Questions

1. A spreadsheet is
    A. a type of word processing document.
    B. a specialized piece of paper on which information is recorded in columns and rows.
    C. an additional program that enhances Lotus 1-2-3.
    D. a macro.

2. Wysiwyg
    A. is a 1-2-3 database.
    B. is a publishing add-in provided with 1-2-3 Releases 2.3 and 2.4.
    C. stands for "where-you-sit-is-what-you-get."
    D. is an action performed on a specified cell or group of cells.

3. A pie graph
    A. typically is used to show the trend of numeric data across time.
    B. often compares two or more items.
    C. is a shorthand method of using formulas.
    D. shows only one data series, in which the parts total 100 percent of a specific numeric category.

An Overview of 1-2-3

4. A cell is
    A. the highlighted bar that enables you to enter data into the worksheet.
    B. a device that attaches to your computer and enables you to point and click.
    C. the intersection of a row and column in the 1-2-3 worksheet.
    D. a menu selection used to carry out an operation within the worksheet.
5. Lotus 1-2-3
    A. has spreadsheet, graphics, and data management capabilities.
    B. is desktop publishing software.
    C. is word processing software.
    D. is a communications package.

Fill-in-the-Blank Questions

1. The 1-2-3 worksheet contains ____256____ columns.
2. The 1-2-3 worksheet contains ____8,192____ rows.
3. All columns in the worksheet are assigned ____Letters____ to identify them.
4. All rows in the worksheet are assigned ____Numbers____ to identify them.
5. The intersection of a row and column in the 1-2-3 worksheet is called ____Cells____.

Review: Short Projects

1. Manual Spreadsheet Layout

    Study your own checkbook register to become familiar with the layout of a manual spreadsheet. Notice how it is set up in columns and rows.

2. Layout Comparison

    Briefly study a phone book and compare how it is set up to your check book.

3. Ledger Sheet Layout

    Look at an accountant's ledger sheet, noticing that it contains both descriptive text and numbers and calculations.

Testing Your Knowledge

Review: Long Projects

1. Creating a Budget

    On a sheet of paper, create a three-month budget for yourself of your family. Notice how difficult it is to make changes to this manual budget.

2. Entering Data Manually

    On a sheet of paper, enter the names of four bowlers down the left side of the page. Enter their bowling scores for three games. Add their scores to show their total. Average their scores to give a three-game average.

Getting Started

2

This chapter helps you get started using 1-2-3 and Wysiwyg. Before you begin, be sure that 1-2-3 is installed on your computer system. Follow the instructions in your Lotus documentation.

Objectives

1. To Start Lotus 1-2-3
2. To Exit Lotus 1-2-3
3. To Use Keyboard
4. To Use a Mouse in 1-2-3
5. To Understand the 1-2-3 Screen
6. To Learn the Icons in Release 2.4
7. To Understand 1-2-3's Menu System
8. To Use the 1-2-3 Help System and On-Line Tutorial

Getting Started

2

Key Terms in This Chapter	
Lotus 1-2-3 Access Menu	The Lotus menu system that links all 1-2-3's different programs. It includes options for accessing the main 1-2-3 program, printing graphs, modifying installation settings, and translating files between 1-2-3 and other software programs.
Alphanumeric keys	The keys in the center section of the computer keyboard. Most of these keys resemble those on a typewriter keyboard.
Numeric keypad	The keys on the right side of the Personal Computer AT and enhanced keyboards. This keypad is used for entering and calculating numbers, for moving the cell pointer in the worksheet area, or for moving the cursor and menu pointer in the control panel.
Function keys	The 10 keys on the left side of the Personal Computer AT keyboard or the 12 keys at the top of the enhanced keyboard. These keys are used for special 1-2-3 functions, such as accessing help, editing cells, and recalculating the worksheet.
Control panel	The area above the frame containing column letters of the 1-2-3 worksheet. The control panel contains three lines that display important information about the contents of a cell, command options and explanations, special prompts or messages, and mode indicators.
Worksheet area	The largest part of the 1-2-3 screen, where data that has been entered into the worksheet is displayed.
Status line	A single line located at the bottom of the 1-2-3 screen that displays information, such as the file-and-clock indicator, error messages, and status indicators.
Icon panel or palette	The area on the right side of the screen containing icons for use with a mouse or the keyboard.

Objective 1: To Start Lotus 1-2-3

Getting into 1-2-3 is quite easy. Starting from DOS, you can go directly to a fresh worksheet, or you can enter 1-2-3 by using the Lotus 1-2-3 Access Menu, which provides several menu options. The following sections describe both methods.

Starting 1-2-3 from DOS

Starting 1-2-3 directly from DOS is a shortcut and requires less memory than using the Lotus 1-2-3 Access Menu.

Exercise 1.1: Starting 1-2-3 from DOS

In the following instructions, the assumption is that the 1-2-3 program is on drive C of your hard disk, in a subdirectory named \123. To start 1-2-3, follow these steps:

1. With the C> system prompt displayed on-screen, change to the \123 directory by typing **cd \123** and pressing ⏎Enter.
2. Start 1-2-3 by typing **123** and pressing ⏎Enter.

After a few seconds, the 1-2-3 logo appears. The logo remains on-screen for a few seconds. Then the worksheet appears, and you're ready to use 1-2-3. (If you are using 2.3 or 2.4 and Wysiwyg is loaded, the Wysiwyg logo will appear before the worksheet appears.)

If these steps did not work, it is probably because the subdirectory is named something besides 123, such as 123R24. To find out what it is named on your system, type **dir/p** from the C> prompt and look for the correct name. Repeat Exercise 1.1.

Starting 1-2-3 from the Lotus 1-2-3 Access Menu

Lotus devised the Lotus 1-2-3 Access Menu as a way to move quickly between the programs in the 1-2-3 package. The Lotus 1-2-3 Access Menu, for example, contains a series of menus that enable you to convert data between 1-2-3 and other programs, such as dBASE, Symphony, and Multiplan.

Getting Started

Exercise 1.2: Starting 1-2-3 from the Access Menu

Starting 1-2-3 from the Access Menu gives you options, other than just using the spreadsheet. To start 1-2-3 from the Access Menu, follow these steps:

1. With the C> system prompt displayed on-screen, change to the \123 directory by typing **cd\123** and pressing `Enter`.
2. Start the Lotus 1-2-3 Access Menu by typing **lotus** and pressing `Enter`. The Lotus 1-2-3 Access Menu screen appears (see fig. 2.1).
3. Press `Enter` with 1-2-3 highlighted, and you see the main program screen (see fig. 2.2).

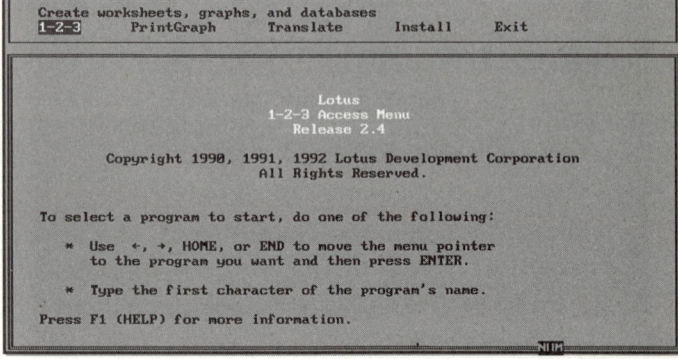

Fig. 2.1
The 1-2-3 Access Menu.

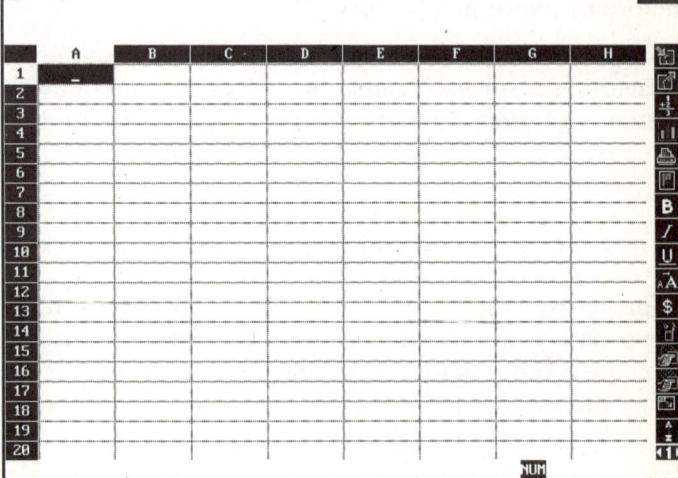

Fig. 2.2
The main 1-2-3 program screen.

The other options on the Access Menu include Printgraph (for printing graphs), Translate (for accessing the utility that translates files from other software), Install (which changes the options set during installation), and Exit (which quits the 1-2-3 program and returns you to DOS).

Objective 2: To Exit Lotus 1-2-3

Once you are successfully in the 1-2-3 program and want to end the session, you will have four or five steps to follow depending on which method you used to start the program. The **Quit** command on the 1-2-3 main menu enables you to exit both the worksheet and the 1-2-3 program if you typed **123** to start the program (as in Exercise 1.1). If you typed **lotus** (as in Exercise 1.2), you are returned to the Access Menu, and you must choose the **Exit** option (see fig. 2.3). If you have done some work in the spreadsheet, you need to save it, or it will be lost. Because you probably don't have anything to save at this point, just verify that you want to leave 1-2-3 by choosing **Yes**.

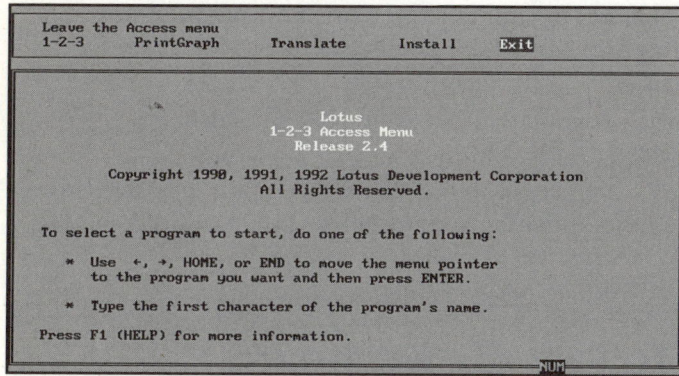

Fig. 2.3
Exit quits the 1-2-3 program and returns you to DOS.

Exercise 2.1: Exiting 1-2-3

When you are finished working with 1-2-3, follow these steps to exit the program:

1. Call up the 1-2-3 menu by pressing [/] or moving the mouse pointer to the top of the screen.
2. Select **Q**uit (see fig. 2.4).

Getting Started

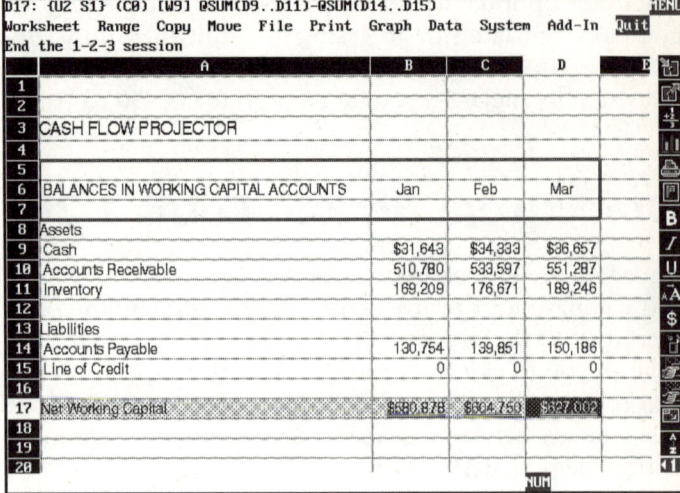

Fig. 2.4
The Quit command is highlighted.

3. You are asked to verify that you want to exit. Select **Y**es.

   If you have made changes in your current worksheet but have not saved them by using /**F**ile **S**ave, 1-2-3 beeps and displays a reminder when you try to exit.

4. Select **Y**es to exit the program without saving the spreadsheet.

5. If you started 1-2-3 from the Lotus 1-2-3 Access Menu, you are returned to the Lotus 1-2-3 Access Menu. To exit the Lotus 1-2-3 Access Menu and return to the operating system, select **E**xit. **E**xit quits the 1-2-3 program and returns you to DOS.

Objective 3: To Use the Keyboard

Before you begin learning 1-2-3, you need to get to know your keyboard. Each of the two most popular keyboards consists of these sections: the alphanumeric keys in the center, the numeric keypad with direction keys on the right, and the function-key section on the left or across the top. The enhanced keyboard, the standard keyboard for all new IBM personal computers and most compatibles, also has a separate grouping of direction keys.

Figure 2.5 shows the original IBM personal computer AT keyboard, and figure 2.6 shows the enhanced keyboard.

To Use the Keyboard

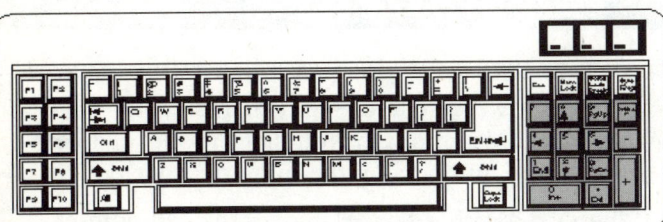

Fig. 2.5
The original IBM personal computer AT keyboard.

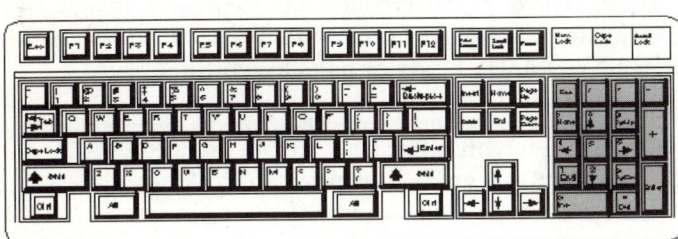

Fig. 2.6
The enhanced keyboard.

The Alphanumeric Keys

Most of the alphanumeric keys on the computer keyboard perform the same actions as those on a typewriter. When you use 1-2-3, several of the keys have special functions. The slash (/) key, for example, accesses the 1-2-3 menu, the colon (:) key accesses the Wysiwyg menu, and the period (.) key helps you to define a range of cells. Table 2.1 highlights each of these important keys.

Table 2.1	1-2-3 Special Keys
Key	*Action*
Esc	Returns to the previous menu; erases the current entry during editing, or the range or command specification; returns from a help screen; clears error messages from the screen.
Tab	Moves the cell pointer one screen to the right.
Shift + Tab	Moves the cell pointer one screen to the left.
Caps Lock	Activates capitalization of all alphabetic characters when keys for those characters are pressed. Displays the CAPS indicator in the status line when active. This key is a toggle, which means that capitalization stays activated until you press this key again.

continues

Getting Started

Table 2.1 Continued	
Key	*Action*
Shift	Changes lowercase letters and characters to uppercase. When not in Num Lock mode, enables you to type numbers on the numeric keypad.
Ctrl	When used with ← or →, moves the cell pointer one screen to the left or right in READY mode or moves the cursor five characters to the left or right in EDIT mode; when used with Break, returns 1-2-3 to READY mode or halts execution of a macro.
Alt	When used with other keys, invokes macros, activates STEP mode, performs an Undo, or executes other commands.
Spacebar	Inserts a space within a cell entry, moves the menu pointer one item to the right when selecting commands from a menu, and enables you to make selections in dialog boxes.
Backspace	Erases the previous character in a cell during cell definition; erases the character to the left of the cursor during editing. Cancels a range during some prompts that display the old range.
Enter	Accepts an entry into a cell or selects a highlighted menu command.
.	Defines a range of cells or anchors one corner when defining a range. Also used as a decimal point.
:	Calls up the Wysiwyg menu.
/	Calls up the 1-2-3 main menu; also functions as a division sign in formulas.
<	Used as an alternative to the slash (/) for calling up the 1-2-3 main menu; also used in logical formulas.
Scroll Lock	Scrolls the entire window one row or column when the cell pointer is moved. Displays the SCROLL indicator in the status line when active. Acts as a toggle.

To Use the Keyboard

Key	Action
[Pause]	Pauses a macro, a recalculation, and some commands until you press any key. On AT keyboards, press [Ctrl]+[Num Lock] to get same effect.
[Num Lock]	Activates the numeric representation of keys in the numeric keypad. Displays the NUM indicator in the status line when active. Acts as a toggle.
[Ins]	Changes 1-2-3 from insert mode to overtype mode during editing. When pressed, causes the OVR indicator to appear in the status line and enables new characters to overwrite existing text. Acts as a toggle.
[Del]	Erases the cell entry at the cell pointer in READY mode (similar to the /Range Erase command). Also deletes the character above the cursor during the editing process.

Using the Numeric Keypad and Direction Keys

The keys in the numeric keypad are used mainly for data entry and for moving the cell pointer or cursor. The enhanced keyboard has separate direction keys for this movement function.

Using the Function Keys

You use the function keys **F1** through **F10** for special tasks, such as accessing Help, editing cells, and recalculating the worksheet. Although the enhanced keyboard has 12 function keys (**F1** through **F12**), 1-2-3 uses only the first 10.

In addition to using the function key alone, you also can use the **Alt** key in conjunction with function keys. To use the **Alt**+function key combination, first hold down **Alt**, and then press the function key. If you use the **Ctrl** key with the **F1** key, you can display the last Help screen that was viewed.

A plastic function-key template that describes the actions of each function key or **Alt**+function key combination on the enhanced keyboard is provided with

Getting Started

the Lotus software. Another version of the template is provided for users with AT or compatible keyboards. The operations of the function keys are summarized inside the back cover of this book.

Using the Keyboard

As you start entering data into your worksheet, you need some easy ways to move the cell pointer quickly and accurately.

Remember that the cell pointer and the cursor are two different features. The *cell pointer* is the bright rectangle that highlights an entire cell in the worksheet area. The *cursor* is the underscore that is sometimes inside the cell pointer and sometimes in the control panel.

When you start 1-2-3, the cell pointer appears automatically in cell A1 of the worksheet (see fig. 2.7).

You control the cell pointer by using the keyboard or the mouse. (To use a mouse, you must have Release 2.3 or 2.4, a mouse driver loaded, and a mouse attached to the computer.)

Using the Keyboard To Move the Cell Pointer

When 1-2-3 is in READY mode, the program is ready for you to enter data into the highlighted cell. To enter data into another cell, move the cell pointer to the new location by using the direction keys, as shown in table 2.2.

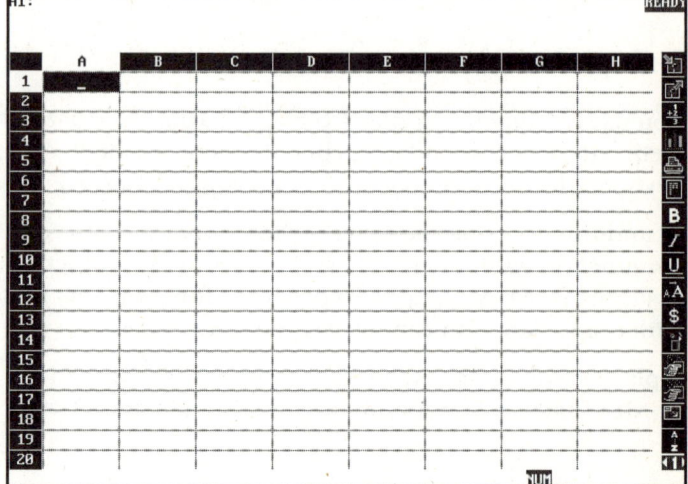

Fig. 2.7
The opening 1-2-3 screen.

To Use the Keyboard

Table 2.2 Direction Keys

Key	Action
←	Moves the cell pointer one column to the left in the worksheet; in the control panel, moves the cursor one character to the left in EDIT mode or the menu pointer one item to the left in MENU mode
→	Moves the cell pointer one column to the right in the worksheet; in the control panel, moves the cursor one character to the right in EDIT mode or the menu pointer one item to the right in MENU mode
↑	Moves the cell pointer up one row
↓	Moves the cell pointer down one row
Tab or Ctrl+→	Moves the cell pointer one screen to the right in the worksheet; in the control panel, moves the cursor five characters to the right in EDIT mode
Shift+Tab or Ctrl+←	Moves the cell pointer one screen to the left in the worksheet; in the control panel, moves the cursor five characters to the left in EDIT mode
PgUp	Moves the cell pointer up one screen
PgDn	Moves the cell pointer down one screen
Home	Returns the cell pointer to cell A1 from any location in the current worksheet; when used after End, positions the pointer at the lower right corner of the active area of the worksheet
End	When used before any arrow key, moves the cell pointer (in the direction of the arrow key) to the next boundary between a blank cell and a cell containing data
F5 (GoTo)	Moves the cell pointer to the cell coordinates (or range name) you specify

Getting Started

Using the Basic Direction Keys

The arrow keys on the numeric keypad (or on the separate pad of the enhanced keyboard) are the basic keys for moving the cell pointer with the keyboard. The cell pointer moves in the direction of the arrow on the key for as long as you hold down the key. When you reach the edge of the screen, the worksheet continues scrolling in the direction of the arrow.

Exercise 3.1: Moving the Cell Pointer around the Worksheet

Start Lotus 1-2-3, as described earlier in the chapter. Then follow these steps:

1. Press [→] several times to move the cursor to the right. Notice that the letters at the top of the worksheet change.
2. Now hold down [→]. The cell pointer continues moving to the right.
3. Try pressing [←], [↓], and [↑].
4. Press [Home]. The cell pointer moves to A1, the normal home position.
5. Press [Tab]. The cell pointer moves one screen to the right each time you press it.
6. Hold down [Shift] and press [Tab] at the same time. This key combination has the opposite effect of [Tab]; that is, the cell pointer moves one screen to the left.
7. Press [PgDn]; notice that this key works like [Tab] except that [PgDn] moves you down one screen at a time.
8. Now press [PgUp] to move up one screen at a time.
9. Press [End], let up on it, and press [→]. Your cell pointer jumps all the way to column IV. Notice that 1-2-3 displays the END status indicator at the bottom of the screen after you press [End].
10. Press [End], let up on it, and press [↓]. Your cell pointer is now in cell IV8192, the bottom right corner of the worksheet (see fig. 2.8)

    When you press an arrow key after you have pressed and released [End], the cell pointer moves in the direction of the arrow key to the next boundary between a blank cell and a cell containing data. Because you had no data between your current location and the far right of the worksheet, the cell pointer went all the way to column IV and for the same reason it went all the way to the bottom.

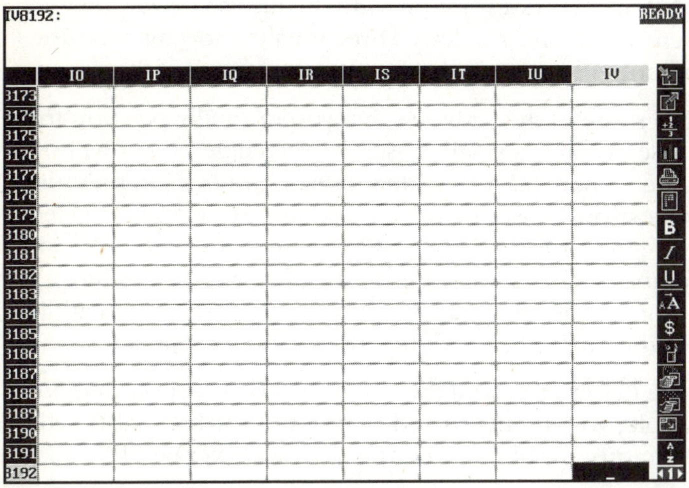

To Use a Mouse in 1-2-3

Fig. 2.8
The cell pointer is in the bottom right corner of the worksheet, cell IV8192.

11. Press `F5`. 1-2-3 prompts you for the new cell address. Disregard the current location that 1-2-3 shows you and type `z100` (see fig. 2.9). Press `Enter`. Your cell pointer jumps directly to cell Z100.

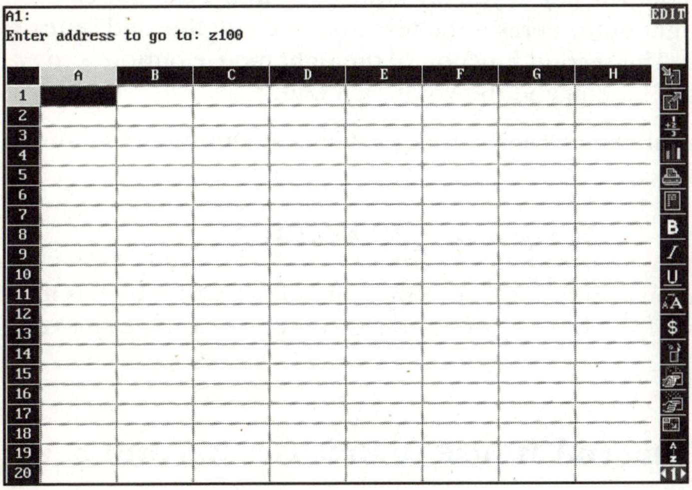

Fig. 2.9
Using the **F5** key enables you to move the cell pointer directly to a cell.

Objective 4: To Use a Mouse in 1-2-3

Lotus Releases 2.3 and 2.4 enable you to use a mouse to make menu choices and to move around the worksheet. To use a mouse, you must load a mouse

33

Getting Started

driver before starting 1-2-3. 1-2-3 does not provide the mouse driver; the company that manufactures the mouse does. Directions for adding a mouse driver are in the documentation you received with your mouse.

Your mouse can replace some of the activities that you normally perform from the keyboard. The mouse pointer, a small on-screen rectangle or arrow, points to the center of the screen when 1-2-3 is loaded. Pressing either the right or left mouse button enables you to use the mouse and mouse pointer to select commands, switch between the 1-2-3 and Wysiwyg menus, move the cell and menu pointers, select ranges, choose options on dialog boxes, and select SmartIcons. Before using the mouse, you should become familiar with additional terms, such as point, click, click-and-drag, icon, and icon panel.

To *point* means to move the mouse until the tip of the arrow is pointing on something. If, for example, you are instructed to point to (or highlight) cell B5, you must move the mouse until the tip of the arrow is over cell B5.

When you *click* the mouse, you press and immediately release one of the two buttons on the mouse. (If your mouse has three buttons, only the two outside buttons are active. The center button is not used in 1-2-3.) Normally, you click a mouse button only after you point with the mouse. The left button on the mouse acts as the **Enter** key. The right button has two functions. The right button usually acts as the **Esc** key; if you are typing text into a cell, for example, pressing the right button erases the text from the edit line and returns 1-2-3 to READY mode. The second function of the right mouse button is to switch between the 1-2-3 menu and the Wysiwyg menu.

Click-and-drag is a combination of pointing, clicking, and moving the mouse.

Using the Mouse To Move the Cell Pointer

You can use the left mouse button to move the cell pointer when 1-2-3 is in READY or POINT mode. 1-2-3 offers several ways to use the mouse to move the cell pointer.

Exercise 4.1: Using the Mouse in Releases 2.3 and 2.4

When you are using 1-2-3 Release 2.3 or 2.4 and you have not loaded the SmartIcons, you can use the mouse to move the cell pointer around the worksheet. Follow these steps:

1. With the left mouse button, click the triangle that points to the right. This action moves the cell pointer one cell to the right (see fig. 2.10). Repeat this step, using the other arrows.

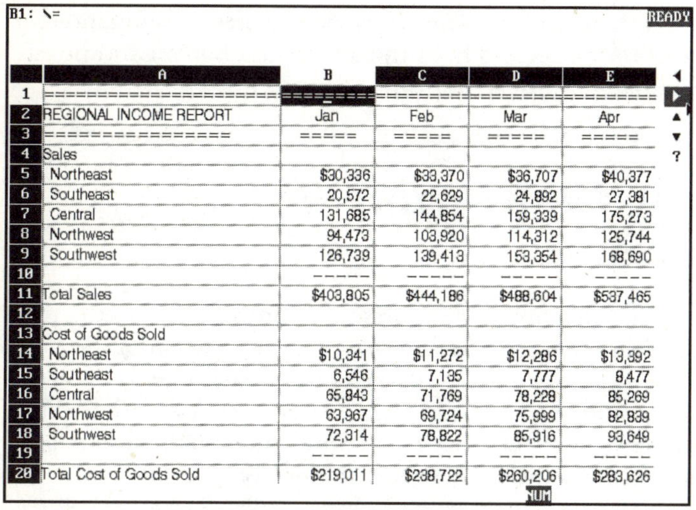
B1: \= READY

	A	B	C	D	E
1	====================	=========	=========	=========	=========
2	REGIONAL INCOME REPORT	Jan	Feb	Mar	Apr
3	===============	=====	=====	=====	=====
4	Sales				
5	Northeast	$30,336	$33,370	$36,707	$40,377
6	Southeast	20,572	22,629	24,892	27,381
7	Central	131,685	144,854	159,339	175,273
8	Northwest	94,473	103,920	114,312	125,744
9	Southwest	126,739	139,413	153,354	168,690
10		-----	-----	-----	-----
11	Total Sales	$403,805	$444,186	$488,604	$537,465
12					
13	Cost of Goods Sold				
14	Northeast	$10,341	$11,272	$12,286	$13,392
15	Southeast	6,546	7,135	7,777	8,477
16	Central	65,843	71,769	78,228	85,269
17	Northwest	63,967	69,724	75,999	82,839
18	Southwest	72,314	78,822	85,916	93,649
19		-----	-----	-----	-----
20	Total Cost of Goods Sold	$219,011	$238,722	$260,206	$283,626

NUM

Fig. 2.10
The icon palette contains four scroll triangles and one Help icon.

2. With the mouse pointer on the triangle that points to the right, press and hold down the left mouse button; the cell pointer keeps moving to the right. Repeat this technique, using the other arrows.
3. Press and release End, and then click the triangle that points to the right. This action moves the cell pointer to the next boundary between a blank cell and a cell containing data. If there is no data between the current cell location and the far right boundary, the cell pointer goes all the way to column IV.

Another important use of the mouse is to highlight a group of cells on the worksheet. If you want to do things to groups of cells, such as format or print, you can choose the cells ahead of time with the mouse.

Exercise 4.2: Learning To Click and Drag the Mouse

The click-and-drag movement of the mouse is used to highlight a worksheet range. Follow these steps:

1. Move the mouse pointer to the desired beginning location, such as the upper left corner of a range.
2. Press and hold the left mouse button; don't release the button at this time. (This step anchors the cell pointer.)
3. Move the mouse to the desired ending location, such as the lower right corner of a range, and release the mouse button. The desired range is highlighted.

Getting Started

To select a range from B5 through D10 while performing menu commands, for example, point to cell B5, press and hold the left mouse button and point to cell D10; then release the left mouse button.

Objective 5: To Understand the 1-2-3 Screen

The 1-2-3 display is divided into three main parts: the control panel at the top of the screen, the worksheet area, and the status line at the bottom of the screen (see fig. 2.11). If you have a mouse, the screen also includes an icon panel located on the right side of the screen. The worksheet frame separates the control panel from the worksheet area. This frame contains the letters and numbers that mark the columns and rows of the worksheet area.

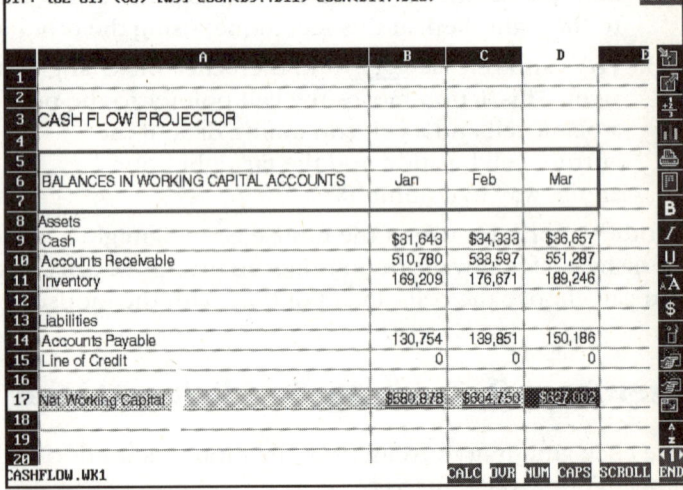

Fig. 2.11
The 1-2-3 screen with Wysiwyg and SmartIcons add-ins attached.

To Understand the 1-2-3 Screen

The Control Panel

The *control panel*, the area above the frame containing column letters, can show three lines of information. The control panel contains data about the current cell as well as the menu commands.

The left corner of the first line of the control panel shows information about the current cell (the cell highlighted by the cell pointer) (see fig. 2.12).

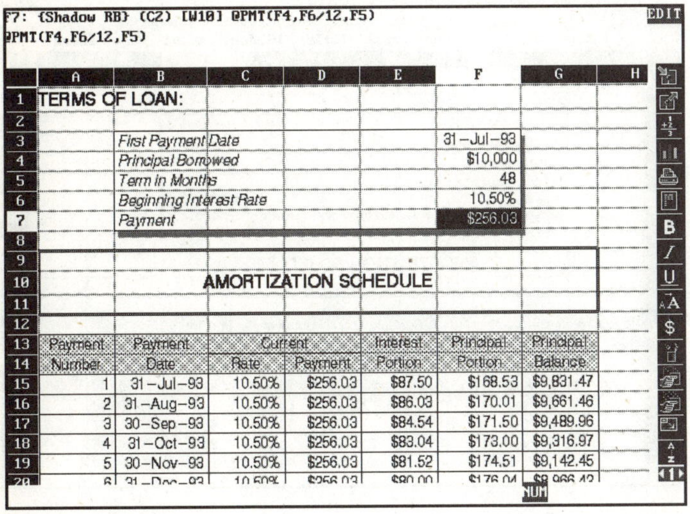

Fig. 2.12
The control panel includes the following cell information: the cell address, formatting information, the column width, and the contents of the cell.

The right corner of the first line always displays the mode indicator (EDIT in this example). Mode indicators appear in reverse video and change depending on the action you are taking. The READY mode appears whenever data can be entered into the worksheet or whenever the menu can be invoked.

The second line of the control panel displays characters you are entering from the keyboard or that you are editing. If you are going to make a menu choice, the second line can also display options in a menu.

Figure 2.13 shows the 1-2-3 main menu with the **W**orksheet menu option highlighted.

The third line of the control panel provides explanations of the current menu item or the next hierarchical menu. As you move the menu pointer from one item to the next in a command menu, the explanation on the third line of the control panel changes to correspond to the highlighted option.

37

The Worksheet Frame

Immediately below the control panel is the *worksheet frame*. When you first start 1-2-3, the letters A through H appear at the top of each column and the numbers 1 to 20 appear at the left of each row. As you move around the worksheet, the column letters and row numbers change, and 1-2-3 highlights the current column and row to indicate your position.

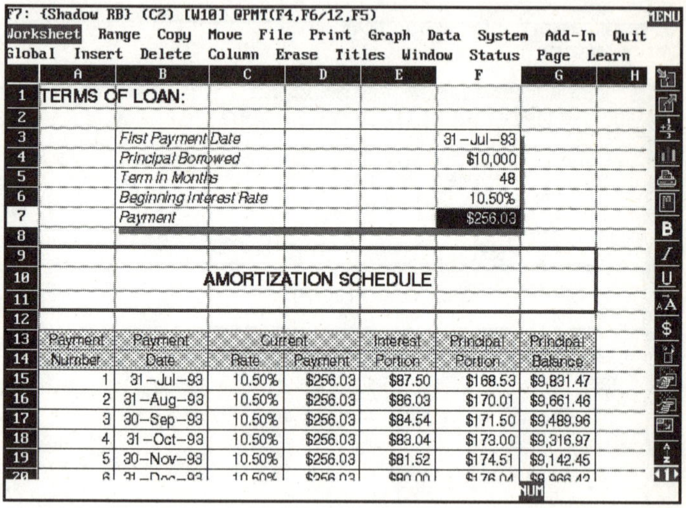

Fig. 2.13
The 1-2-3 main menu.

The Worksheet Area

The largest part of the 1-2-3 screen is composed of the worksheet area, which is made up of rows and columns.

The Status Line

The *status line* is the bottom line of the 1-2-3 screen. This line normally displays the current date and time and status indicators that appear in reverse video. These indicators include general messages such as NUM, telling you that Num Lock is invoked, or error messages such as CIRC, giving you a warning.

Objective 6: To Learn the Icons in Release 2.4

An *icon* is a character that represents an action. These characters are displayed on the right side of the screen in Release 2.4. If you have only the mouse loaded and not the SmartIcons, you will see four triangles and one question mark. When a mouse is installed without SmartIcons, the five mouse icons appear in the icon panel on the right side of the screen (see fig. 2.14).

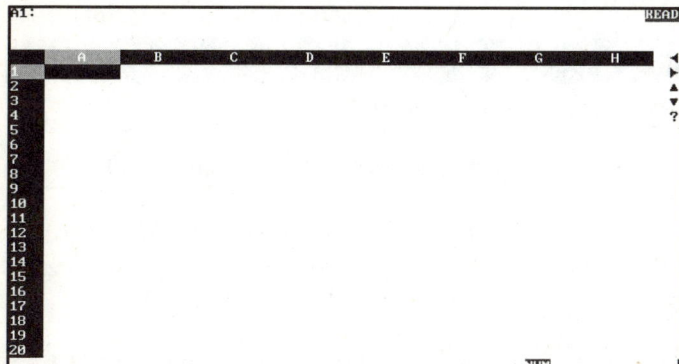

Fig. 2.14

The five mouse icons.

When you load SmartIcons, you have a choice of many more icons (up to 68). When Wysiwyg is loaded, all the icons are active. When Wysiwyg is not loaded, the icons look different and 19 are inactive.

If you select an icon that is not active, you see an error message, indicating that Wysiwyg must be loaded.

SmartIcons are organized into groups that 1-2-3 calls *palettes*. One palette is visible at all times on the right side of the screen. The number of palettes or groups of icons varies depending on the resolution of your graphics monitor and whether Wysiwyg is loaded.

Exercise 6.1: Using Cell-Movement SmartIcons

You can use a mouse or the keyboard to choose SmartIcons. To use a mouse to choose cell-movement SmartIcons, follow these steps:

1. Click the arrows by the number at the bottom of each palette to move to the desired palette.

Getting Started

2. Click an icon (shown in table 2.3) to move the cell pointer.

To use the keyboard to choose cell-movement SmartIcons, follow these steps:

1. Press the add-in key assigned to SmartIcons. Press [Alt]+[F7], for example.
2. Use [→] and [←] to move to the palette that contains the SmartIcon you want to use.
3. Use [↑] and [↓] to move to the icon you want, and then press [⏎Enter].

Table 2.3 shows cell-movement SmartIcons. They appear differently on the screen if Wysiwyg is not loaded.

Table 2.3	Movement SmartIcons	
Wysiwyg	*Non-Wysiwyg*	*Description*
←	◀	Moves left one cell or name on list.
→	▶	Moves right one cell or name on list.
↑	▲	Moves up one cell or name on list.
↓	▼	Moves down one cell or name on list.
⌐	⌐	Moves to cell A1; choosing this SmartIcon is the equivalent of pressing [Home].
⌐	⌐	Moves to the last active cell in the worksheet; choosing this SmartIcon is the equivalent of pressing [End], [Home].
∥↓	∥↓	Moves down to the last cell in the range; choosing this SmartIcon is the equivalent of pressing [End], [↓].
∥↑	∥↑	Moves up to the last cell in the range; choosing this icon is the equivalent of pressing [End], [↑].
→⁼⁼	→⁼⁼	Moves right to the last cell in the range; choosing this SmartIcon is the equivalent of pressing [End], [→].

To Understand 1-2-3's Menu System

Wysiwyg	Non-Wysiwyg	Description
	= = ←	Moves left to the last cell in the range; choosing this icon is the equivalent of pressing End, ←.
	GOTO	Moves to the indicated cell or range; choosing this SmartIcon is the equivalent of pressing Goto (F5).

Objective 7: To Understand 1-2-3's Menu System

To choose a command from the 1-2-3 main menu, make certain that 1-2-3 is in READY mode, and then press /.

When you press /, the mode indicator in the upper right corner of the screen changes to MENU, and the 1-2-3 main menu appears on the second line of the control panel (see fig. 2.15).

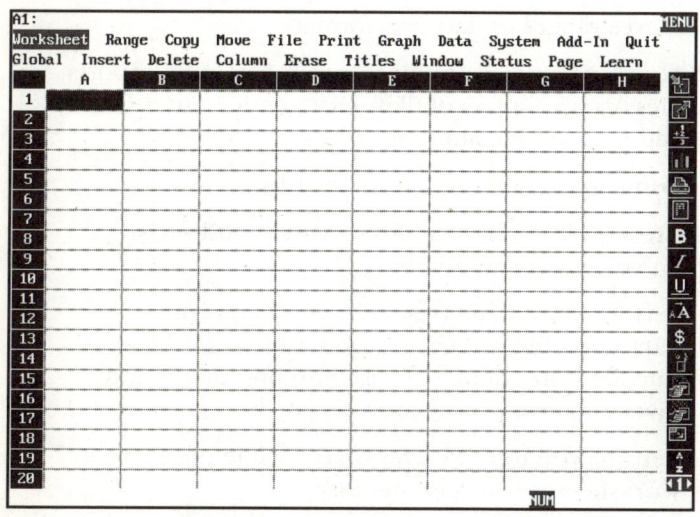

Fig. 2.15
The 1-2-3 menu.

The third line of the control panel contains either a brief explanation of the highlighted command or the menu that results from choosing the highlighted command. As you move the menu pointer across the menu and point to

Getting Started

different commands, 1-2-3 highlights each command and provides an explanation (or menu) for that command. This assistance appears at all levels of menus.

The 1-2-3 main menu provides the command options for building and modifying your worksheet and graphics applications. Table 2.4 summarizes the selections on the 1-2-3 main menu.

Table 2.4 Selections on the 1-2-3 Main Menu	
Selection	*Description*
Worksheet	Changes global worksheet settings; inserts and deletes columns or rows; sets column widths, windows, and titles; erases the worksheet from memory; displays worksheet status; inserts page breaks; and records keystrokes in the worksheet
Range	Formats, erases, names, justifies, protects, and searches ranges of data; aligns labels; restricts data entry; converts formulas to values; and transposes columns and rows
Copy	Copies ranges of data and formats
Move	Moves ranges of data and formats
File	Accesses, saves, combines, erases, lists, and imports files; extracts parts of files; changes current directory; and controls file administration
Print	Prints worksheets to a printer or file
Graph	Creates, resets, views, saves, names, and adds enhancements to graphs
Data	Performs sorts, queries, and regressions on 1-2-3 databases; fills a range; creates tables of values; calculates frequency distribution; multiplies and inverts matrixes; and converts labels
System	Returns you to DOS temporarily while the current worksheet remains in memory
Add-In	Loads, activates, or removes 1-2-3 add-in programs
Quit	Quits 1-2-3 (ends the 1-2-3 session)

To Understand 1-2-3's Menu System

To point to a command on the menu, use ← and → on the keyboard. After you highlight the command you want, press **Enter**.

If you move the menu pointer to the last command of a menu and press → again, the menu pointer reappears on the first command of the menu. Similarly, if the menu pointer is on the first command of a menu, press ← to move to the last command. Note that you also can move the menu pointer to the end of the command line by pressing **End** or to the beginning of the line by pressing **Home**.

Another way to choose a command from the keyboard is to type the command's first letter. When you become familiar with the commands in 1-2-3's various menus, you will find that typing is much faster than pointing. To choose a menu command from the keyboard, you can either point or type.

Exercise 7.1: Pointing to Commands

You can make menu selections by pointing to the command with the arrow keys. Follow these steps:

1. Display the 1-2-3 menu by pressing [/].
2. Use [←] or [→] to move the menu pointer until you have highlighted **R**ange command. Then press [↵Enter].
3. Use [→] to move to the **L**abel command and press [↵Enter].
4. Press [Esc] once to take you back to the **R**ange menu and again to take you back to the main menu.

   Note: Any time you press [Esc] from within a menu, 1-2-3 returns you to the preceding menu.

Exercise 7.2: Typing the First Letter of Commands

You can make menu selections by typing the first letter of the command you want to use. Follow these steps:

1. Display the 1-2-3 menu by pressing [/].
2. Choose **R**ange **L**abels by pressing [R] and [L].
3. Return to the main menu by pressing [Esc] two times.

Getting Started

Exercise 7.3: Making Menu Selections with a Mouse

You can make menu choices with a mouse. You can display the menu by moving the mouse into the control panel. Then, move the mouse to highlight the command you want and click the left mouse button. Repeat exercise 7.2, but this time use the mouse to choose the menu selections.

Using the Wysiwyg Menu in Releases 2.3 and 2.4

In addition to the 1-2-3 menu, Releases 2.3 and 2.4 include a Wysiwyg menu to enhance your 1-2-3 worksheets. As with other add-in programs that are available for 1-2-3, the Wysiwyg menu is not available for use until you load and start the program, unless you installed Wysiwyg when you loaded 1-2-3. To choose a command from the Wysiwyg menu, make certain that 1-2-3 is in READY mode, and press :.

When you press :, the mode indicator in the upper right corner of the screen changes to WYSIWYG, and the Wysiwyg main menu appears in the second line of the control panel.

The format of the Wysiwyg menu is similar to the 1-2-3 main menu, and you make menu selections the same way. You use first letters of commands, or highlight and press **Enter**, or use a mouse. Table 2.5 summarizes the selections on the Wysiwyg main menu.

Table 2.5 Selections on the Wysiwyg Main Menu	
Selection	*Description*
Worksheet	Sets column widths, row heights, and page breaks
Format	Adds boldface, italic, lines, shading, colors, fonts, and drop shadows
Graph	Inserts a graph into a worksheet range, enhances and sizes the graph and lets you edit a graph
Print	Prints the formatted worksheet or graph and specifies page layout and enhancement options
Display	Alters screen characteristics, such as colors, cell size, grid lines, and intensity; enables you to save Wysiwyg default settings
Special	Copies, moves, imports, and exports formats

Selection	Description
Text	Enables you to edit and align text as if you were using a miniature word processor
Named-Style	Assigns names to commonly used format combinations
Quit	Returns to READY mode

Objective 8: To Use the 1-2-3 Help System and On-Line Tutorial

The 1-2-3 Help System

1-2-3 has a context-sensitive help system. In other words, when you need clarification on a particular topic, you can press **F1** at any time and read the displayed information or select the topic you need from the list that appears. If you press **F1** while in READY mode, the Help Index appears. Choose any of the topics in the Help Index to get to the other Help screens. You can use the keyboard or the mouse to navigate through Help.

The On-Line Tutorial

Lotus offers a series of self-paced lessons in an on-screen tutorial called *1-2-3-Go!* The lessons are arranged in order of increasing difficulty and build on each other. The tutorial does not cover all 1-2-3's functions and commands, but it includes enough information to give you a basic understanding of the program. Before you use the tutorial, you must successfully install 1-2-3 on your hard disk; then you can invoke the tutorial from the C> prompt by typing **learn123** or **learnwys** (for the Wysiwyg tutorial).

Getting Started

Summary

This chapter presented the information you need to start and to exit 1-2-3. Accessing help, starting the on-line tutorial, and learning about your keyboard and mouse were also explained. You are now ready to build a spreadsheet, which is discussed in Chapter 3.

Testing Your Knowledge

True/False Questions

~~FALSE~~ 1. The largest part of the 1-2-3 screen is the control panel.
~~TRUE~~ 2. Most of the alphanumeric keys on the computer keyboard perform the same actions as those on a typewriter.
~~TRUE~~ 3. The control panel is the area on the screen above the frame.
~~FALSE~~ 4. The status indicators report the mode that is currently in effect.
~~TRUE~~ ~~FALSE~~ 5. The letters A to Z appear at the top of the screen when you start 1-2-3.

Multiple Choice Questions

1. The 1-2-3 display is divided into three main parts:
    A. worksheet, columns, and rows.
    B. control panel, worksheet area, and status line.
    C. worksheet, function keys, and help.
    D. worksheet area, frame, and rows.
2. The function keys
    A. resemble those on the typewriter.
    B. are used for entering numbers.
    C. are used for making menu choices.
    D. are used for special 1-2-3 functions.
3. The second line of the control panel displays the menu. The third line of the control panel
    A. displays the letters A to H.
    B. provides explanations of the current menu item.
    C. displays two different types of indicators.
    D. is the worksheet frame.

Testing Your Knowledge

4. To access the Help Index
   - A. press `F1` while in READY mode.
   - B. press `F1` after typing **@pmt**
   - C. type a **?** from the keyboard.
   - D. from the C> prompt, type **help**
5. To run the on-screen tutorial that comes with 1-2-3,
   - A. type **help** while at the C> prompt.
   - B. type **1-2-3help** while at the C> prompt.
   - C. type **learn123** while at the C> prompt.
   - D. press `F1` from anywhere in 1-2-3.

Fill-in-the-Blank Questions

1. _____ *F1* _____ [123 main menu / context-sensitive] help means that you can get clarification of a particular topic, not just general topics.
2. The _____ *cell* _____ [worksheet area] is where data that has been entered is displayed on the screen.
3. A single line located at the bottom of the 1-2-3 screen that displays information is called the _____ *status line* _____.
4. The _____ *control panel* _____ [READY] mode indicator will appear in the top right corner of the screen when data can be entered into the worksheet or whenever the menu can be invoked.
5. To access Help while in 1-2-3, you press the _____ *F1* _____ key.

Review: Short Projects

1. Using the 1-2-3 On-Line Tutorial

   Start the on-line tutorial. Walk through several menu choices to familiarize yourself with 1-2-3.

2. Starting and Exiting 1-2-3

   Start 1-2-3 using both methods described in exercises 1.1 and 1.2. Exit 1-2-3 using the methods described in exercise 2.1.

3. Using the 1-2-3 Help System

   Access the 1-2-3 Help System. Choose topics from the index that interest you.

Getting Started

Review: Long Projects

1. Becoming Familiar with the Keyboard

    Using the three-month budget that you created on paper in the Chapter 1 long project, enter the data into a 1-2-3 spreadsheet. Press `Enter` after each entry and use the arrow keys to move to the next location.

2. Using the Keyboard

    Using the bowling score spreadsheet that you created on paper in the Chapter 1 long project, enter the data into the 1-2-3 spreadsheet. Press `Enter` after each entry and use the arrow keys to move to the next location. Notice that you must type in the total and average after you have figured it out. The next chapter shows you how to have 1-2-3 perform mathematical tasks for you.

Introducing Worksheet Basics

3

In this chapter, you learn some of the simpler operations in 1-2-3—entering and editing data; using formulas and functions; copying data; and naming, saving, retrieving, and printing files.

In this chapter, you build a sample spreadsheet that uses formulas and functions to compute totals of rows and columns. You also learn to navigate the Lotus 1-2-3 menus by making menu choices, such as printing, saving, and retrieving the sample spreadsheet.

Objectives

1. To Enter and Edit Data
2. To Enter Formulas and Functions
3. To Use the Undo Feature in Releases 2.2, 2.3, and 2.4
4. To Name, Save, Print, and Retrieve Files

Introducing Worksheet Basics

Key Terms in This Chapter	
Cursor	The underscore that appears inside the cell pointer or within the control panel in EDIT mode.
Range name	An alphanumeric name given to a cell or a rectangular group of cells.
Menu pointer	The rectangular bar that highlights menu commands.
Cell pointer	The rectangular bar that highlights the current cell location.
Data	Labels or values entered into a worksheet cell.
Label	A text entry entered in the worksheet.
Value	A number or formula entered in the worksheet.
Label prefix	A single aligning character typed before a label.
Operator	A mathematical or logical symbol that specifies an action to be performed on data.
Order of precedence	The order in which an equation or formula is executed; determines which operators act first.
Wild card	A character, such as a question mark (?) or asterisk (*), that represents any other single character or multiple characters.
Dialog box	A message box that shows you current options for a command and enables you to change those options on-screen.

Objective 1: To Enter and Edit Data

You can enter data into a cell by using the cell pointer to highlight the cell, and then typing the entry into the cell. To complete the entry, press **Enter** or any of the direction keys. If you press a direction key to complete the entry, the cell pointer also moves one cell in the indicated direction. Using this method eliminates one step in data entry operations because you do not need to press **Enter** and a direction key after every entry.

If you enter data into a cell that already contains data, the new data replaces the original data.

1-2-3 has two types of cell entries: labels and values. Labels are text entries, and values can be numbers or formulas (including functions, which 1-2-3 treats as built-in formulas). The first character you enter determines the type of entry. 1-2-3 treats your entry as a value (a number or a formula) when you start with one of the following characters:

0 1 2 3 4 5 6 7 8 9 + - . (@ # $

When you begin your entry with a character other than one of the preceding ones, 1-2-3 treats your entry as a label.

You can use a value—whether a number, formula, or function—for calculating purposes. A label is a collection of characters and cannot logically be used in a calculation.

Entering Labels

Commonly used in 1-2-3 for row and column headings, titles, explanations, and notes, labels play an important role in worksheet development. Without labels in a worksheet, you have no way of knowing what the numbers mean. Not only do labels give the values in a worksheet meaning, they also help you find information quickly.

A label can be up to 240 characters long and can contain any string of characters and numbers. A label that is too long for the width of a cell is displayed across the cells to the right, as long as the neighboring cells contain no other entries. If you enter numbers as labels, you cannot perform any calculations on those numbers.

When you make an entry into a cell and the first character does not indicate a value entry, 1-2-3 assumes that you are entering a label, and 1-2-3 shifts to LABEL mode.

You can control how labels appear in the cell. By preceding a text entry with a label prefix, you can tell 1-2-3 to left-justify (´), center (^), right-justify ("), or repeat (\) a label when it is displayed.

Introducing Worksheet Basics

Aligning Labels

Because the default position for displaying labels is left-justified, you don't have to type the label prefix when entering most labels—1-2-3 automatically supplies it for you after you press **Enter**. When your labels consist of numbers followed by text (as in addresses), you must use a label prefix before 1-2-3 accepts the entry into a cell.

To align labels as you enter them into the worksheet, you must first type a label prefix. Use the following label prefixes for label alignment:

Prefix	Function
'	Left-justifies
"	Right-justifies
^	Centers

Exercise 1.1: Entering Labels into the Spreadsheet

Labels explain the numbers that will be calculated; labels are an important part of any worksheet. To enter the months across the top of a budget, follow these steps:

1. Move the cell indicator to cell B1, type **Jan**, and then press ⏎Enter. Notice that Jan in the control panel has an apostrophe (') in front of it. The apostrophe is the default prefix and denotes that the entry is left-justified.
2. Press →.
3. Type ^**Feb**, and then press →. Notice that you don't need to press ⏎Enter and an arrow—just pressing an arrow saves you a keystroke.
4. Type "**Mar** and then press ⏎Enter. Notice that the three labels are located in their three columns differently because of the label prefixes.
5. Press / to display the menu.
6. Select **R**ange **E**rase.
7. Press ← until Mar, Feb, and Jan are all highlighted, and then press ⏎Enter.
8. In cell B1, type **Jan**, and press →.
9. Type **Feb**, and press →.
10. Type **Mar** and press ⏎Enter.
11. Press / to display the menu, and then choose **R**ange **L**abel **R**ight. Press ← to highlight Feb and Jan, and press ⏎Enter (see fig. 3.1).

To Enter and Edit Data

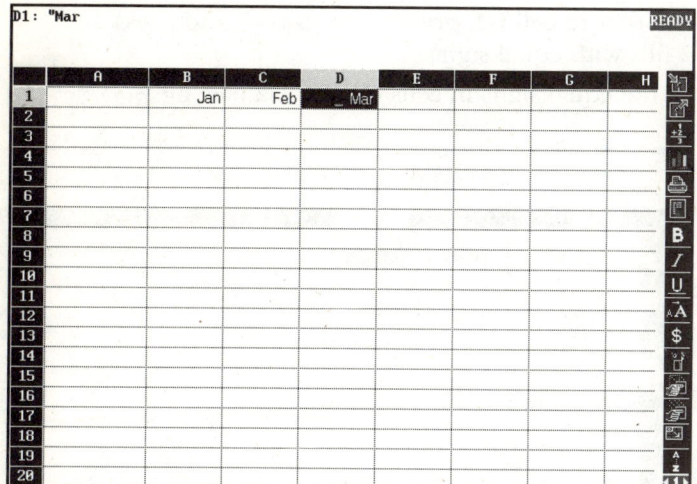

Fig. 3.1
The /Range Label command moves all the highlighted labels at once.

With this method, you can type your text and align it all at one time without having to type label prefixes.

An additional label prefix is available for repeating one or more characters in a single cell. You can use the repeat character—a backslash ( )—to create a separator line that fills an entire cell, for example (see fig. 3.2).

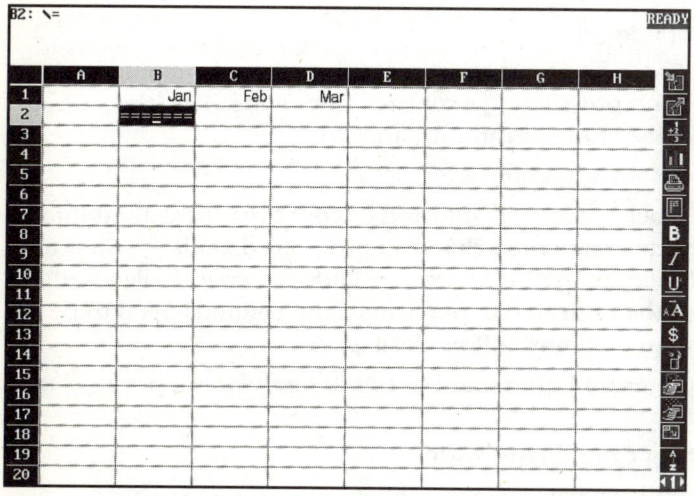

Fig. 3.2
The \ key is the repeat key.

53

Introducing Worksheet Basics

12. Move your cell pointer to cell B2, press [\], press [=], and press [↵Enter]. Cell B2 fills with equal signs.
13. Press [→] and put the equal signs in cells C2 and D2 (see fig. 3.3).

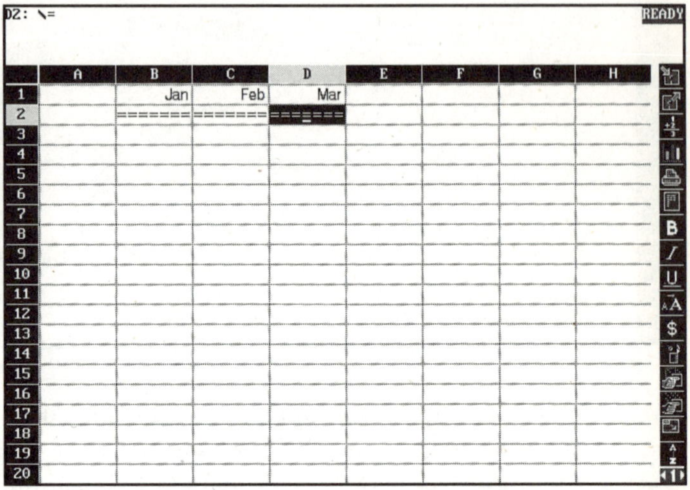

Fig. 3.3
The equal signs appear in all three cells.

Next, you create a budget for the three months.

14. Move the cell pointer to cell A3.
15. Type **Rent**, and press [↓].
16. In cell A4, type **Car**, and press [↓]. Repeat this process by typing the following labels and pressing [↓] after each one: **Food**, **Utilities**, **Student Loan**, **VISA**, **Entertainment**, and **Tuition**.
17. In cell A11, type **Books**, and press [↵Enter].

    Notice that the labels Student Loan and Entertainment extend into column B. All columns are nine characters wide by default. If you want labels that are longer than nine characters and you want to place data in the column to the right of the long labels, the columns need to be widened. To widen columns, follow these steps:

18. With the cell pointer on Entertainment (the longest label), press [/] to display the menu.
19. Choose **W**orksheet **C**olumn **S**et-Width.
20. Press [→] until you have completely highlighted the label Entertainment, and then press [↵Enter]. All of column A is widened (see fig. 3.4).

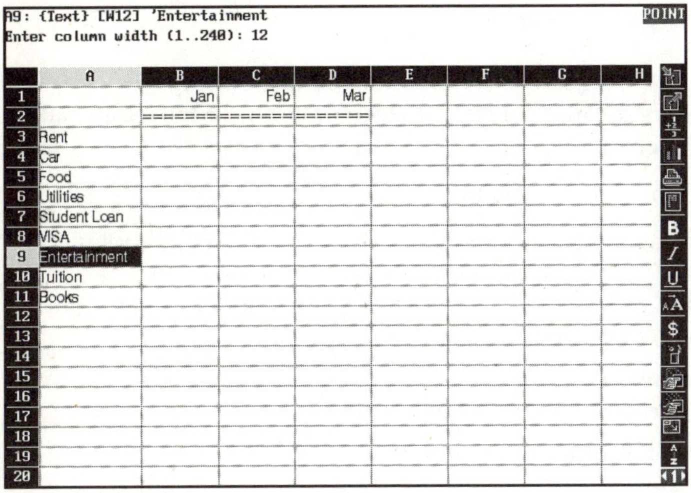

To Enter and Edit Data

Fig. 3.4
Column A is now wide enough for the long text label.

If you are using Release 2.4, you also can align text in a cell by using the mouse and SmartIcons.

Skip

Exercise 1.2: Aligning Text in Release 2.4

Using SmartIcons is a fast way to work in 1-2-3. Follow these steps to align text using SmartIcons:

1. Move the cell pointer to cell B1.
2. Highlight the cells that you want to align by dragging the mouse pointer to cell D1.
3. Choose one of the following alignment SmartIcons:

Wysiwyg	Non-Wysiwyg	Alignment
	←L	Left
	←C→	Center
	R→	Right
		Align across columns

55

Introducing Worksheet Basics

Entering Numbers

As you know, values in 1-2-3 consist of numbers and formulas. 1-2-3 worksheets use numbers for many different types of applications—especially those that involve data entry.

The following rules apply to entering numbers:

- A number must begin with a numeral 0 through 9, a decimal point, a minus sign (–), or a dollar sign ($). If you type a plus sign (+) or dollar sign ($) before a number or if you enter a number in parentheses, the + and the ( ) do not appear in the cell.
- You can end a number with a percent sign (%), which causes 1-2-3 to divide the number preceding the sign by 100.
- A number cannot have more than one decimal point.
- You can enter a number in scientific notation, which is called Sci format in 1-2-3 (for example, 1.234E+06).
- You cannot enter spaces after numbers.
- You cannot begin a number entry with one or more spaces. If you do, 1-2-3 treats the entry as a label. This mistake does not cause an immediate error message, but 1-2-3 treats the cell contents as zero the next time the number is used in a formula.

If you don't follow these rules, 1-2-3 beeps when you press **Enter** and automatically shifts to EDIT mode as if you had pressed Edit (**F2**).

Exercise 1.3: Entering Numbers

To add number data to the budget worksheet, follow these steps:

1. Move the cell pointer to cell B3.
2. Type **600** for January's rent, and press ↓.
3. Type **250** in cell B4, and press ↓. Repeat this process by typing the following entries, and pressing ↓ after each one: **250** in cell B5, **150** in cell B6, **120** in cell B7, **50** in cell B8, **20** in cell B9, **500** in cell B10, and **200** in cell B11.

Notice that all numbers are right-justified in the column (see fig. 3.5). Don't ever edit a worksheet by changing the alignment of the numbers. If 1-2-3 finds a label prefix in front of a number, 1-2-3 treats the number as a label, and you cannot perform calculations on a label.

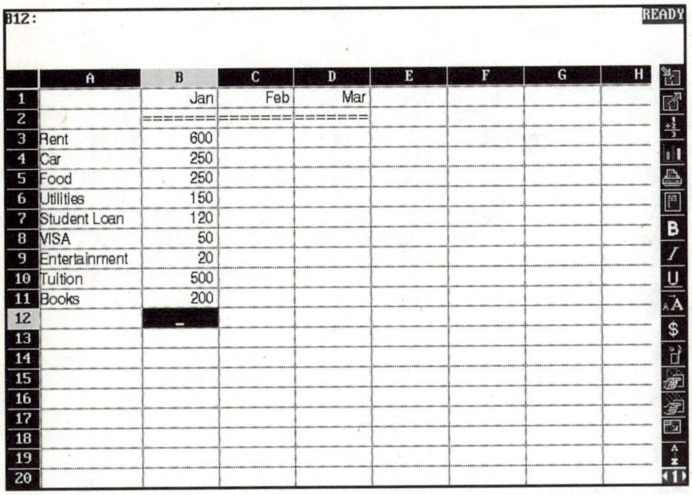

To Enter Formulas and Functions

Fig. 3.5
All numbers are right-justified in the column.

To quickly enter the next two months of numbers into the worksheet, you can use the Copy option. Follow these steps:

1. Move the cell pointer to cell B3, and press [/] to display the menu.
2. Choose Copy. The Copy What? prompt appears in the control panel.
3. Press [↓] until all the numbers in column B are highlighted, that is, to cell B11. Press [↵Enter]. The To Where? prompt appears in the control panel.
4. Press [→] once, moving the cell pointer to cell C3.
5. Type a period (.), press [→] a second time to highlight cell D3, and press [↵Enter]. Your budget should have data for all three months (see fig. 3.6).

Objective 2: To Enter Formulas and Functions

In addition to simple values, you can enter formulas into cells. You can enter formulas by typing the formula into the cell. You also can use the keyboard or the mouse to point to cells; 1-2-3 then enters the cell addresses for you.

57

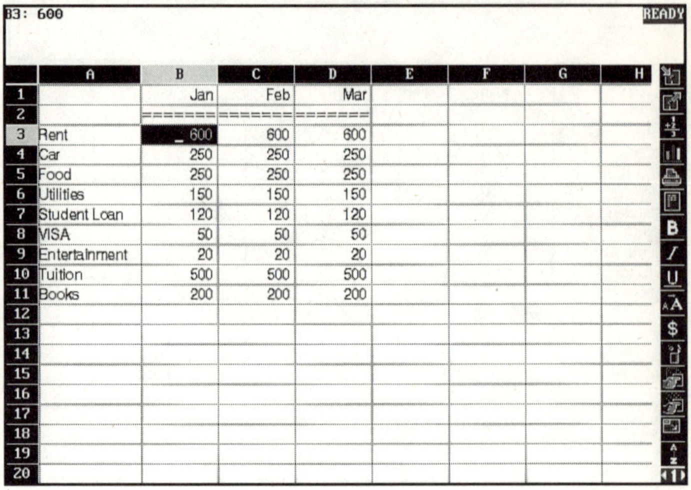

Introducing Worksheet Basics

Fig. 3.6
The first month's contents have been copied to the other two months.

Exercise 2.1: Entering Formulas

When you create a budget using 1-2-3, you don't use a calculator to add the totals. You simply tell 1-2-3 to add the contents of the cell locations. Follow these steps:

1. Move your cell pointer to cell E1, type **Total**, and press ↓.
2. Press \, type =, and press ↓.
3. In cell E3, type + to tell 1-2-3 that a formula is following. Notice that the mode indicator switches to VALUE.
4. Type **B3+C3+D3** and press ↵Enter. Notice that when you press ↵Enter, you see the results in the cell E3, but the control panel shows the formula that gives the results (see fig. 3.7).

   You also can enter a formula with cell addresses by pointing to the cell locations.

5. Move the cell pointer to cell E4 and type +.
6. Press ← to move to cell B4 and type +. Notice that your cell pointer moves immediately from cell B4 back to cell E4.
7. Move the cell pointer to cell C4 and type +.
8. Move to cell D4, and press ↵Enter to complete the formula. Notice that the mode indicator in the upper right corner of the screen changes from VALUE to POINT as you move the cell pointer. Also notice that the second line of the control panel builds the formula as you move the cell pointer and type the plus signs.

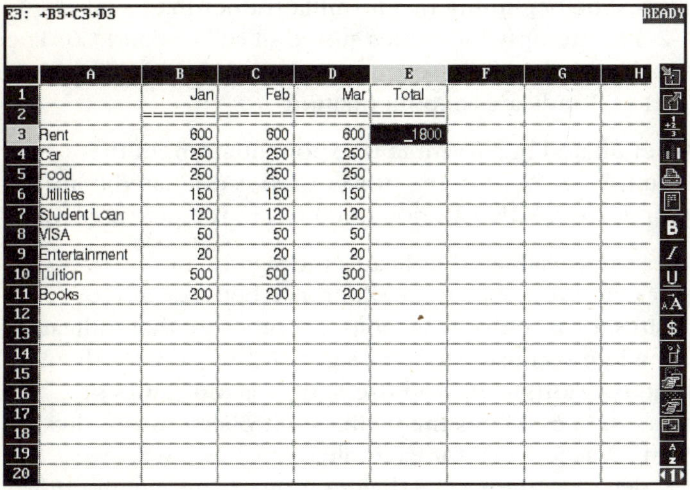

	A	B	C	D	E	F	G	H
1		Jan	Feb	Mar	Total			
2		=======	=======	=======	=======			
3	Rent	600	600	600	1800			
4	Car	250	250	250				
5	Food	250	250	250				
6	Utilities	150	150	150				
7	Student Loan	120	120	120				
8	VISA	50	50	50				
9	Entertainment	20	20	20				
10	Tuition	500	500	500				
11	Books	200	200	200				
12								
13								
14								
15								
16								
17								
18								
19								
20								

Fig. 3.7
The formula is displayed in the control panel and the result is displayed in the spreadsheet.

When you write formulas, use the method that works best for you. You probably will want to use pointing when cells are close to the one you are defining and use typing when referencing distant cells. Both methods produce the same results; you can mix and match the two techniques in the same formula.

Using Mathematical Operators in Formulas

Operators are mathematical or logical symbols that indicate arithmetic operations in formulas. The following list shows the mathematical operators:

Operator	*Meaning*
^	Exponentiation
+,–	Positive, negative
*, /	Multiplication, division
+,–	Addition, subtraction

This list indicates, from the top down, the order of precedence—the order in which these operators are evaluated. Exponentiation (the power of a number) takes place before multiplication, for example, and division occurs before subtraction. Operations inside parentheses are always evaluated first, and operators at the same level of precedence are evaluated in order from left to right.

Consider the following formula:

+F4*C6–G2^C7

Introducing Worksheet Basics

The plus sign (+) indicates the beginning of a formula (rather than a label). The asterisk (*) tells 1-2-3 to multiply the values stored in cells F4 and C6. The minus sign (–) subtracts the results of the second element (G2^C7) from the first (+F4*C6). The caret (^) indicates exponentiation.

The first operator to be evaluated in a formula is exponentiation. In the formula 8+2^3, for example, 2^3 (2 to the power of 3) is evaluated before the addition. The answer is 16 (8+2*2*2), not 1,000 (10 to the power of 3).

The next set of operators to be evaluated indicates the sign of a value (whether it is positive or negative). Notice the difference between a + or – sign that indicates a positive or negative value and a + or – sign that indicates addition or subtraction. When you use + or – as signs, 1-2-3 evaluates them before multiplication and division; when you use + or – as indicators of addition and subtraction, 1-2-3 evaluates them after multiplication and division. 1-2-3 evaluates 5+4/–2 as 5+(–2), for example, with 3 as the answer. The – sign indicates that 2 is negative; then 1-2-3 divides 4 by –2, and finally adds 5 to –2, resulting in the answer of 3.

You can use parentheses to override the order of precedence. Consider the order of precedence in the following formulas, in which cell B3 contains the value 2, cell C3 contains the value 3, and cell D3 contains the value 4. Notice how parentheses affect the order of precedence and the results in the first two formulas.

Formula	Evaluation	Result
+C3–D3/B3	3–(4/2)	1
(C3–D3)/B3	(3–4)/2	–0.5
+D3*C3–B3^C3	(4*3)–(2^3)	4
+D3*C3*B3/B3^C3–25/5	((4*3*2)/(2^3))–(25/5)	–2

Correcting Errors in Formulas

You probably will make errors when you enter formulas—especially when you enter formulas that are complex. 1-2-3 provides ways to help you discover and correct the inevitable errors.

When you try to enter a formula that contains a logical or mathematical error, the program beeps, changes to EDIT mode, and moves the cursor to the section of the formula where the problem most likely exists. You then can correct the error and continue entering the formula.

To Enter Formulas and Functions

Common errors in built-in formulas (functions) include omitting a parenthesis or commas. The error that appears to be a logical one may be only a missing punctuation mark. When 1-2-3 beeps to indicate a formula error, check the formula for a missing parenthesis or comma near the cursor.

Using Functions in Calculations

Like most electronic spreadsheets, 1-2-3 includes built-in functions. These functions fall into the following eight basic categories: Mathematical and trigonometrical, Date and time, Financial, Statistical, Database, Logical, String, and Special.

Entering a 1-2-3 Function

Functions consist of three parts: the @ sign, a function name, and one or more arguments enclosed in parentheses. An argument can contain the range of the cells that the function will use.

Consider the following function:

   @SUM(B3..D3)

The @SUM function computes the total of the values in cells B3 through D3. Notice that you need to type only the beginning and ending locations separated by a period. The @ sign signals that the entry is a function. SUM is the name of the function being used. (You can enter function names by typing upper- or lowercase letters; this book uses uppercase letters to denote 1-2-3 functions.)

A function's arguments, which are always enclosed in parentheses, specify the cell or range of cells on which the function will act. In the example, the argument is the range B3..D3. This function tells 1-2-3 to compute the sum of the numbers in cells B3, C3, and D3. When you enter a function that requires a cell address, you can enter the address by typing or pointing.

Exercise 2.2: Adding Cells with the @SUM Function

You wrote a formula to calculate the first two totals. In 1-2-3, there are built-in functions to perform many mathematical operations. To add a total using a built-in function, follow these steps:

1. Move the cell pointer to cell E5, type @SUM(B5.D5), and press Enter. Notice that the cell displays the results and the control panel displays the formula that makes use of @SUM (see fig. 3.8).

Introducing Worksheet Basics

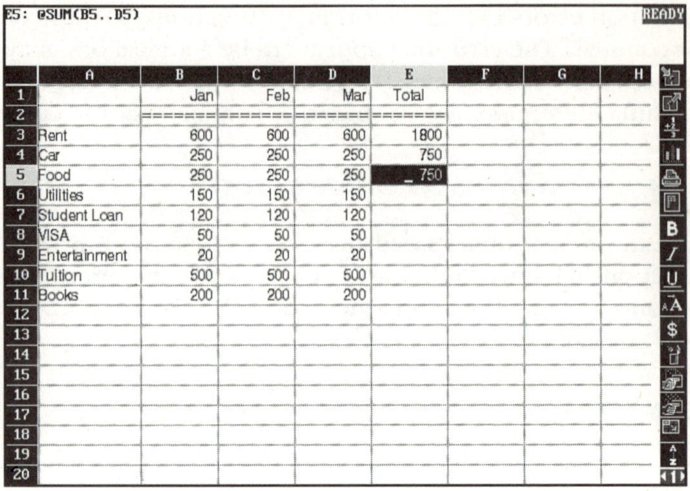

Fig. 3.8
@SUM adds the range in the parentheses.

2. Move the cell pointer to cell E6, and type **@SUM(**.
3. Move the cell pointer to cell B6, and press [.].
4. Press [→] two times.
5. Type the closing parenthesis (**)**), and press [⏎Enter] (see fig. 3.9).

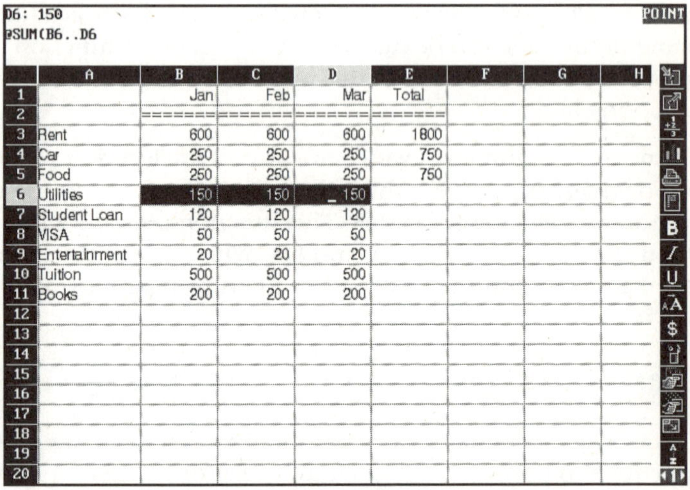

Fig. 3.9
You highlight the range that you want to calculate.

6. If you are using Release 2.4, go on to the next section; otherwise, use each method for calculating the totals previously explained to complete column E's totals (see fig. 3.10).

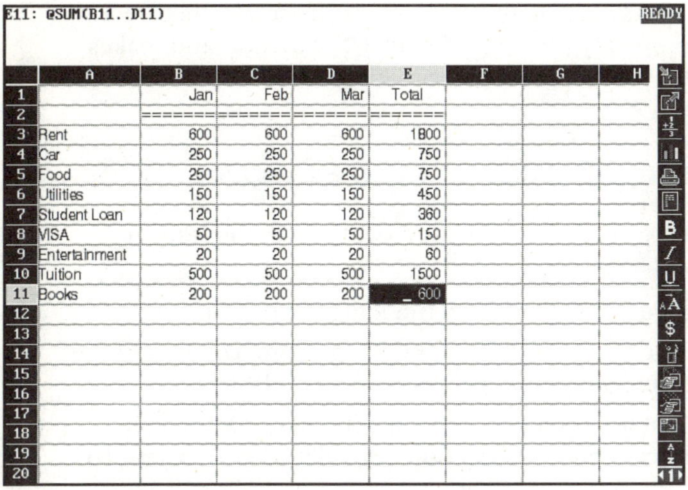

E11: @SUM(B11..D11) READY

	A	B	C	D	E	F	G	H
1		Jan	Feb	Mar	Total			
2		=======	=======	=======	=======			
3	Rent	600	600	600	1800			
4	Car	250	250	250	750			
5	Food	250	250	250	750			
6	Utilities	150	150	150	450			
7	Student Loan	120	120	120	360			
8	VISA	50	50	50	150			
9	Entertainment	20	20	20	60			
10	Tuition	500	500	500	1500			
11	Books	200	200	200	600			
12								
13								
14								
15								
16								
17								
18								
19								
20								

Fig. 3.10
Enter a formula to calculate the total for the rest of the items.

7. Move the cell pointer to cell B12, type **+B3+B4+B5+B6+B7+B8+B9+B10+B11**, and press ↵ to enter a formula to calculate January's budget. Notice how much you had to type to enter this formula. The advantage of the @SUM function is that it reduces the amount of typing you have to do.
8. In cell C12, type **@SUM(C3.C11)**.
9. Use either of the addition methods—the @SUM function or adding the cells individually—to total the values in columns D and E (see fig. 3.11).

F12: READY

	A	B	C	D	E	F	G	H
1		Jan	Feb	Mar	Total			
2		=======	=======	=======	=======			
3	Rent	600	600	600	1800			
4	Car	250	250	250	750			
5	Food	250	250	250	750			
6	Utilities	150	150	150	450			
7	Student Loan	120	120	120	360			
8	VISA	50	50	50	150			
9	Entertainment	20	20	20	60			
10	Tuition	500	500	500	1500			
11	Books	200	200	200	600			
12		2140	2140	2140	6420			
13								
14								
15								
16								
17								
18								
19								
20								

Fig. 3.11
All the columns are now totaled.

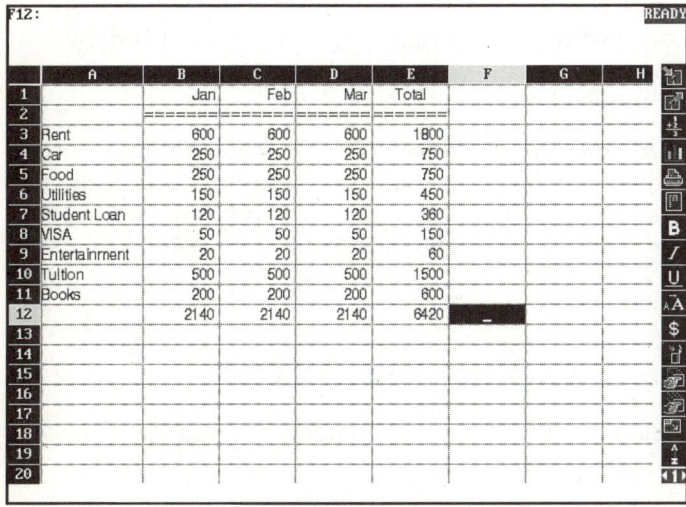

Introducing Worksheet Basics

1-2-3 Release 2.4 offers another method of calculating totals. Release 2.4's Range Sum SmartIcon quickly performs the @SUM function and makes finding the total of the values in a range easy.

Exercise 2.3: Using the Range Sum SmartIcon

To use the Range Sum icon to total rows and columns in the budget worksheet, follow these steps:

1. Highlight the range B7..E7 and click the Range Sum icon.
2. Highlight the range B8..E8 and click the Range Sum icon. Continue this process one cell at a time through range B11..E11.
3. Move the cell pointer to cell B12 and click the Range Sum icon. Continue this process one cell at a time for cells C12, D12, and E12.

Using the Edit Key (F2)

To use the Edit key (F2) to edit data, move the cell pointer to the appropriate cell and press **F2**. The mode indicator changes to EDIT. 1-2-3 copies the contents of the cell to the second line of the control panel (the edit line), the cursor appears at the end of the entry, and 1-2-3 is ready for your edit of the data.

When you first press **F2**, 1-2-3 is in insert mode. 1-2-3 inserts any new characters you type at the cursor and pushes any characters on the right side of the cursor one position to the right. If you activate overtype mode by pressing **Ins**, any new character you type replaces the character directly above the cursor, and the cursor moves one position to the right. When 1-2-3 is in overtype mode, the indicator OVR appears at the bottom of the screen. Pressing **Ins** again toggles 1-2-3 back to insert mode.

If you have a typing error, you don' need to retype the whole formula, just correct the error. You can delete the error and type the correct text, using the same editing and directional keys you use to enter data and move around the spreadsheet. Then press **Enter** to complete the edit and return 1-2-3 to READY mode.

Exercise 2.4: Editing the Contents of a Cell

The F2 (Edit) key is an easy way to change cell contents without having to retype the entry. Follow these steps:

To Use the Undo Feature in Releases 2.2, 2.3, and 2.4

1. Move to cell B8.
2. Press `F2`.
3. Press `Home` to move the cursor to the beginning of the entry.
4. Type **1**, and press `↵Enter` to complete the edit.

Wysiwyg Editing for Releases 2.3 and 2.4 *(Skip)*

The **:Text Edit** command on the Wysiwyg menu (also available with the Edit Text icon) provides you with additional editing features. With this command, you can enter and edit a range of labels in the worksheet (rather than in the control panel). The process is similar to that of editing a paragraph in a word processing program because Wysiwyg treats the range that you specify for editing as a "paragraph." Also, when you select a range to edit, the text wraps to the next line as you type; you don't have to press **Enter** at the end of each line.

When you choose **:Text Edit** and specify a cell or range of cells, a vertical-line cursor appears in front of the first character in the label in the worksheet. The entry does not appear in the control panel. Move the cursor by using the arrow keys on the keyboard or by clicking the triangle icons with the mouse if SmartIcons are not attached. Delete characters by pressing **Del** or **Backspace**; insert characters by typing them from the keyboard. Complete the edit by pressing **Esc** or by clicking the right mouse button. When you finish, the format reference {Text} appears in the cell contents line of the control panel.

By using the **:Text Edit** command, you can edit a range of data in the worksheet area (see fig. 3.12).

Objective 3: To Use the Undo Feature in Releases 2.2, 2.3, and 2.4

When you use electronic spreadsheet packages, you can destroy hours of work by using the wrong commands or typing over existing entries.

The Undo feature, which you can activate by pressing **Alt+F4** (hold down **Alt** and press **F4**), in most cases returns the worksheet to its previous appearance and condition before the most recent command or entry. You can undo only the last command. If you change your mind about what was just undone, you can press Undo (**Alt+F4**) again to reverse the undo.

Introducing Worksheet Basics

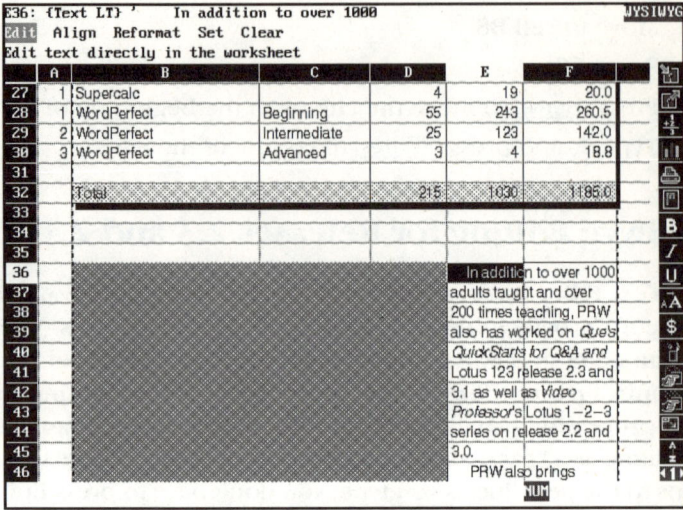

Fig. 3.12
Editing a range of cells.

In Release 2.4 you can choose the Undo SmartIcon to undo an action. You cannot use the keyboard to access the Undo SmartIcon, however.

Activating and Deactivating Undo

Initially, the Undo feature is disabled. To turn on the Undo feature, choose /**W**orksheet **G**lobal **D**efault **O**ther **U**ndo **E**nable.

To make the change permanent—so that the Undo feature is active each time you access 1-2-3—you must choose /**W**orksheet **G**lobal **D**efault **U**pdate before you exit 1-2-3. You can use the /**W**orksheet **G**lobal **D**efault **S**tatus command to determine whether the Undo feature is enabled, or you can look at the Default Settings dialog box. When the Undo feature is available, the UNDO status indicator appears when 1-2-3 is in READY mode (see fig. 3.13).

For the Undo feature to work, 1-2-3 creates a temporary backup copy of the entire worksheet whenever you start a command or cell entry. This information is stored in your computer's temporary memory (RAM). Storing this data takes up space and limits the size of the worksheet you can build.

If you become accustomed to the Undo feature and rely on it heavily for security, avoid building worksheets so large that they prevent your use of Undo. An alternative to using Undo is to make sure that you save your file before attempting a command with which you are not familiar.

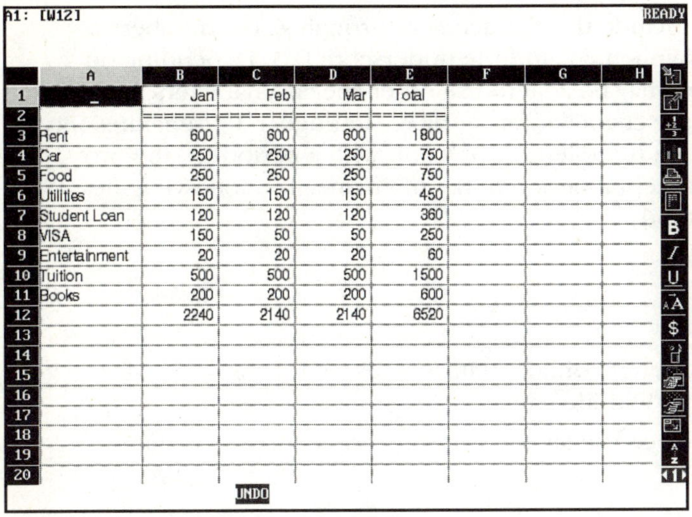

Fig. 3.13
The UNDO status indicator.

What Cannot Be Undone?

You cannot undo some commands. You cannot "unerase," "unsave," or "unextract" a disk file; nor can you "unprint" your last printed output.

You can undo most other commands, however, including the entire sequence of commands associated with creating graphs, setting up ranges for data query commands, and all "undo-able" steps embedded in a macro.

Objective 4: To Name, Save, Print, and Retrieve Files

The sections that follow explain file operations that beginning 1-2-3 users need most often: naming, saving, printing, and retrieving files.

Naming Files

1-2-3 file names can be up to eight characters long with a three-character extension (see fig. 3.14).

Adhere to the following basic rules when naming files:

Introducing Worksheet Basics

- File names can include the characters A through Z, the numbers 0 through 9, the hyphen (-), and the underscore (_). Depending on your system, you may be able to use other special characters, but 1-2-3 will not accept the characters <,>, or *. Although 1-2-3 separates the file name from the three-letter extension with a period (.), the program does not accept a period in the file name. The following file names are not valid:

    CH<15>.Wk1
    TOM*BBS.PRN
    SALES.91.WK1

- File names should not contain blank spaces. SALES RPT.WK1, for example, is not a valid file name.
- 1-2-3 converts lowercase letters to uppercase letters in file names.

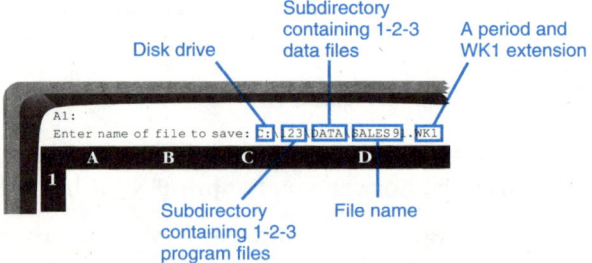

Fig. 3.14
Parts of a file name.

You determine the eight-character file name, but 1-2-3 creates the extension based on the file format. The following is a list of the basic file extensions 1-2-3 uses:

- WK1 is the extension automatically added to names of worksheet files saved with the /File Save command. If you choose to back up an existing file while you save it, -2-3 assigns the BAK extension to the previous version of the file.
- PRN is the extension automatically added to names of 1-2-3 files that you save in text (ASCII) format with the /Print File command. PRN files can be printed or imported into 1-2-3 and other programs.
- PIC is the extension 1-2-3 automatically adds to names of graph files saved with the /Graph Save command. You must issue this command after creating the file in 1-2-3 and before printing the graph from 1-2-3's PrintGraph program.
- FMT is the extensions that 1-2-3 automatically adds to the names of files when you have Wysiwyg loaded. 1-2-3 creates both an FMT and WK1 file when you use :File Save with Wysiwyg.

ENC is the extension 1-2-3 automatically adds to names of files that you save in encoded format with the /Print Encoded command. Encoded files can be printed from DOS.

Note: Release 2.4 can read older 1-2-3 worksheets with WKS extensions, but 1-2-3 writes the new files with WK1 extensions when you save the worksheet. If you want to run WK1 files with earlier versions of 1-2-3, you need to use the Translate Utility. If you want to use a Release 3.*x* file (extension WK3) in Release 2.4, the file must first be saved with the WK1 extension from in 1-2-3 Release 3.*x*. If you use this procedure, however, certain formatting created in Release 3.*x* may be lost in the translation.

Remember to be descriptive when you think of a name for the new file. Choose a file name that tells something about the file's contents. This practice prevents confusion after you have created several different files and need to access a particular file quickly. Figure 3.15 shows some good examples of file names.

Fig. 3.15
Examples of valid file names.

If you work with many different worksheets that contain basically the same information, you should use similar file names. If you use the name SALES92 for a sales worksheet for the year 1992, for example, you could use SALES93 and SALES94 as the names for the sales worksheets for 1993 and 1994, respectively. This naming technique will help you recall file names later.

Saving Files

With electronic spreadsheets—and with computer files in general—the risks of power outages or human errors can be costly in terms of data and time loss. If you exit 1-2-3 without saving your file, any work you have done since the last time you saved the file is lost. You can recover the data only by retyping it into the worksheet. You should make an effort, therefore, to save your files frequently—at least once every 30 to 60 minutes (depending on how many changes are made).

Introducing Worksheet Basics

Exercise 4.1: Using the Keyboard To Save a New File

To save a file in 1-2-3, follow these steps:

1. Choose /**F**ile **S**ave. When you save a new worksheet file, 1-2-3 automatically supplies a list of the worksheet files on the current drive and directory (see fig. 3.16).

Fig. 3.16
List of worksheet files on the current directory.

	A	B	C	D	E	F	G	H
		Jan	Feb	Mar	Total			
1		======	======	======	======			
2								
3	Rent	600	600	600	1800			
4	Car	250	250	250	750			
5	Food	250	250	250	750			
6	Utilities	150	150	150	450			
7	Student Loan	120	120	120	360			
8	VISA	150	50	50	250			
9	Entertainment	20	20	20	60			
10	Tuition	500	500	500	1500			
11	Books	200	200	200	600			
12		2240	2140	2140	6520			

(Control panel: `List ◄ ► ▲ ▼ ? .. A: B: C: H:` FILES / `Enter name of file to save: C:\123R24\DATA\*.wk1` / `92BUDGET.WK1  93BUDGET.WK1  94BUDGET.WK1  94SALES.WK1  AMORTSCH.WK1`)

2. Type **BUDGET**, and press ⏎**Enter**. 1-2-3 automatically supplies a WK1 extension for a new file and saves the file on disk.

   Notice that the drive on which the file is to be saved automatically precedes the file name BUDGET. 1-2-3 displays A:\, B:\, C:\123R24\DATA\ or the other disks or directories that, during installation, you instructed 1-2 3 to use when it saves your files.

To save a file that has already been saved, follow these steps:

1. Choose /**F**ile **S**ave. BUDGET.WK1 appears in the control panel. Press ⏎**Enter**. Another menu appears with the options **C**ancel, **R**eplace, and **B**ackup.

2. Choose **R**eplace, which updates the current file on disk.

You choose the **B**ackup option if you want to save the last changes made to an existing file. **B**ackup renames the older version of your file, using the same file name but adding BAK as the file extension. The current version of your file is then saved with the WK1 extension. This feature ensures that your two most recent worksheet versions are always available.

To Name, Save, Print, and Retrieve Files

In Release 2.4, you can save a file with an existing name by using the Save SmartIcon. This icon is usually the first icon on the icon palettes.

Printing the Worksheet

To print a worksheet that is in memory, you must specify what range you want to print and send it to the printer.

Exercise 4.2: Printing the Budget

To print the budget worksheet, follow these steps:

1. Make sure that your computer is attached to a printer and that the printer is turned on and is ready to print.
2. Press [Home] and choose /**P**rint **P**rinter **R**ange.
3. Type a (.), press → to highlight through column E, press ↓ to highlight through row 12 and press [↵Enter] (see fig. 3.17).

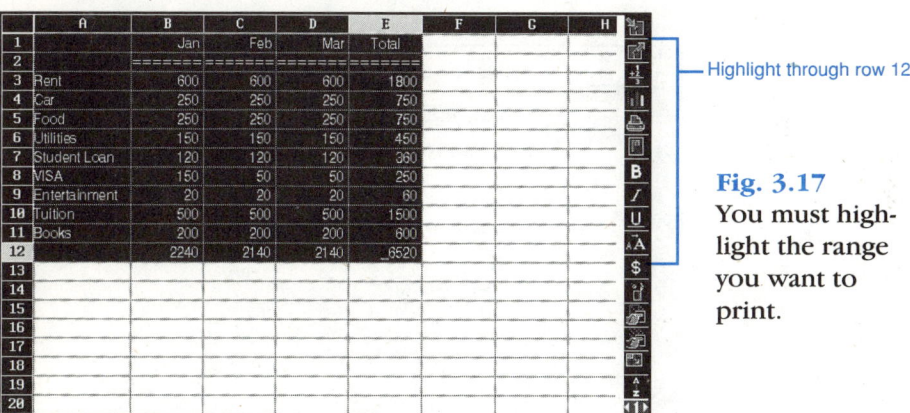

— Highlight through row 12

Fig. 3.17
You must highlight the range you want to print.

4. Choose **A**lign, which ensures that printing begins at the top of the page.
5. Choose **G**o to begin printing.

   You can choose **P**age (to advance the paper) and **Q**uit to return to READY mode.

71

3

Retrieving a File

When you return to 1-2-3 at another time, you may want to call a file back into memory from disk. If you are just starting 1-2-3, this command brings a new file into memory. Otherwise, the /File Retrieve command replaces the current file with the new file. Therefore, be sure that you have saved the current file with /File Save before you retrieve a new file. Releases 2.3 and 2.4 provide a prompt to warn you to save the file.

Warning: Releases 2.01 and 2.2 don't warn you to save the file before you load a different or new one.

Exercise 4.3: Retrieving a File

To retrieve the budget file from your disk to the screen, follow these steps:

1. Choose /File Retrieve, or click the Retrieve SmartIcon. 1-2-3 displays a partial list of worksheet files in the current drive and directory.
2. Move the highlight to BUDGET.WK1, and press ↵Enter (see fig. 3.18).

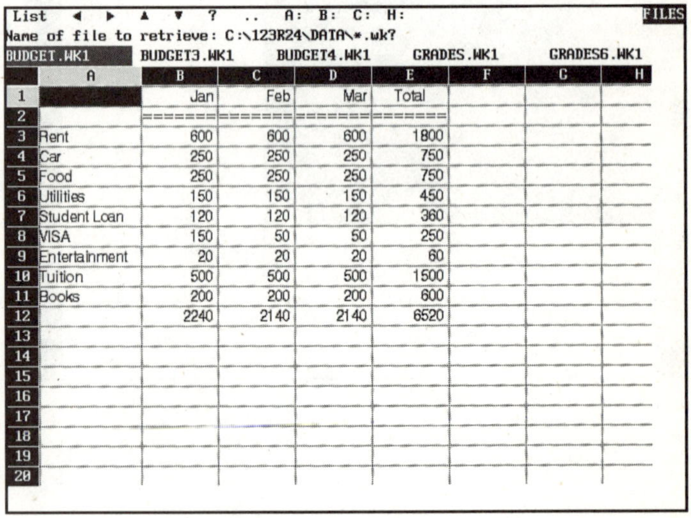

List ◄ ► ▲ ▼ ? .. A: B: C: H: FILES
Name of file to retrieve: C:\123R24\DATA*.wk?
BUDGET.WK1 BUDGET3.WK1 BUDGET4.WK1 GRADES.WK1 GRADES6.WK1

	A	B	C	D	E	F	G	H
1		Jan	Feb	Mar	Total			
2		=======	=======	=======	=======			
3	Rent	600	600	600	1800			
4	Car	250	250	250	750			
5	Food	250	250	250	750			
6	Utilities	150	150	150	450			
7	Student Loan	120	120	120	360			
8	VISA	150	50	50	250			
9	Entertainment	20	20	20	60			
10	Tuition	500	500	500	1500			
11	Books	200	200	200	600			
12		2240	2140	2140	6520			
13								
14								
15								
16								
17								
18								
19								
20								

Fig. 3.18
Highlight the name of the file you want to retrieve.

Retrieving Files from Subdirectories

1-2-3 keeps track of subdirectory names as well as file names. When you issue the /**F**ile **R**etrieve command, for example, 1-2-3 displays subdirectories of the current directory along with the file names. The backslash (\) symbol following a name (in a list of file names) indicates a subdirectory name.

When you select a subdirectory name, 1-2-3 displays the list of files in that subdirectory.

When you need to access a file that is on a different drive or a file that is in a different directory, choose /**F**ile **R**etrieve and press **Esc** or **Backspace**. When you press **Esc** while the default path name shows in the control panel, 1-2-3 changes to EDIT mode. You then can edit the file specification just as you edit any label entry. When you press **Esc** a second time, 1-2-3 erases the current drive and directory specification. You then can enter the specification for the drive and directory you want.

The following list illustrates some valid file names, including their drive and directory specifications:

File name	Description
B:\SAMPLE1.WK1	Worksheet file on drive B
C:\123R24\SAMPLE1.WK1	Worksheet file in subdirectory \123R24 on drive C
C:\123R24\DATA*.PIC	List of all PIC files in subdirectory DATA of subdirectory \123R24 on drive C. (1-2-3 displays the list and waits for you to select a specific file name.)
A:*.*	List of all files on drive A. (1-2-3 displays all file names and waits for you to select a specific file name.)

Summary

This chapter covers many important concepts that are essential for beginning 1-2-3 users, such as entering and editing data, formulas, and labels; and naming, saving, printing, and retrieving 1-2-3 files.

Introducing Worksheet Basics

Testing Your Knowledge

True/False Questions

 1. You can begin number entries with a ', ", or ^ to align them in the column.

 2. You can type a formula to add a group of cells by starting with a + sign and including all cell locations or by starting with @SUM and including the beginning and ending locations in parentheses.

 3. If you type the formula **+A3+B3*B12**, the contents of cell B3 are multiplied by the contents of cell B12 and the result added to cell A3.

 4. If you type the formula **(A3+B3)*B12**, the contents of cell A3 are added to the contents of cell B3 and the result is multiplied by the contents of cell B12.

 5. When you use **/F**ile **R**etrieve to load a file from disk, 1-2-3 adds that file to the file currently on-screen.

Multiple Choice Questions

1. When you save a file using **/F**ile **S**ave, 1-2-3 automatically gives it the three-letter extension
    - A. PIC.
    - B. WK1.
    - C. PRN.
    - D. DOC.

2. The Undo feature available in Releases 2.2, 2.3, and 2.4
    - A. remembers the last three commands.
    - B. must be used immediately because it remembers only the last command.
    - C. can undo absolutely everything you do.
    - D. doesn't require much memory to run.

3. To add the contents of the cells A4, A5, A6, and A7, you would use which of the following:
    - A. @SUM(A4.A7).
    - B. +A4+A5+A6+A7.
    - C. +A4.A7
    - D. either A or B.

Testing Your Knowledge

4. The function of [F2] is to
   A. activate Undo.
   B. act as the GoTo key.
   C. activate EDIT mode.
   D. replace the mouse for pointing.
5. The valid 1-2-3 file name in the list below is
   A. My file.wk1.
   B. My_file.wk1.
   C. My*file.wk1.
   D. My,file.wk1.

Fill-in-the-Blank Questions

1. When 1-2-3 is in ___READY___ mode, the program is waiting for you to enter data into the highlighted cell.
2. When you begin entering numerical data, 1-2-3 changes to ___EDIT___ mode. Value
3. To save the file on the screen over the file on the disk with the same name, choose ___REPLACE___ to update the file on disk.
4. When you press the ___F2___ key, 1-2-3 waits for you to change the contents of the highlighted cell.
5. The ___UNDO___ is a feature that enables you to bring back erased cells.

Review: Short Projects

1. Creating a Budget

   Create a small three-month budget of your own. Save the worksheet to disk as BUDGET94 and print it.
2. Creating a Bowling Spreadsheet

   Keep track of a bowling team's scores. Create a small worksheet listing the names of the players in column A and placing their three game scores in columns B, C, and D. Total the scores for each player and for each game. Save the worksheet to disk as GAME and print it.
3. Editing a Spreadsheet

   Retrieve either BUDGET94 or GAME. Edit the worksheet using [F2] to change entries. For example, change one of the bowler's names and scores. Save the spreadsheet under a different name and print it.

75

Introducing Worksheet Basics

Review: Long Projects

1. Creating a Checkbook Register

   Create a checkbook register that automatically adds deposits and deducts checks to create a running total (see fig. 3.19).

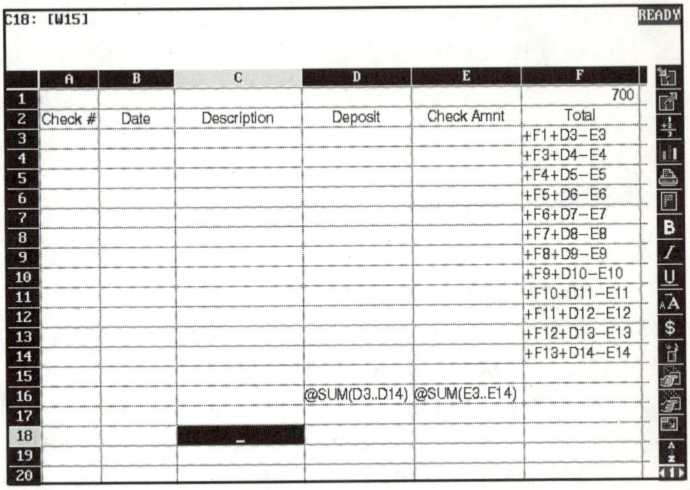

   Fig. 3.19
   Create a Checkbook register.

   You should start with a balance of $700, and include Check Number, Date, Description, Deposit Amount, Check Amount, and Total categories. Also total the deposits for the month, at the bottom of the worksheet. Save the blank (formulas and labels only) file to disk as CHKBOOK.WK1. Then put in at least 12 checks and 3 deposits. Save this as the current month, such as SEPT93.WK1, and print it.

2. Creating a Budget Worksheet

   Create a 12-month budget with formulas and labels only, and save it to disk as BUDFORM.WK1. Enter the values for the year, and save the worksheet with a different name, such as BUD94.WK1. Print the worksheet.

Modifying the Spreadsheet or a Range

4

This chapter shows you how to change part or all of the spreadsheet you are working on. You can, for example, erase all or just part of the spreadsheet; you can format the entire spreadsheet and change the format for smaller sections; you can widen all columns or just one or a few.

Objectives

1. To Understand the Range Concept in 1-2-3
2. To Understand the Worksheet Commands
3. To Format the Worksheet
4. To Insert and Delete Columns and Rows
5. To Recalculate the Worksheet

4

Modifying the Spreadsheet or a Range

Key Terms in This Chapter	
Range	A rectangular group of cells used in a worksheet operation.
Range commands	Commands used to manipulate cells in ranges. You can access the **R**ange commands through the /**R**ange option on the 1-2-3 main menu.
Worksheet commands	1-2-3 commands that affect the entire worksheet or certain defined areas of the worksheet. The /**W**orksheet command is found on the 1-2-3 main menu.
Range name	An alphanumeric name of up to 15 characters given to a rectangular group of cells.
Formatting	The process of changing the way data is displayed in the worksheet. Formatting is accomplished with the /**R**ange Format or /**W**orksheet **G**lobal **F**ormat commands, Wysiwyg, or SmartIcons.
Windows	Two separate screens that appear, either horizontally or vertically, after you execute the /**W**orksheet **W**indow command.
Automatic recalculation	A default 1-2-3 setting—the worksheet is calculated each time a cell's content changes.

Objective 1: To Understand the Range Concept in 1-2-3

1-2-3's definition of a *range* is a rectangular block of adjacent cells. The smallest possible range is one cell, and the largest is the entire worksheet. Ranges are specified by the cells in the upper left and lower right corners of the range, as shown in figure 4.1

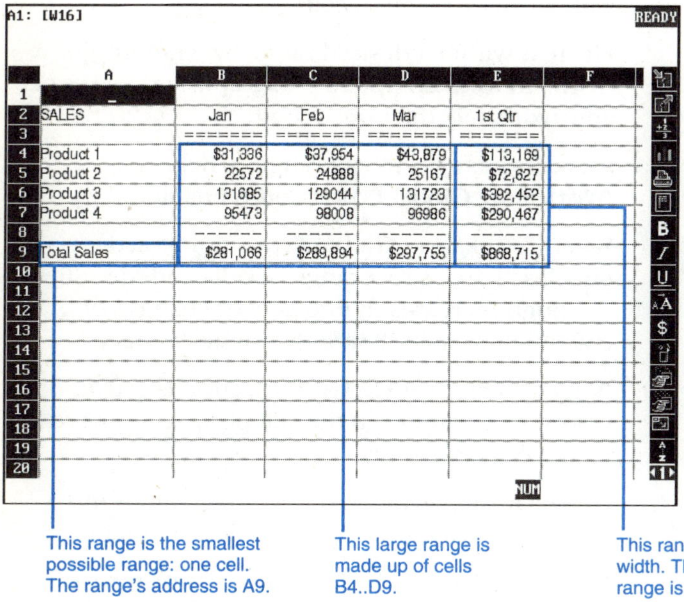

Fig. 4.1
Defining ranges.

This range is the smallest possible range: one cell. The range's address is A9.

This large range is made up of cells B4..D9.

This range is one column in width. The address for the range is E4..E9.

Access the range commands by selecting /**R**ange from the 1-2-3 main menu. You see the following menu of commands:

Format **L**abel **E**rase **N**ame **J**ustify **P**rot **U**nprot **I**nput **V**alue **T**rans **S**earch

Table 4.1 provides a brief description of the actions of each of these commands.

Modifying the Spreadsheet or a Range

Table 4.1 Selections on the /Range Menu	
Selection	*Description*
Format	Changes the display of values or formula results in a cell or range of cells
Label	Aligns text labels in a cell or range of cells
Erase	Deletes the contents of a cell or range of cells
Name	Assigns, modifies, or deletes a name associated with a cell or range of cells
Justify	Fits text within a desired range by wrapping words to form complete paragraphs with lines of approximately the same length
Prot (Protect)	Prevents changes to cell ranges when /Worksheet Global Protection is enabled
Unprot (Unprotect)	When /Worksheet Global Protection is active, enables changes to a range of cells and identifies (through increases in intensity or changes of color) which cells' contents can be changed
Input	When /Worksheet Global Protection is active, restricts movement of the cell pointer to unprotected cells in a range
Value	Copies formulas in a range to their values in another specified range (or the same range)
Trans (Transpose)	Reorders columns of data into rows or rows of data into columns
Search	Finds or replaces a string of data in a specified range

Designating a Range

Many commands act on ranges. The /Range Erase command, for example, prompts you for the range to erase. You can point to and highlight a range in commands and functions just as you can point to a single cell in a formula.

To Understand the Range Concept in 1-2-3

Following the prompt to enter a range, 1-2-3 displays the address of the cell pointer in the control panel. This single cell, shown as a one-cell range, is anchored. The default range with most /Range commands is an anchored one-cell range. When the cell is anchored, you highlight a range as you move the cell pointer. If the cell is not anchored, you can press the period key (.) to anchor the cell.

When a range is highlighted, the cells of the range appear in reverse video (or in a different color if you have a color monitor). Reverse video, or the use of a different color, allows ranges to be specified easily, with little chance for error. As you move the cell pointer, the reverse-video or colored rectangle expands until you finish specifying the range.

To clear an incorrectly highlighted range, press **Esc** or **Backspace**. If you press **Esc**, the highlight collapses to the anchored cell only, and the anchor is removed. If you press **Backspace**, the highlight collapses and the cell pointer moves to where you were when you started the command. In either case, you can then move the cell pointer to the correct location at the beginning of the range.

Exercise 1.1: Erasing a Range of Cells

When you have information in a spreadsheet that you want to erase, use the /Range Erase option. Follow these steps:

1. Retrieve the Budget spreadsheet that you created in the exercises in Chapter 3.

    The tuition and book expenses were entered incorrectly. That is, they were copied to Feb and Mar, but they are a one time expense in Jan, so the Feb and Mar entries should be erased.

2. Move the cell pointer to cell C10.
3. Choose **/R**ange **E**rase.
4. Press ⏎Enter to erase the contents of the single cell range C10. (You can erase more than one cell at a time by highlighting a range of cells.) Leave the cell pointer in cell C10.
5. Choose **/R**ange **E**rase.
6. Press →, ↓, and ⏎Enter. Notice that all the formulas recompute as the cells are erased, as shown in figure 4.2.

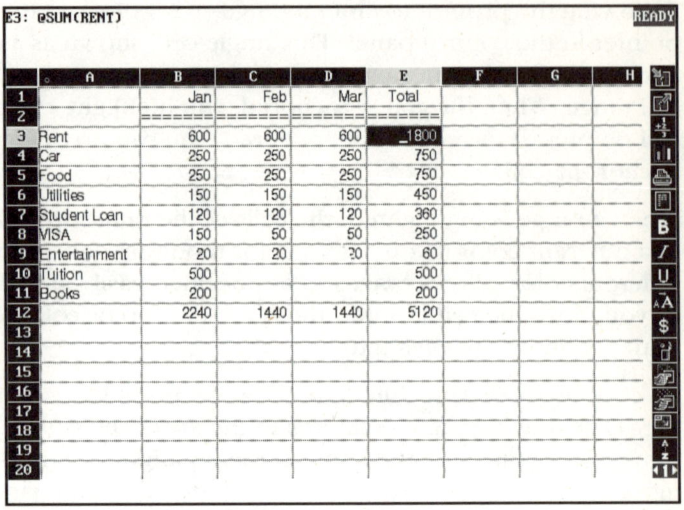

Modifying the Spreadsheet or a Range

Fig. 4.2
The Budget spreadsheet with Tuition and Book entries erased for Feb and Mar.

	A	B	C	D	E
		Jan	Feb	Mar	Total
1					
2		======	======	======	======
3	Rent	600	600	600	1800
4	Car	250	250	250	750
5	Food	250	250	250	750
6	Utilities	150	150	150	450
7	Student Loan	120	120	120	360
8	VISA	150	50	50	250
9	Entertainment	20	20	20	60
10	Tuition	500			500
11	Books	200			200
12		2240	1440	1440	5120

Naming a Range of Cells in the Spreadsheet

Range names can contain as many as 15 characters and should describe the range's contents. The advantage of naming ranges is that they are easier to understand than cell addresses. Naming a group of cells that contain information on rent costs as RENT is a more understandable way of describing the range than its coordinates, B3..D3.

Range names can be useful tools for processing commands and generating formulas. Whenever you must designate a range that has been named, you can use the range name instead of entering cell addresses or pointing to cell locations. 1-2-3's **/R**ange **N**ame command enables you to give a specific range of the worksheet any name you choose. After naming the range, you can type the name and press **Enter** instead of typing the cell addresses that indicate the range's boundaries. After you establish a range name, 1-2-3 automatically uses that name, rather than the cell addresses, throughout the worksheet.

Exercise 1.2: Using a Range Name in a Formula

Instead of cell addresses, you can use range names in formulas. Follow these steps:

1. Move the cell pointer to cell E3.
2. Choose **/R**ange **E**rase, and press ↵Enter.

To Understand the Range Concept in 1-2-3

3. Move the cell pointer to cell B3.
4. To give the cells B3, C3, and D3 the name RENT, choose **/R**ange **N**ame **C**reate. Type **rent**, and press `Enter`. Press `→` twice, and press `Enter`.
5. Move the cell pointer to E3.
6. Type the formula **@SUM(RENT)**, and press `Enter`.

Deleting Range Names

You can delete range names individually or all at once. The **/R**ange **N**ame **D**elete command enables you to delete a single range name, and the **/R**ange **N**ame **R**eset command causes all range names to be deleted. Note that these commands delete only the range names, not the actual ranges.

If you delete a range name, 1-2-3 no longer uses that name and reverts to using the range's cell address. @SUM(RENT), for example, returns to @SUM(B3..D3). The contents of the cells in the range, however, remain intact. To erase the contents of ranges, use the **/R**ange **E**rase command.

Listing Range Names

You can use the F3 (Name) function key to produce a list of the range names in the current worksheet.

Exercise 1.3: Moving to a Named Range

Using the F3 (Name) in conjunction with the F5 (Goto) is an easy way to move around a large spreadsheet. Follow these steps:

1. Press `PgDn` to move away from the current spreadsheet.
2. Press `F5` (Goto).
3. Press `F3` (Name).
4. Select RENT—move the cursor to highlight it if necessary, and press `Enter`. The cell pointer should jump to the top left corner of the RENT range (cell B3).

Modifying the Spreadsheet or a Range

Objective 2: To Understand the Worksheet Commands

1-2-3 offers a group of commands that perform some tasks similar to the /Range commands, but which affect the entire worksheet or preset segments of the worksheet. /Worksheet is the first command option on the 1-2-3 main menu. When you select /Worksheet, 1-2-3 offers the following group of commands:

Global Insert Delete Column Erase Titles Window Status Page Learn

Table 4.2 provides a brief description of the actions of each of these commands.

Table 4.2	Selections on the /Worksheet Menu
Selection	*Description*
Global	Sets formats that affect the entire worksheet
Insert	Inserts blank columns and rows into the worksheet
Delete	Deletes entire columns and rows from the worksheet
Column	Sets column widths; hides and redisplays columns
Erase	Removes the entire worksheet from memory
Titles	Freezes or unfreezes the display of titles
Window	Splits the screen into two windows or restores the original screen
Status	Displays the current status of the global worksheet settings and hardware configuration. In Releases 2.3 and 2.4, also displays the hardware configuration and circular references
Page	Inserts a character that controls page breaks in a printed worksheet
Learn	Records keystrokes used in macros

To Understand the Worksheet Commands

Erasing the Entire Worksheet from Memory

The /Worksheet Erase command clears the worksheet from the screen and memory. The effect is the same as if you quit 1-2-3 and restarted from the operating system. This command does not erase the worksheet file stored on disk. Be sure that you understand the difference between the /Worksheet Erase and the /Range Erase command.

Exercise 2.1: Erasing the Worksheet from Memory

Erasing the worksheet from the screen and memory is dangerous if the worksheet is not saved on the disk. To erase the worksheet, follow these steps:

1. Save the Budget file. Choose /**F**ile **S**ave. Press ⏎Enter, and choose **R**eplace.
2. Select /**W**orksheet **E**rase.
3. To erase the worksheet, select **Y**es. (You could change your mind by selecting **N**o.)
4. If you did not save the worksheet, 1-2-3 warns you again. Select **Y**es. (You could again change your mind by selecting **N**o.)

   Note: In versions before 2.2, there is no way to get back the spreadsheet just erased if it was not saved. In versions 2.2 and later, however, if Undo is active, you can press Alt + F4 immediately before issuing any other command to bring the spreadsheet back.

Objective 3: To Format the Worksheet

You now know that 1-2-3 expects you to enter data in a certain way. If, for example, you try to type **1,234**, the program beeps, switches to EDIT mode, and waits for you to remove the comma. You get the same result if you try to type **10:08 AM**—in this case, the colon and the AM are the offenders. If you try to type **$9.23**, the program accepts the entry, but removes the dollar sign.

1-2-3 would have limited usefulness if you could not change the way data is displayed on-screen. You can, however, control the display of data with commas, time, and currency, and with a variety of other formats. You determine formats with one of the options of the /**R**ange **F**ormat or /**W**orksheet **G**lobal **F**ormat command, or SmartIcons.

85

Modifying the Spreadsheet or a Range

Table 4.3 shows examples of the formats that are available in 1-2-3. These formats primarily affect the way numeric values are displayed in a worksheet.

Cell formats specified with /Range Format are automatically displayed in parentheses in the first line of the control panel. The worksheet's default cell format, however, does not appear in the control panel. You can use the /Worksheet Global command to view the current default worksheet format. (If you are using Release 2.01 or 2.2, use /Worksheet Status.)

Table 4.3   1-2-3 Format Options

Format	Description	Example Data entered	Example Result*
Fixed	Controls the number of decimal places displayed	15.56	16
Sci	Displays large or small numbers, using scientific (exponential) notation.	−21034567	-2E+07
Currency	Displays currency symbols and commas.	234567.75	$234,568
, (Comma)	Inserts commas to mark thousands and multiples of thousands.	1234567	1,234,567
General	Displays values with up to 10 decimal points or uses scientific notation; the default format in a new worksheet.	26.003	26.003
+/−	Creates horizontal bar graphs or time-duration graphs; useful for computers that cannot display graphs	4.1 −3	++++ - - -
Percent	Displays a decimal number as a whole number with a % sign.	0.25	25%
Date	Displays serial-date numbers. /Range Format Date Time sets time formats.	@DATE(91,8,1) @NOW	01-Aug-91 07:48 AM

To Format the Worksheet

Format	Description	Example Data entered	Example Result*
Text	Displays formulas as text, not the computed values that 1-2-3 normally displays.	+B5+B6 @SUM(C4..C8)	+B5+B6 @SUM(C4..C8)
Hidden	Hides contents from the display and does not not print them; hidden contents are still evaluated.	289	
Reset	Returns the format to the current /Worksheet Global format.		

The data displayed when formatted with no decimal places.

Exercise 3.1: Formatting with SmartIcons in Release 2.4

[handwritten: skip]

The most used formats are assigned to SmartIcons. To format a range of numbers with a SmartIcon, follow these steps:

1. Highlight the range you want to format by dragging the mouse or pressing `F4` and using the arrow keys.
2. Select one of the icons shown in table 4.4.

Setting Range and Worksheet Global Formats

Although you frequently use the /Range Format command to format individual ranges in your worksheet, you also can change the default format for the entire worksheet. The /Worksheet Global Format command controls the format of all cells in the worksheet, and the /Range Format command controls specific ranges.

Generally, you use the /Worksheet Global Format command when you are just starting to enter data into a worksheet. Be sure to choose a format that the majority of cells will use. After you set all the cells to that format, you can use the /Range Format command to override the Global format setting for specific cell ranges.

Modifying the Spreadsheet or a Range

Table 4.4   Formatting SmartIcons

Wysiwyg	Non-Wysiwyg	Description
$	$	Formats as currency (two decimal places)
0,0	0,0	Formats with commas (zero decimal places)
%	%	Formats as a percent (two decimal places)
(date icon)	DATE	Formats with today's date in the form mm/dd/yy, or leaves the existing date format

The /Range Format command takes precedence over the /Worksheet Global Format command. This means that whenever you change the global format, all the affected numbers and formulas will change automatically unless you formatted them previously with the /Range Format command. In turn, when you format a range, the format for that range will override any already set by /Worksheet Global Format.

Although the /Range Format command is generally used on cells that contain data, you can choose to select a format for cells that are now blank but will eventually contain data. Any information put in these cells later will be displayed according to the format you chose with /Range Format.

After you use /Range Format, the cells may display asterisks (*****). The asterisks indicate that the column is too narrow to display the formatted values and must be widened.

Exercise 3.2: Formatting the Spreadsheet or a Range

Most spreadsheets need a default setting for most cells in the spreadsheet and another format setting for special cells. To set formatting, follow these steps:

1. With the Budget spreadsheet on the screen, select /Worksheet Global Format comma (,) 2 decimal places.

    Notice that all entries change to the format.

2. Move the cell pointer to cell E3.
3. Select **/Range Format Currency**.
4. Press ↵Enter on 2 decimal places.
5. Press ↓ nine times to highlight all the entries in column E, and press ↵Enter. Notice the dollar sign in the totals column (see fig. 4.3).

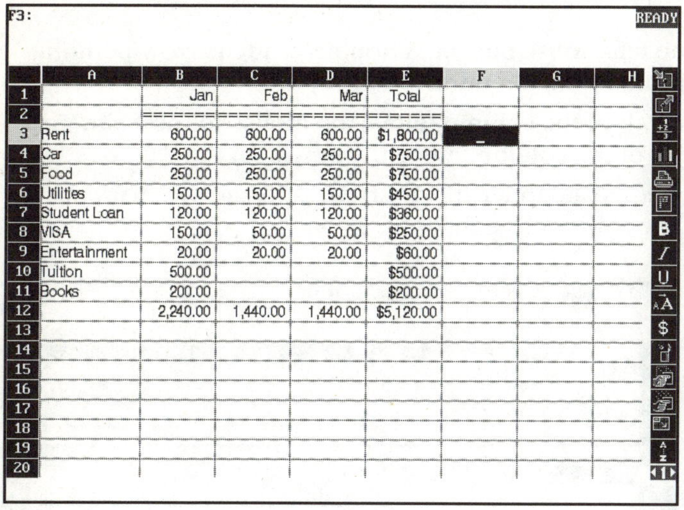
F3: READY

	A	B	C	D	E	F	G	H
1		Jan	Feb	Mar	Total			
2		=======	=======	=======	=======			
3	Rent	600.00	600.00	600.00	$1,800.00			
4	Car	250.00	250.00	250.00	$750.00			
5	Food	250.00	250.00	250.00	$750.00			
6	Utilities	150.00	150.00	150.00	$450.00			
7	Student Loan	120.00	120.00	120.00	$360.00			
8	VISA	150.00	50.00	50.00	$250.00			
9	Entertainment	20.00	20.00	20.00	$60.00			
10	Tuition	500.00			$500.00			
11	Books	200.00			$200.00			
12		2,240.00	1,440.00	1,440.00	$5,120.00			
13								
14								
15								
16								
17								
18								
19								
20								

Fig. 4.3
The Totals column has dollar signs because of the **/Range Format Currency** command. The rest of the worksheet is set to **/Worksheet Global Comma** format.

Adjusting Column Widths in the Spreadsheet

You can control the worksheet's column widths to accommodate data entries that are too wide for the default column width. You also can reduce column widths to give the worksheet a better appearance when a column contains narrow entries. With 1-2-3, you have several options for setting column widths: one column at a time with the keyboard, one column at a time with the mouse, all the columns in the worksheet at once, or a range of contiguous columns.

Setting the Width of a Single Column

In Chapter 3, to change the width of a single column, you used the **/Worksheet Column Set-Width** command to widen column A to accomodate the long entry *Entertainment* in the Budget spreadsheet.

Modifying the Spreadsheet or a Range

Exercise 3.3: Widening Columns in 2.3 and 2.4

If Wysiwyg is loaded, you can use the mouse to change a column width, as follows:

1. Position the mouse pointer in the top frame of the worksheet and point to the vertical line that marks the right side of the column to be sized.
2. Press and hold the left mouse button. A double-headed arrow pointing left and right appears in the top frame.
3. To increase the width of the column, move the mouse to the right. To decrease the width of the column, move the mouse to the left.

   A thin vertical line appears under the double-headed arrow, marking the boundary of the column (see fig. 4.4).

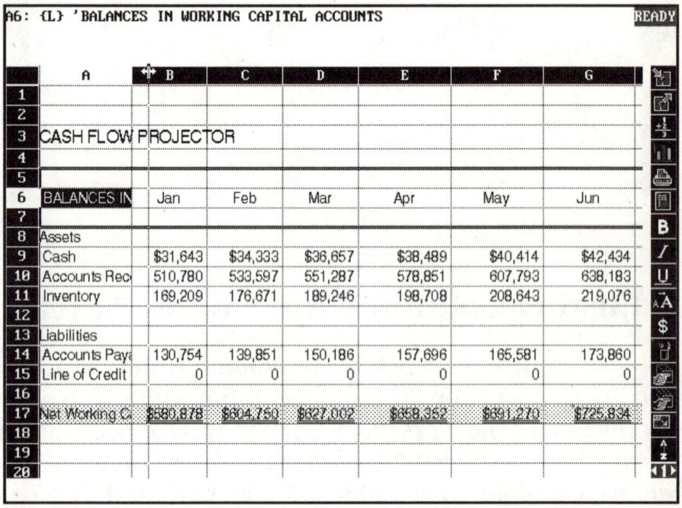

Fig. 4.4
A thin vertical line marks the boundary of the column.

4. Release the left mouse button when the desired column width is marked.

To use a mouse to return a column to the default width of nine characters, move the mouse pointer to the vertical line that marks the right side of the column. Press and hold **Shift** and click the left mouse button.

To Format the Worksheet

Setting the Widths of All Columns at Once

You can set all the column widths in the worksheet at one time by using the /Worksheet Global Column-Width command. Many of the /Worksheet Global commands have corresponding /Range commands that affect only certain areas of the worksheet; in this case, however, the corresponding commands are the /Worksheet Column Set-Width and /Worksheet Column Column-Range Set-Width commands.

Exercise 3.4: Setting the Widths of All Columns at Once

You can change the widths of all columns in the worksheet at one time.

1. Select /Worksheet Global.

   If you are using 2.3 or 2.4, the Global Settings dialog box appears. Press F2 or click the left mouse button in the dialog box to edit the settings.

2. Select Column-Width.

3. Type the column width between 1 and 240, and press ↵Enter. Instead of typing the column width, you can use the → to expand the column width and the ← to contract the column, if you are editing the setting in the control panel.

   In this example type 11 (see fig. 4.5).

   Note: The /Worksheet Global Column-Width command does not alter the width of columns already set with either the /Worksheet Column Set-Width or /Worksheet Column Column-Range commands.

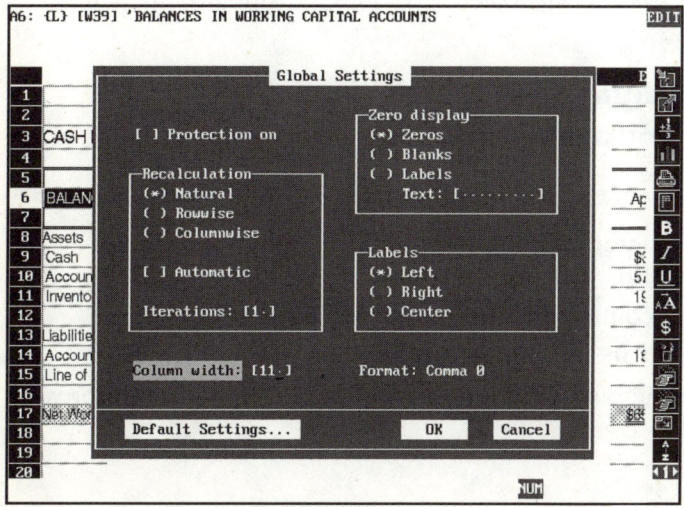

Fig. 4.5
Enter the width of the column.

Modifying the Spreadsheet or a Range

4. If you are using 2.3 or 2.4, Select the OK command button at the bottom of the dialog box. Press `Esc` or the right mouse button until you return to READY mode.

All the columns (except column A) have a width of 11 characters (see fig. 4.6).

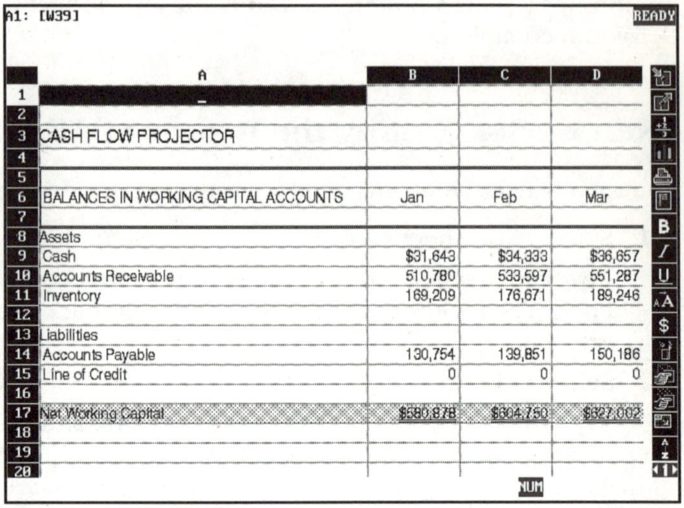

Fig. 4.6
The columns have a width of 11.

Setting the Width of Contiguous Columns

If you want to set a group of adjacent columns to the same width, use the /Worksheet Column Column-Range Set-Width command. This command keeps you from having to set each adjacent column individually.

Exercise 3.5: Changing the Width of Contiguous Columns

To change the widths of contiguous columns, follow these steps:

1. Position the cell pointer on the first or last column in the range of columns whose widths you want to change.
2. Select /Worksheet Column Column-Range Set-Width.
   The Enter range for column width change: prompt appears.
3. Highlight cells in the range of columns you want to change; then press `Enter`.

To Format the Worksheet

In this example, highlight the range B6..D6, and press `⏎Enter` (see fig. 4.7).

4. At the `Select a width for range of columns:` prompt, either enter a width between 1 and 240, or press `←` or `→` until the desired column width appears; then press `⏎Enter`.

   In this example, type **11**, and press `⏎Enter` (see fig. 4.8).

   Note: The **R**eset-Width option, on the same menu as **S**et-Width, does not prompt you for a specific width, but returns the widths of all selected columns to the default column-width setting.

To verify the global column-width setting, use the /Worksheet Status command. For Release 2.3 or 2.4, use the Global Settings dialog box (select/Worksheet Global) to check the global column width setting.

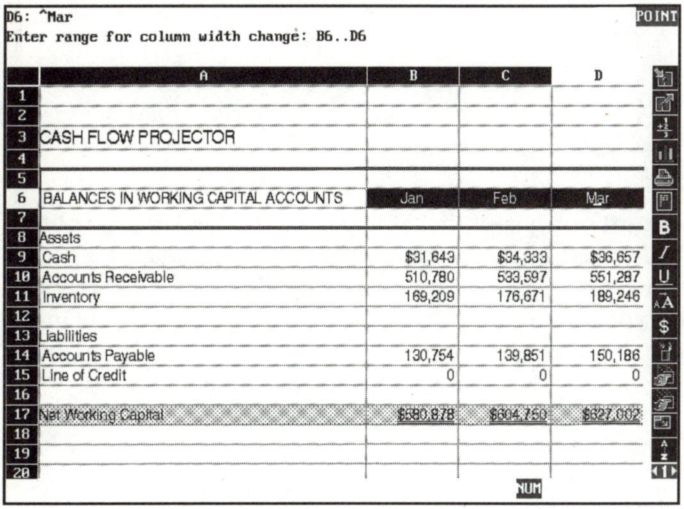

Fig. 4.7
Highlight the range B6..D6 and press **Enter**.

Splitting the Screen Display for Viewing Two Sections of the Spreadsheet

Sometimes the size of a 1-2-3 worksheet can be unwieldy. If, for example, you want to compare data in column A with data in column N, you need to be able to "fold" the worksheet so that you can see both parts at the same time. To do this, you can split the 1-2-3 screen display into two windows, either horizontally or vertically. This feature helps you to overcome some of the inconvenience of not being able to see the entire worksheet at one time. By splitting the screen with the /**W**orksheet **W**indow command or the mouse, you

Modifying the Spreadsheet or a Range

can make the changes in one area and immediately see their effects in the other area.

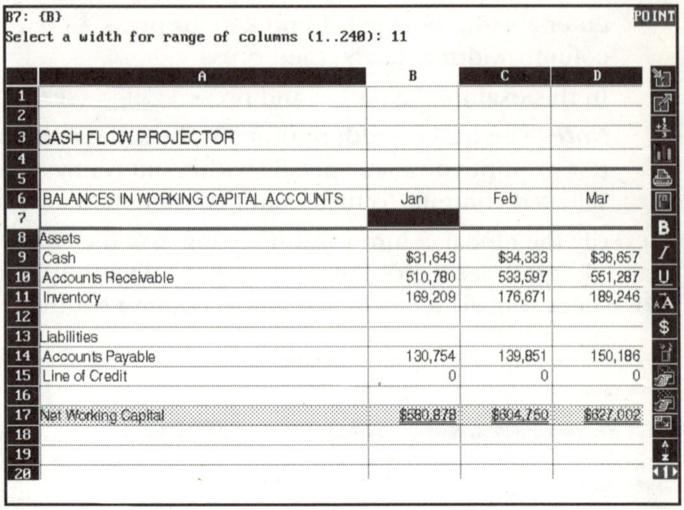

Fig. 4.8
Type **11**, and press **Enter**.

```
B7: {B}                                                              POINT
Select a width for range of columns (1..240): 11

           A                              B         C         D
 1
 2
 3  CASH FLOW PROJECTOR
 4
 5
 6  BALANCES IN WORKING CAPITAL ACCOUNTS  Jan       Feb       Mar
 7
 8  Assets
 9  Cash                                  $31,643   $34,333   $36,657
10  Accounts Receivable                   510,780   533,597   551,287
11  Inventory                             169,209   176,671   189,246
12
13  Liabilities
14  Accounts Payable                      130,754   139,851   150,186
15  Line of Credit                        0         0         0
16
17  Net Working Capital                   $580,878  $604,750  $627,002
18
19
20
```

The **Horizontal** and **Vertical** options of the **/Worksheet Window** menu split the screen in the manner indicated by their names. The screen splits at the point at which the cell pointer is positioned when you select the command **Horizontal** or **Vertical**. In other words, you don't have to split the screen exactly in half. Remember that the dividing line requires specifying either one row or one column, depending on whether you split the screen horizontally or vertically.

Exercise 3.6: Splitting the Screen

To use the keyboard to split the screen into two horizontal windows, follow these steps:

1. Position the cell pointer at the location where you want to split the screen. In the Budget spreadsheet move to cell A11.
2. Select **/Worksheet Window**.
3. Select **Horizontal** to split the screen into two horizontal windows, as shown in figure 4.9.
4. Press `F6` (the Window key) to jump back and forth between windows.
5. Use the arrow keys to move around in each window.
6. To clear the window, use **/Worksheet Window Clear**.

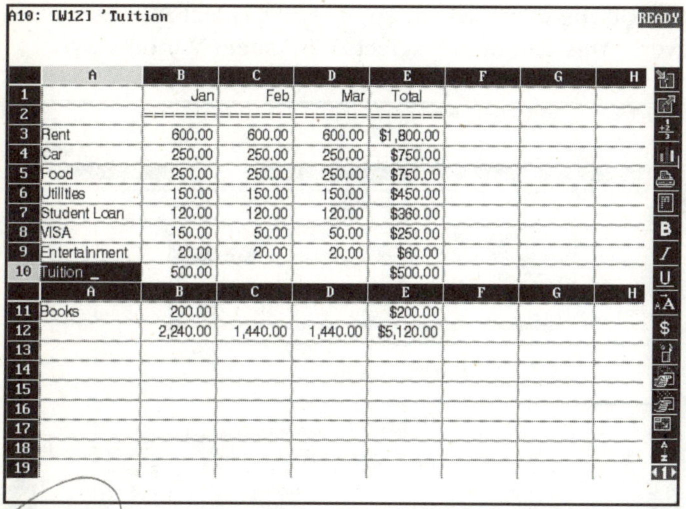

To Format the Worksheet

Fig. 4.9
The Budget worksheet appears in two windows.

(handwritten: Skip)

Exercise 3.7: Splitting the Screen in 2.3 or 2.4 with the Mouse

To use the mouse to split the screen into two horizontal or two vertical windows, follow these steps:

1. Position the mouse pointer in the upper left corner of the worksheet frame. For a horizontal window, move to the line above row number 1. For a vertical window, move to the line to the left of column letter A.

2. Press and hold the left mouse button. A double-headed arrow appears. The arrow points up and down for horizontal windows, left and right for vertical windows.

3. To create two horizontal windows, move the mouse down (see fig. 4.10). To create two vertical windows, move the mouse to the right.

4. Release the left mouse button when you reach the desired position of the window (see fig. 4.11).

After you use the **H**orizontal or **V**ertical option to split the screen, the cell pointer appears in one window. To jump the division between the windows, use the **F6** (Window) function key, or click the left mouse button on a cell in the opposite window.

After the screen is split, you can change the screen display so that the windows scroll independently rather than together. (The default is scrolling

Modifying the Spreadsheet or a Range

windows together.) To scroll the windows independently, select /Worksheet Window Unsync. To reverse this command, select /Worksheet Window Sync.

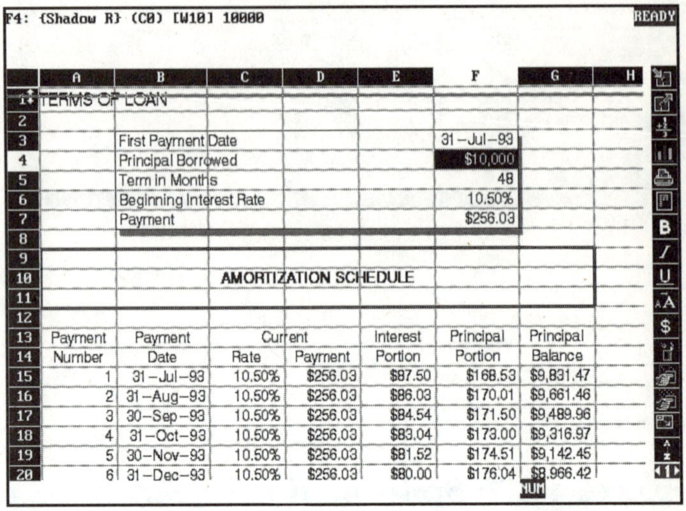

Fig. 4.10
Moving the mouse down displays a horizontal line—indicating the position of the horizontal window.

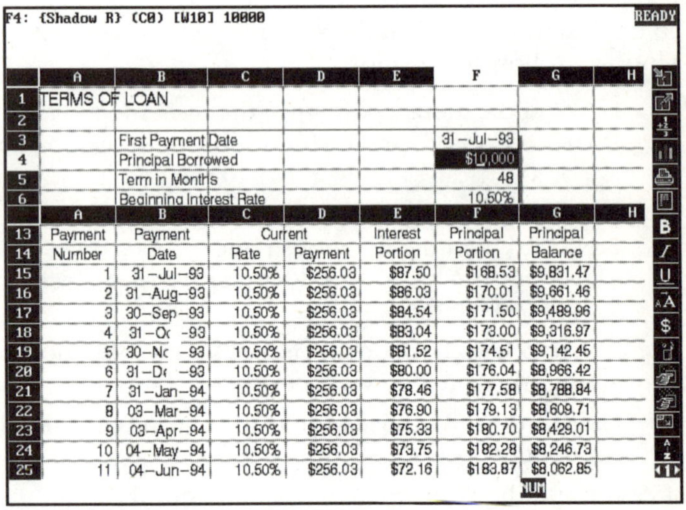

Fig. 4.11
The screen is split horizontally into two windows, and the cell pointer is moved to show two different parts of the worksheet.

Freezing the Titles On-Screen

If you need to freeze rows or columns along the top and left edges of the worksheet so that they remain in view as you scroll to different parts of the

To Format the Worksheet

worksheet, use the /Worksheet Titles command. This command is similar to the /Worksheet Window command. Both commands enable you to see one area of a worksheet while you work on another area. The unique function of the /Worksheet Titles command, however, is that it freezes all the cells to the left or above (or both) the cell pointer's position so that those cells cannot move off the screen.

Because the default screen shows 20 rows by 8 columns (with the original column widths and row heights), you must shift the screen if your data is outside this screen area. In fact, you may have to scroll the screen several times in order to enter or view all the information.

Exercise 3.8: Freezing the Titles on the Screen

To freeze worksheet titles on-screen, follow these steps:

1. Position the cell pointer one cell below and to the right of the rows or columns you want to freeze. In the Budget spreadsheet move the cell pointer to cell B3.
2. Select /Worksheet Titles.
3. Select Both. The Both option allows you to freeze rows and columns above and to the left of the cell pointer.
4. Press Ctrl + →. Notice that the titles in column A remain on the screen.
5. Press Home. Notice that the Home position is cell B3.
6. Press PgDn and then press End and ↓. Notice that the months and the underline remain along the top (see fig. 4.12).

   When you freeze columns or rows, you cannot move the cell pointer into the frozen area while 1-2-3 is in READY mode. If you try to move the cell pointer into the frozen area, 1-2-3 beeps. You can avoid this restriction, however, by using the GoTo (F5) key to move the cell pointer to the frozen titles area.

7. To unlock the frozen worksheet titles, use the /Worksheet Titles Clear command. Now you can move the cell pointer freely throughout the worksheet.

Suppressing the Display of Zeros in the Worksheet

The /Worksheet Global Zero command enables you to suppress the display in the worksheet of all cells that have a numeric value of zero. This technique is

Modifying the Spreadsheet or a Range

useful, for example, for preparing reports for a presentation in which cells showing $0.00 would look odd. As an alternative, you may choose to have zero-value cells display a label (such as No Charge).

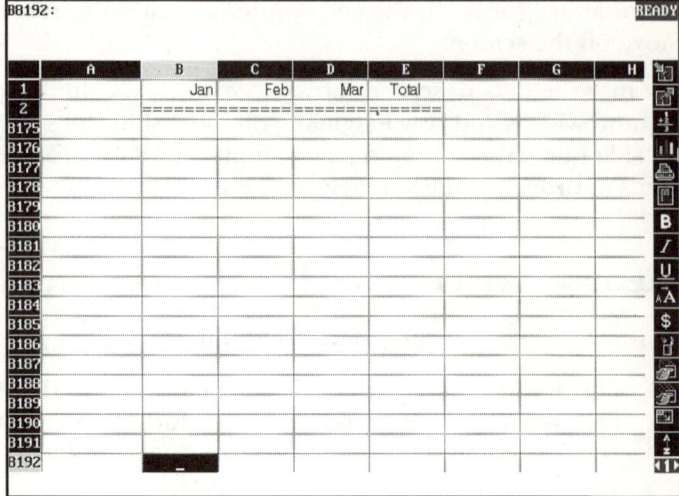

Fig. 4.12
The months and line are frozen on the screen; the cell pointer is in row 8,192.

You can enter formulas and values for all the items in the report, including the zero items, and then display the results with all the zeros removed or replaced by a label. The actual formula or value is displayed in the control panel when the cell pointer highlights a cell that contains a zero, or a formula that evaluates to zero.

Exercise 3.9: Suppressing Zeros

To suppress the display of zeros or to substitute a label for zero entries, follow these steps:

1. Select /Worksheet Global.

    In Releases 2.3 and 2.4 the Global Settings dialog box appears. Press F2 or click the left mouse button in the dialog box to edit the settings.

2. Select Zero.

3. In Releases 2.2 and earlier, you should choose Yes to suppress zeros, or choose Label and type a label, and press ↵Enter.

To Insert and Delete Columns and Rows

Skip

4. In Releases 2.3 or 2.4 with the keyboard or mouse, select one of the following options:

Selection	Description
Zeros	Displays zeros (the default)
Blanks	Suppresses zeros
Labels	Displays a specified label

If you choose **L**abels, select **T**ext. Type the label to appear in place of zeros in the worksheet, and press `↵Enter`.

Select the OK command button at the bottom of the dialog box; then press `Esc` or the right mouse button until you return to READY mode.

If you want the zeros visible again, use the command /**W**orksheet **G**lobal **Z**ero **N**o. When you use the /**F**ile **S**ave command to save your worksheet, the zero suppression or label substitution features of this command are not saved with the worksheet. Therefore, these features are not present when you retrieve a file.

Objective 4: To Insert and Delete Columns and Rows

Suppose that you are finished creating a worksheet, but you want to enhance its general appearance. You can improve it by inserting blank columns and rows in strategic places to highlight headings and other important items. Whether you want to insert additional data or add blank rows or columns to separate sections of your worksheet, you can use the /**W**orksheet **I**nsert command to insert columns or rows. You can insert multiple adjacent columns and rows each time you invoke this command.

Exercise 4.1: Inserting and Deleting Columns and Rows

To insert a new column or row into the worksheet, follow these steps:

1. Position the cell pointer at the location of the new column or row to be inserted. For example, in the Budget spreadsheet move the cell pointer to cell A12.

Modifying the Spreadsheet or a Range

2. Select **/W**orksheet **I**nsert.
3. Select **R**ow.
4. Press ⏎Enter.

   In this example, when you press ⏎Enter, a blank row appears, setting the totals off from the data in the budget (see fig. 4.13).

When you insert rows, 1-2-3 inserts a blank row; all data located below the new row is automatically shifted down one row, and any formulas are modified. 1-2-3 does not have the capability to insert or delete partial columns and rows. When you insert columns 1-2-3 automatically shifts all data to the right of the new column—one column to the right—and modifies all cell formulas for the change.

Fig. 4.13
The totals for the months have been moved down one row.

	A	B	C	D	E	F	G	H
		Jan	Feb	Mar	Total			
1								
2		=======	=======	=======	=======			
3	Rent	600.00	600.00	600.00	$1,800.00			
4	Car	250.00	250.00	250.00	$750.00			
5	Food	250.00	250.00	250.00	$750.00			
6	Utilities	150.00	150.00	150.00	$450.00			
7	Student Loan	120.00	120.00	120.00	$360.00			
8	VISA	150.00	50.00	50.00	$250.00			
9	Entertainment	20.00	20.00	20.00	$60.00			
10	Tuition	500.00			$500.00			
11	Books	200.00			$200.00			
12								
13		2,240.00	1,440.00	1,440.00	$5,120.00			

Deleting Columns and Rows

You can delete single (or multiple) columns or rows by using the **/W**orksheet **D**elete command the same way you used **/W**orksheet **I**nsert. After you select this command, choose **C**olumn or **R**ow from the menu that appears on-screen. If you choose **R**ow, 1-2-3 asks you to specify a range of rows to be deleted; the range you specify needs to include only one cell from each row to be deleted.

If you plan to use the command **/W**orksheet **D**elete to delete a column or row containing values, keep in mind that all formulas in the worksheet that still refer to these cells will then result in ERR. Also remember that when you use the **/W**orksheet **D**elete command, the columns or rows you delete may be gone forever. This command deletes entire columns or rows, not just the range of cells you specify in those columns or rows.

If the Undo feature is enabled, you can undo the deletion by pressing **Alt+F4** before executing another command. Otherwise, the only remedies are to re-create the missing data or retrieve the worksheet file again. The latter approach works only if you have saved a copy of your worksheet that contains the missing data.

Deleting and Inserting with SmartIcons in 2.4

You also can use SmartIcons to delete or insert rows or columns. Follow these steps:

1. Highlight one cell in each row or column you want to delete or insert. Columns or rows will be inserted to the left or above the highlighted range.
2. Select one of the icons shown in table 4.5.

Table 4.5   SmartIcons for Deleting and Inserting

Wysiwyg	Non-Wysiwyg	Description
	+ROW	Inserts row(s)
	+COL	Inserts column(s)
	−ROW	Deletes row(s)
	−COL	Deletes column(s)

Objective 5: To Recalculate the Worksheet

One of the primary functions of a spreadsheet program is to recalculate cells that contain formulas when a value or formula in one of the cells changes. 1-2-3 provides two basic recalculation methods: automatic and manual. When you use automatic recalculation—which is the default—1-2-3 recalculates the formulas that are affected whenever a cell in the worksheet changes. In

101

Modifying the Spreadsheet or a Range

manual recalculation, the worksheet is recalculated only when the user requests it, either from the keyboard with the **F9** (Calc) key, with the Recalculate SmartIcon, or from a macro.

1-2-3 also provides three orders of recalculation: the natural order and two linear orders, either columnwise or rowwise. Natural order is the default, but you can choose any of the three orders. You also can choose the number of times worksheets are recalculated. You select the recalculation options by using the **/W**orksheet **G**lobal **R**ecalculation command. The recalculation options are described in table 4.6.

Exercise 5.1: Recalculating the Worksheet

You do not need to change the recalculation settings when you are beginning to use 1-2-3. To see spreadsheet recalculate, follow these steps:

1. Move the cell pointer to cell C3.
2. Suppose that your rent went up in February. Type **650**, and press ↵Enter.
3. Suppose that your rent went up again in March. Type **700**, and press ↵Enter.

   Notice that the Total for Rent and the Grand Total of all your expenses are recalculated, as shown in figure 4.14.

Fig. 4.14
The spreadsheet recalculates automatically when data is changed.

	A	B	C	D	E
		Jan	Feb	Mar	Total
3	Rent	600.00	650.00	700.00	$1,950.00
4	Car	250.00	250.00	250.00	$750.00
5	Food	250.00	250.00	250.00	$750.00
6	Utilities	150.00	150.00	150.00	$450.00
7	Student Loan	120.00	120.00	120.00	$360.00
8	VISA	150.00	50.00	50.00	$250.00
9	Entertainment	20.00	20.00	20.00	$60.00
10	Tuition	500.00			$500.00
11	Books	200.00			$200.00
13		2,240.00	1,490.00	1,540.00	$5,270.00

Summary

Table 4.6 Selections on the /Worksheet Global Recalculation Menu

Selection	Description
Order of Recalculation	
Natural	Does not recalculate any cell until the cells it depends on have been recalculated. **Natural** is the default setting
Columnwise	Begins recalculation at cell A1 and continues down column A; then goes to cell B1, down column B, and so forth
Rowwise	Begins recalculation at cell A1 and proceeds across row 1; then goes across row 2, and so forth
Method of Recalculation	
Automatic	Recalculates the worksheet whenever a cell changes. **Automatic** is the default setting
Manual	Recalculates the worksheet only when you press [F9] (Calc)
Number of Recalculations	
Iteration	Recalculates the worksheet a specified number of times when you change cell contents in automatic recalculation or press [F9] (Calc) in manual recalculation. The default is one iteration per recalculation.

Summary

In this chapter, you have learned to work with the entire worksheet using the /Worksheet commands and with a portion of the worksheet using the /Range commands.

Modifying the Spreadsheet or a Range

Testing Your Knowledge

True/False Questions

1. Automatic recalculation is a default setting indicating that the worksheet is calculated each time a cell's content changes.
2. The comma format puts commas and a dollar sign in each cell.
3. The default column width in 1-2-3 is 12.
4. Suppressing zeros in the worksheet means rounding numeric entries to the nearest whole number.
5. 1-2-3's definition of a range is a rectangular block of adjacent cells.

Multiple Choice Questions

1. When a range is highlighted in 1-2-3,
   A. the cells of the range disappear from the screen.
   B. the cells of the range appear in reverse video (or in a different color if you have a color monitor).
   C. the highlighting can be cancelled with the F3 key.
   D. zeros will not appear in the range.

2. The percent format for numeric entries in 1-2-3
   A. is the default format.
   B. multiplies entries by 100.
   C. creates a horizontal bar "graph" of plus or minus signs in the cell.
   D. displays formulas as they are entered in the command line, not the computed values that 1-2-3 normally displays.

3. The /Worksheet Erase command
   A. has the same effect as /Range Erase.
   B. erases the file on disk.
   C. clears the worksheet from the screen and memory.
   D. can be undone at any time you are using 1-2-3.

4. Range names
   A. can be useful tools for processing commands and generating formulas.
   B. can be up to three characters long.
   C. cannot be deleted once named.
   D. are useful, but cannot appear in formulas.

Testing Your Knowledge

5. The width of columns in 1-2-3
    A. cannot be changed.
    B. can be widened but not made narrower.
    ✗C. can be changed only one at a time.
    D. can be widened and made narrower either one at a time, as a group, or for the entire worksheet.

Fill-in-the-Blank Questions

1. If you need to keep the titles from moving off the screen as you move around a large worksheet, you can choose the /Worksheet _____TITLE_____ command.
2. The /Worksheet Global ___FORMAT___ and the /Range ___FORMAT___ commands change the way data is displayed on the screen.
3. To clear an incorrectly highlighted range, press ___F4___ ESC, BACKSPACE or ___the ARROWS___.
4. When the pointer is anchored to a cell, you highlight a range by pressing an arrow key. If the pointer is not anchored, you must press the ___PERIOD___ key to anchor it.
5. ___Worksheet/Global___ allow you to view different parts of the worksheet at the same time. WINDOWS

Review: Short Projects

1. Using /Range Format

   In a empty worksheet with your cursor in cell A1, enter **15.7523**, and press [↵Enter]. To copy this to other cells select /Copy, and press [↵Enter], [↓], [.], [↓] 10 times, and [↵Enter].

   Now starting at A2, use /Range Format, choosing each format for one of the copied numbers. If asked for decimal places, choose two each time. The result will be a list of same number all looking different because of the 1-2-3 formatting option. Label what each one is in column C and print the list.

2. Formatting the Spreadsheet

   Retrieve one of the worksheets that you created for Chapter 3 and format the cells using both /Worksheet Global Format and /Range Format, use any of the other features from this chapter to fix it up. Save the worksheet to disk, replacing the old one with the updated one, and print it.

Modifying the Spreadsheet or a Range

3. **Recalculating the Spreadsheet**

   Retrieve one of the worksheets that you created in Chapter 3. Change the numeric entries. Notice how the formulas recalculate each time a number is entered.

Review: Long Projects

1. **Formatting a Worksheet**

   Retrieve the check book register created in Chapter 3. Format the entire spreadsheet for comma (,) 2 decimal places, and format the totals for currency 2 decimal places. Widen or narrow columns for better display. Suppress zeros so that empty formulas don't compute to $0.00. Save the spreadsheet, replacing the old one with this new one, and print the spreadsheet.

2. **Using Ranges**

   Create a worksheet that tracks the mileage your car is currently getting. List the dates of gas fill-ups in column A, the number of gallons of the fill-up in column B, and the number of miles driven in column C. Write a formula to compute miles per gallon in column D. Place appropriate column headings over each column. Use the **/R**ange **N**ame **C**reate command to create a named range, and then write one of your formulas using the range name. Place formulas in cells for future dates and suppress zeros. Format as necessary, and widen or narrow columns as necessary. Save the worksheet to disk, and print it.

Modifying a Worksheet

5

1-2-3 includes tools for modifying a spreadsheet that can speed up entering data or that can change existing data. In this chapter you learn about three valuable tools.

Objectives

1. To Move Data or Formulas in the Spreadsheet
2. To Copy Cells in the Spreadsheet

Modifying a Worksheet

Key Terms in This Chapter	
Relative cell address	A cell reference that adjusts for a new location when used in a formula copied to that location. This type of cell address is the default.
Absolute cell address	A cell reference that does not adjust when used in a formula copied to that location.

5

Objective 1: To Move Data or Formulas in the Spreadsheet

In the days of manual spreadsheets, the process of moving data around on the page was called cutting and pasting because scissors and glue were used to move sections of the spreadsheet. With 1-2-3, you can cut and paste sections of the worksheet on-screen.

With the /Move and /Copy commands and SmartIcons, you can move and copy the contents of cells and ranges of cells from one part of the worksheet to another. The difference between moving and copying is that data moved from one location to another disappears from the first location; data that is copied appears in both locations.

Exercise 1.1: Using the SmartIcons in 2.4 To Move Data or Copy Data

The SmartIcons in Release 2.4 can greatly speed up the process of moving data to a different location in the spreadsheet or copying data to another location in another part of the spreadsheet. Follow these steps:

1. Select the range you want to move or copy. You can select a range by dragging the mouse pointer.

   Or press [F4] (Abs) in READY mode. The control panel requests that you enter a range. Use the arrow keys to expand the range, and press [Enter] when the range is selected.

To Move Data or Formulas in the Spreadsheet

2. Select one of the following SmartIcons:

Wysiwyg	Non-Wysiwyg	Description
	COPY	Copy
	MOVE	Move

3. Select the range you want to move or copy to.
4. Click the left mouse button or press `Enter` to finish the copy process.

Using the Keyboard To Copy and Move

In all releases of 1-2-3 you can select to move and copy from the main menu using the keyboard.

Exercise 1.2: Using the Keyboard and the Move Command

To move a range in a single worksheet, follow these steps:

1. On a blank screen, move the cell pointer to cell A1.
2. Type the following, pressing the keys indicated:

   Jan →
   Feb →
   Mar `Enter`

   Now, move back to cell A1.
3. Select /Move. The Move what? prompt appears.
4. Specify the range you want to move by pressing → twice, and pressing `Enter` (see fig. 5.1).
5. At the To where? prompt, highlight the upper left cell of the new location (that is, move the cell pointer to cell B1, and press `Enter`).

   Note: You don't need to highlight the entire range at the To where? prompt.

   The range moves to the new location. The cell pointer returns immediately to where it was when you initiated the /Move command (see fig. 5.2).

109

Modifying a Worksheet

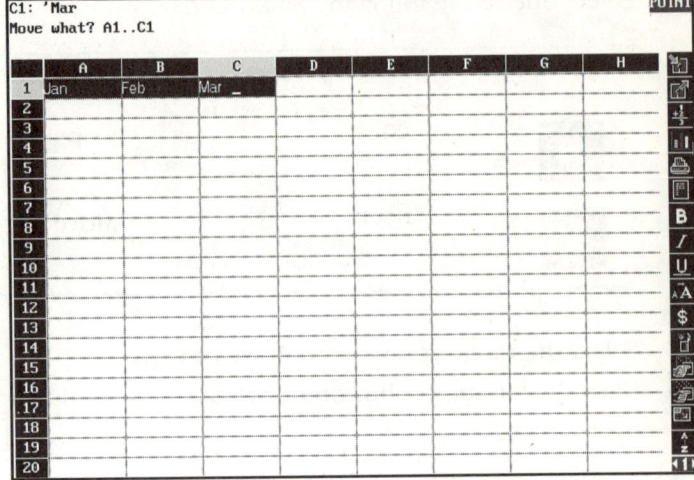

Fig. 5.1
The range to be moved is highlighted.

Remember that the cell pointer does not have to be positioned at the beginning of the starting range when you start the /Move command. You can always press **Esc** (or the right mouse button) to free the cell pointer and move it to the correct location.

Tips for Moving

Remember the following tips whenever you intend to move data:

- When you move a range of cells, the range to which the cells are copied is completely overwritten by the range that is moved. Any cell contents are lost. If you move data into the upper left or lower right cell of a range that a formula references, the reference in the formula evaluates to ERR, and the formula itself evaluates to ERR.

- If the Undo feature is enabled (with the /Worksheet Global Default Other Undo Enable command), you can reverse the effects of a /Move operation by pressing **Alt+F4** before executing another command.

- Highlight ranges (rather than typing ranges) to be moved to help avoid errors. Remember that you also can use the click-and-drag mouse technique to highlight the ranges when moving data.

- Use the **End** key and the arrow keys for pointing to large ranges quickly. This method usually reduces the number of required keystrokes for a move operation. If there are gaps (blank cells) in the blocks of data, however, the **End** key procedure is less useful because the cell pointer goes to the boundaries of each gap.

To Copy Cells in the Spreadsheet

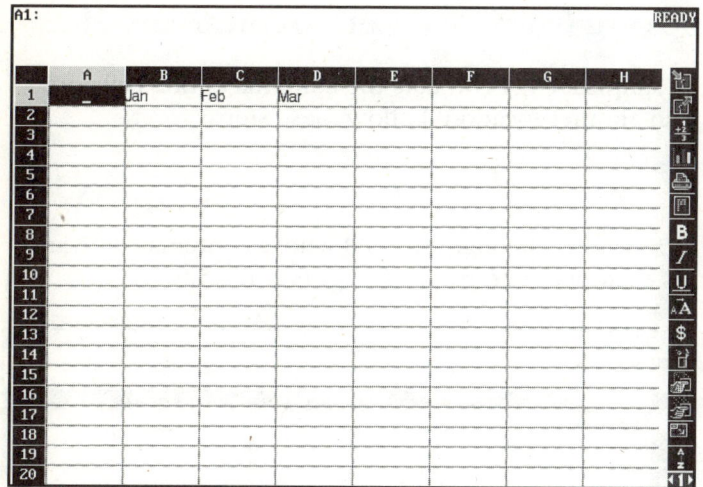

Fig. 5.2
The range moves to the new location.

Objective 2: To Copy Cells in the Spreadsheet

You often will want to copy the contents of cells to other locations in a worksheet. When you copy data, you also copy the cell formats. 1-2-3 lets you copy data in the following ways:

- Copy the contents of one cell to another cell.
- Copy the contents of one cell to every cell in a range.
- Copy from one range to another range of equal size.
- Copy from one range to a larger range.

The procedure used for each copy operation is basically the same. To copy a range, follow these steps:

1. Select /Copy.
2. At the Copy what? prompt, specify the cell or range you want to copy.
3. At the To where? prompt, specify the cell or range to which the data is to be copied.

The only elements that change are the dimensions and locations of the Copy what? and To where? ranges. Remember that you can type the coordinates of each range from the keyboard, type a range name, or highlight (point to) the ranges in POINT mode (with the keyboard or a mouse).

111

Modifying a Worksheet

Exercise 2.1: Copying from One Cell to Another Cell

This first method is the simplest copy—to take the contents of one cell and make a duplicate copy in another location. Follow these steps:

1. In cell A1, type **123**.
2. Select **/C**opy.
3. At the Copy what? prompt, highlight the cell whose contents you want to copy (A1 in this example), and press ↵Enter (see fig. 5.3).

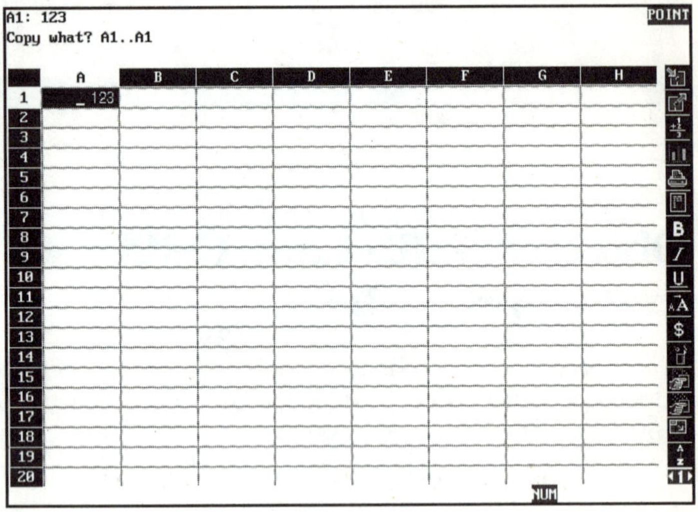

Fig. 5.3
Select cell A1 as the range to copy.

4. At the To where? prompt, highlight the cell to which you want the data copied (A2 in this example), and press ↵Enter. The contents of cell A1 are copied to cell A2 (see fig. 5.4).

Exercise 2.2: Copying from One Cell to Many Cells

To copy the contents of one cell to a group of cells, follow these steps:

1. Move to cell A2. Select **/R**ange **E**rase and press ↵Enter.
2. Move the cell pointer to cell A1.
3. Select **/C**opy.
4. At the Copy what? prompt, highlight the cell whose contents you want to copy (A1 in this case), and press ↵Enter.

To Copy Cells in the Spreadsheet

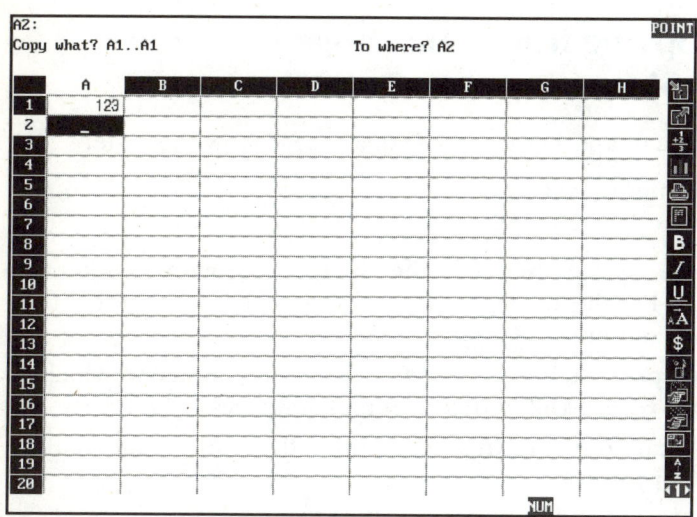

Fig. 5.4
Cell A1 is copied to cell A2.

5. At the To where? prompt, move the cell pointer to cell B1 by pressing →.
6. To highlight a range, the cursor must be anchored; press the . key.
7. Press → six times to highlight to cell H1.
8. Press ↵Enter to complete the copy process (see fig. 5.5).

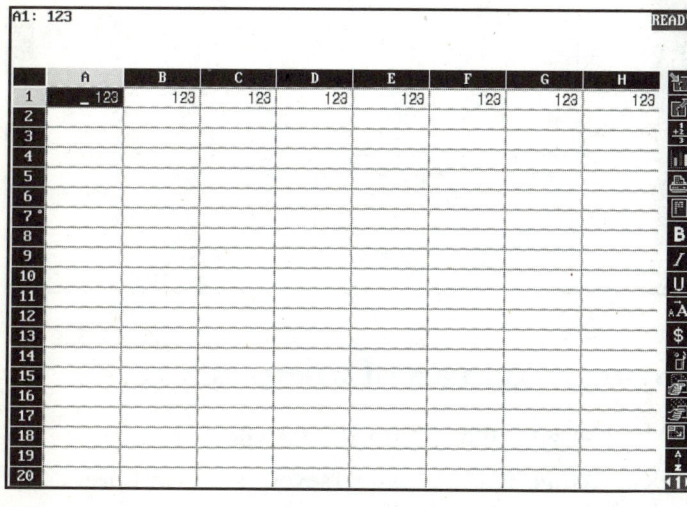

Fig. 5.5
All cells now contain the contents of A1.

113

Modifying a Worksheet

Exercise 2.3: Copying from One Range to Another Range of Equal Size

To copy from one range to another range of equal size, follow these steps:

1. Move the cell pointer to cell A1.
2. Select /Copy.
3. At the Copy what? prompt, highlight the range of cells whose contents you want to copy. For this example, press → seven times to highlight the range A1..H1, and press ↵Enter.
4. At the To where? prompt, highlight the first cell of the range to which you want the data copied (A2 in this example), and press ↵Enter.

   Note: With this method of copying, highlighting the entire range that will receive the copy is not necessary.

   The range A1..H1 is copied to the range A2..H2 (see fig. 5.6).

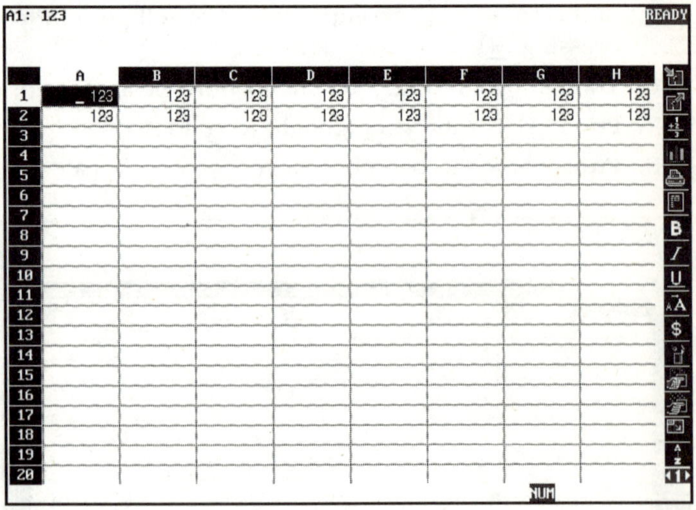

Fig. 5.6
The old range is copied to the new range.

Exercise 2.4: Copying to Ranges of Unequal Size

To copy from one range to a larger range, follow these steps:

1. Move to cell A2, select /Range Erase, press → seven times, and press ↵Enter.
2. Move the cell pointer to cell A1.

To Copy Cells in the Spreadsheet

3. Select /Copy.

4. At the Copy what? prompt, highlight the range of cells whose contents you want to copy. For this example, press → five times to highlight the range A1..F1, and press ↵Enter.

5. At the To where? prompt, highlight the first cell in the column to which you want the information copied (A2 in this example), press . to anchor the cursor, and press ↓ to highlight down to cell A20.

6. Press ↵Enter to complete the copy process.

   The range A1..F1 is copied to the larger range A2..F20 (see fig. 5.7).

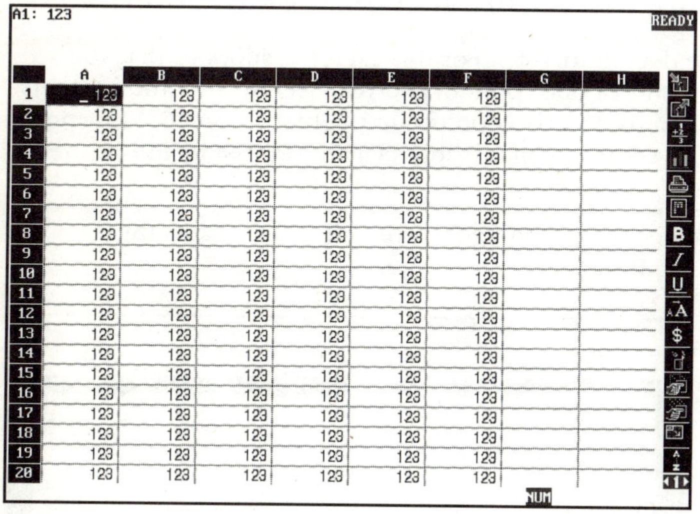

Fig. 5.7
The old range is copied to the new, larger range.

The best way to learn how the copy command works with different ranges is to experiment. After a while, the rules of copying will become second nature.

Addressing Cells

Although the connection may not be obvious, the way you address cells is tied closely to copy operations. Two different methods of addressing cells can be used when copying: relative and absolute. These two methods of referencing cells are important for building formulas. The type of addressing you use when you reference cells in formulas can affect the results produced by these formulas when you copy them to different locations in the worksheet. The following sections cover relative and absolute addressing as well as the combination of both methods—known as *mixed addressing*.

115

Modifying a Worksheet

Referencing Cells with Relative Addressing

Relative addressing, 1-2-3's default for referencing cells, means that when you copy a formula, unless you specify otherwise, the addresses of the cells in the formula are adjusted automatically to fit the new location.

For example, suppose that you have the formula +B3+B4 in cell B5. With relative addressing, when you copy this formula to cell C5, the formula adjusts to become +C3+C4.

Exercise 2.5: Copying Formulas with Relative Address

Relative address is the default in 1-2-3. For this exercise, suppose that you have summed the contents of one column, and you need to sum the contents of several adjacent columns, but you don't want to enter the @SUM function over and over again. To copy formulas using relative addressing, follow these steps:

1. Create the worksheet shown in figure 5.8. Cell B11 contains the formula @SUM(B5.B9).

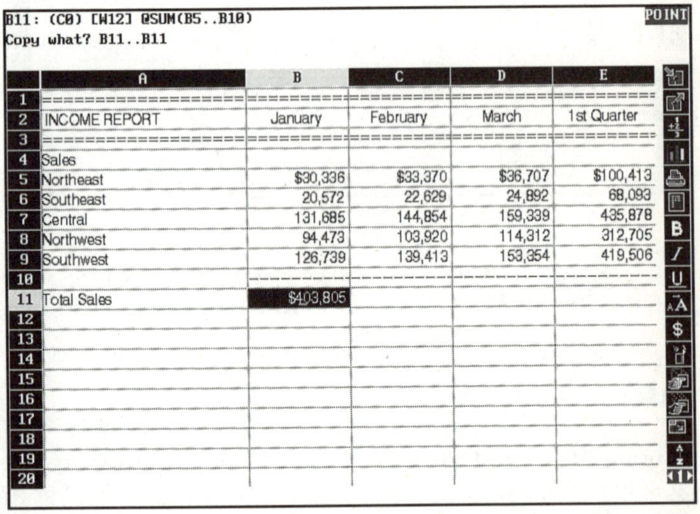

Fig. 5.8
Create this spreadsheet.

2. Move the cell pointer to cell B11.
3. Select /Copy.
4. At the Copy what? prompt, highlight the cell containing the formula to be copied (B11 in this example), and press [↵Enter].

To Copy Cells in the Spreadsheet

5. At the To where? prompt, move the cell pointer to cell C11. Press `.` to anchor the cursor, and press → two times to highlight the range C11..E11 to which you want the formula copied (see fig. 5.9). Press ⏎Enter.

```
E11: (C0) [W12]                                              POINT
Copy what? B11..B11        To where? C11..E11

            A           B          C          D          E
   1  ================================================
   2  INCOME REPORT    January   February    March    1st Quarter
   3  ================================================
   4  Sales
   5  Northeast       $30,336   $33,370    $36,707   $100,413
   6  Southeast        20,572    22,629     24,892     68,093
   7  Central         131,685   144,854    159,339    435,878
   8  Northwest        94,473   103,920    114,312    312,705
   9  Southwest       126,739   139,413    153,354    419,506
  10                  --------  --------   --------   --------
  11  Total Sales    $403,805
```

Fig. 5.9 Highlight the range to copy to.

1-2-3 copies the @SUM function to all the cells in the specified To where? range (see fig. 5.10).

Note: In figure 5.10, the range of formulas appears in Text format to show how each copied formula adjusts to its new location. Your spreadsheet will show the results, but you can see the formula in the control panel.

6. Save as Income.

```
B11: (T) [W12] @SUM(B5..B10)                                  READY

            A           B          C          D          E
   1  ================================================
   2  INCOME REPORT    January   February    March    1st Quarter
   3  ================================================
   4  Sales
   5  Northeast       $30,336   $33,370    $36,707   $100,413
   6  Southeast        20,572    22,629     24,892     68,093
   7  Central         131,685   144,854    159,339    435,878
   8  Northwest        94,473   103,920    114,312    312,705
   9  Southwest       126,739   139,413    153,354    419,506
  10                  --------  --------   --------   --------
  11  Total Sales   @SUM(B5..B10) @SUM(C5..C10) @SUM(D5..D10) @SUM(E5..E10)
```

Fig. 5.10 The @SUM function is copied to the specified range.

117

Modifying a Worksheet

Notice that the cell references in the original function @SUM(B5..B9) refer to column B. When you copy the formula one column to the right, the cell references also change one column to the right. The cell references in the copy change from column B in the original formula to column C (C5..C9) in the copied formula. Cell references in formulas copied to cells D11 and E11 also change.

Referencing Cells with Absolute Addressing

In some cases, a formula has an important address that should not be changed when the formula is copied. To keep an address *absolute*, enter a dollar sign ($) before the cell's column letter and before the cell's row number. For example, $E$11 is an absolute address.

Now that you have summed the contents of several columns of sales, you want to calculate the percentage of sales represented by each month of the quarter. In this example, the best way to do this is to copy a formula that contains an absolute address. When you create the formula in cell B13, place a $ before the E and before the 11 in the second part of the formula. You place the $ in the formula by typing an actual dollar sign or by pressing **F4** (Abs) while pointing to the cell or while using **F2** (Edit).

Exercise 2.6: Copying a Formula with an Absolute Address

To make a formula point to one specific cell location and still be able to use copy, you must make use of absolute referencing. Follow these steps:

1. Move to cell A13 and label the row Percent of 1st Quarter.
2. Move to cell B13, type the formula **+B11/$E$11**, and press ⏎Enter.
3. Select/**R**ange **F**ormat **P**ercent **2** decimal places, and press ⏎Enter twice.
4. Select/**C**opy.
5. At the Copy what? prompt, highlight the cell containing the formula with an absolute address to be copied (B13 in this example) (see fig. 5.11). Press ⏎Enter.

    Note that cell B13 contains an absolute address ($E$11) in the formula +B11/$E$11.

6. At the To where? prompt, move the cell pointer to cell C13, press the [.] key to anchor the cursor. Highlight the range of cells to which you want the formula copied (C13..E13 in this example) by pressing → twice (see fig. 5.12). Press ⏎Enter.

To Copy Cells in the Spreadsheet

7. Save as Income

   Note that, in figure 5.13, the range of formulas in row 13 is displayed in text format to show how each copied formula is adjusted to its new location. The first address of each formula varies, but the second address remains absolute as $E$11 in all four formulas. Your spreadsheet should show the results in percents.

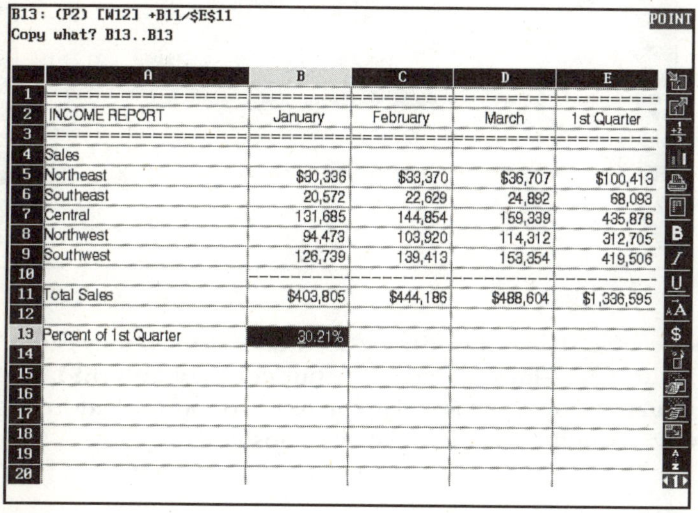

Fig. 5.11
Highlight the cell to be copied.

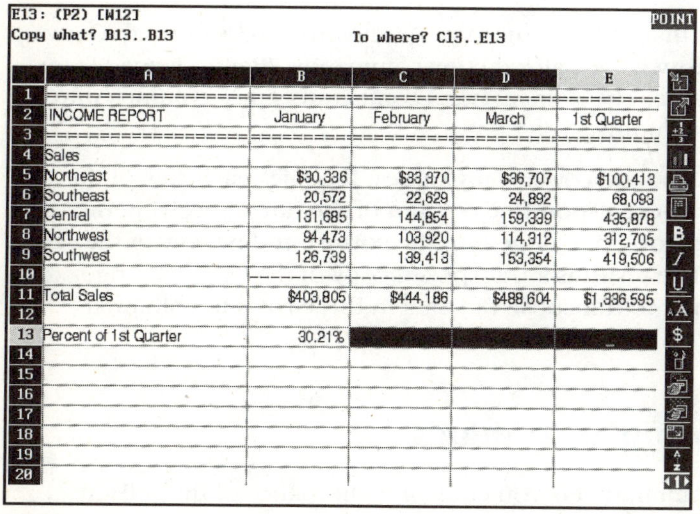

Fig. 5.12
Highlight the range to copy to.

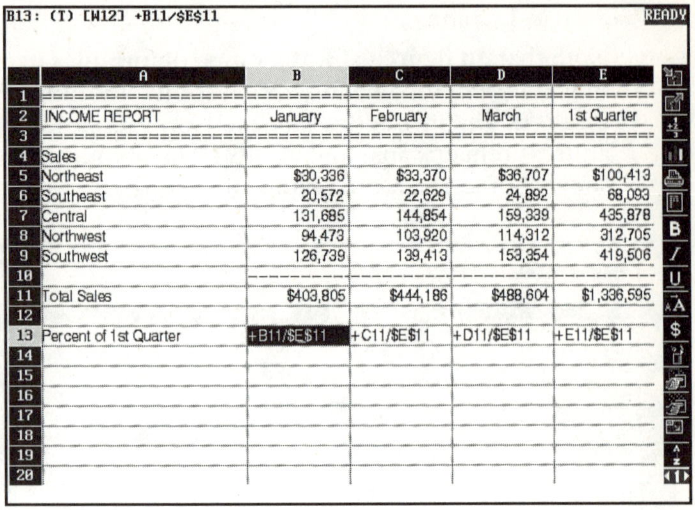

Modifying a Worksheet

Fig. 5.13
The copied formulas adjust to their new location.

B13: (T) [W12] +B11/$E$11					READY
	A	B	C	D	E
1	============	============	============	============	============
2	INCOME REPORT	January	February	March	1st Quarter
3	============	============	============	============	============
4	Sales				
5	Northeast	$30,336	$33,370	$36,707	$100,413
6	Southeast	20,572	22,629	24,892	68,093
7	Central	131,685	144,854	159,339	435,878
8	Northwest	94,473	103,920	114,312	312,705
9	Southwest	126,739	139,413	153,354	419,506
10	------------	------------	------------	------------	------------
11	Total Sales	$403,805	$444,186	$488,604	$1,336,595
12					
13	Percent of 1st Quarter	+B11/$E$11	+C11/$E$11	+D11/$E$11	+E11/$E$11

Cell locations can be relative (B11); they can be absolute ($E$11); they can make use of mixed addressing—locked into a row but not a column (E$11); or locked into a column but not a row ($E11). The last two forms of addressing are not used nearly as often as regular relative or absolute.

Transposing Rows and Columns

For copy operations that are difficult to perform with 1-2-3's normal /Copy commands, 1-2-3 has two specialized copy commands: /Range Trans (Transpose) and /Range Value. The /Range Trans command copies columns into rows and rows into columns.

The /Range Trans command copies only values. It copies each row of the original range into the corresponding column of the range receiving the copy, or each column of the original range into the corresponding row of the range receiving the copy. The result is a transposed copy of the original range. Suppose that you want to transpose the data in three rows to columnar format.

Converting Formulas to Values

The /Range Value command lets you copy only the values of the cells in one range to another range. This command is useful whenever you want to preserve the current formula values of a range of cells instead of having

To Copy Cells in the Spreadsheet

only the changed values after the worksheet has been updated. An important function of the /**R**ange **V**alue command is its capability to convert formulas to values. You don't have to worry, therefore, about formulas that depend on cell references.

Exercise 2.7: Converting Formulas to Values

To convert formulas to values when copying, follow these steps:

1. Retrieve the Budget worksheet created in Chapter 3.
2. Move to cell E3.
3. Select /**R**ange **V**alue.
4. At the `Convert what?` prompt, highlight the range of formulas to be copied by pressing ↓ to highlight through E11, and press ↵Enter.
5. At the `To where?` prompt, move the cell pointer to G3, and press ↵Enter.

Notice that the numbers are repeated, but if you look in the control panel the formulas are gone (see fig. 5.14).

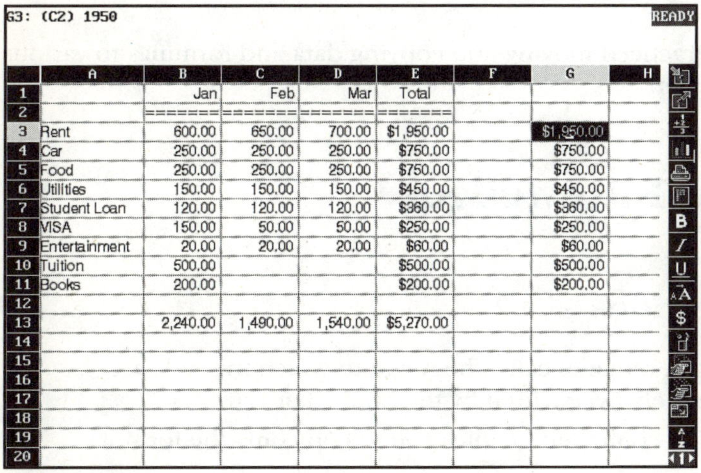

Fig. 5.14
The formulas have been converted to values.

Tips for Copying

Remember the following tips whenever you intend to copy data in the worksheet:

121

Modifying a Worksheet

- When you copy a cell, 1-2-3 automatically copies the format of the cell. This automatic format-copying feature saves you from having to set the format for an entire range of cells before (or after) copying to them.
- Sometimes the original and destination ranges overlap when you copy. The general rule is to avoid overlapping the end points of both ranges to prevent problems with the copy operation. If you do overlap them, you may get mixed results. You can, however, overlap ranges without error when the original and destination ranges have the same upper left boundary (such as when using /Range Value to copy the values of formulas onto themselves).
- Note particularly the finality of the /Copy command when you disable the Undo feature. If you copy over the contents of a cell, you have no way to retrieve the contents. Make sure that you have properly designated your ranges before you complete the command. You can retrieve the worksheet again if it has already been saved, but all changes made since the last save are lost.

Summary

In this chapter you practiced moving and copying data and formulas to various parts of the spreadsheet.

Testing Your Knowledge

True/False Questions

1. When you move a range of cells, the range to which the cells are copied is completely overwritten by the range that is moved.
2. The /Range Value command enables you to copy only the formula in a cell.
3. Absolute addressing of formulas is the default for 1-2-3.
4. The /Range Transpose command copies only values.
5. Dollar signs in a formula indicate that a cell reference is absolute.

Testing Your Knowledge

Multiple Choice Questions

1. You anchor the cursor in a cell to highlight adjacent cells by pressing the
    - A. $ key.
    - B. F4 key.
    - C. Alt key.
    - **(D.)** . key. *connect*
2. A relative cell address
    - A. is a cell reference that does not adjust for a new location when used in a formula copied to that location.
    - B. is a character string.
    - C. is a cell reference that adjusts for a new location when used in a formula copied to that location.
    - D. is designated by using the F4 key.
3. Which one of the following is absolute?
    - A. A7.
    - B. $A7.
    - C. A$7.
    - D. $A$7.
4. Which one of the following is relative?
    - A. A7.
    - B. $A7.
    - C. A$7.
    - D. $A$7.
5. When you copy a cell,
    - A. 1-2-3 deletes the original.
    - B. 1-2-3 also copies the format of the cell.
    - C. 1-2-3 tries to overlap ranges.
    - D. you cannot undo it even if Undo is enabled.

Fill-in-the-Blank Questions

1. The two different methods of addressing cells are ___RELATIVE___ and ___ABSOLUTE___.
2. If you use the ___MOVE___ command, data in the first location disappears.

Modifying a Worksheet

3. If you use the \COPY command, data appears in both locations.
4. If you use the RANGE / TRANS command, data that was in a row will appear in a column.
5. If you use the /R /V command, data that was a formula will now just be values.

Review: Short Projects

1. Using Absolute References

    Retrieve the Budget worksheet created in Chapter 3. At the bottom of the worksheet, figure what percent of the total expenses is represented by each month. Remember absolute referencing before copying the formula and formatting the cells correctly.

2. Using the Copy Command

    Make use of the Copy command in any worksheet created so far in this book to enter formulas before entering data. You also can suppress zeros for a better looking spreadsheet.

3. Using Copy and Move

    Enter any numbers into cells A1 to A10. Move the column of numbers from column A to column C. Copy the numbers from column C to columns D and E. Write a formula in cell C11 to add the column of numbers. Copy the formulas from cell C11 to cells D11 and E11.

Review: Long Projects

1. Copying Values

    Retrieve the checkbook project you created in Chapter 3. Use /Range Value to copy only the values from your Total column to another range.

2. Using Absolute References

    Retrieve the 12-month budget created in the Chapter 3 long project. At the bottom, create a formula that figures what percent of the total expenses is represented by each month. Use /Copy to copy to all 12 months. Remember absolute referencing and formatting the cells.

Using Functions

In addition to creating formulas, you can use a variety of ready-made formulas provided by 1-2-3. These built-in formulas—called *functions*—enable you to take advantage of 1-2-3's analytical capability. Functions are helpful when used with business, engineering, scientific, and statistical applications.

Objectives

1. To Learn To Use Statistical Functions
2. To Learn To Use Financial Functions
3. To Learn To Use Date and Time Functions
4. To Learn To Use Logical Functions
5. To Learn To Use Special Functions

Using Functions

Key Terms in This Chapter	
Functions	1-2-3's built-in formulas that perform many different types of calculations.
Arguments	Inputs needed by most functions to perform their calculations.
Syntax	The format of a specific function.

Entering a 1-2-3 Function

This chapter does not include numbered steps for entering each function because you have already used the @SUM function several times, and you enter all functions with the same procedure. To enter a 1-2-3 function in a worksheet, follow this general four-step process:

1. Press @, the character that identifies a function.
2. Type the function name.
3. Enter, in parentheses, any inputs or arguments that the function needs.
4. Press ↵Enter.

An example of a function is @SUM. If you type the function **@SUM(B3.D3)**, 1-2-3 returns the calculated result.

Some functions don't require arguments. The date function @NOW, for example, returns the current system date; and the mathematical function @RAND produces a random decimal number between 0 and 1.

Objective 1: To Learn To Use Statistical Functions

A set of seven statistical functions enables you to perform all the standard statistical calculations on data in your worksheet or in a 1-2-3 database. You can find minimum and maximum values, calculate averages, and compute the standard deviation and variance.

To Learn To Use Statistical Functions

The attribute of all statistical functions is a list that can be value(s), cell reference(s), range(s), and formula(s). If the list contains more than one item, separate the items with commas, as in the following example:

@SUM(B5..B20,B30..B40,B55,10%*B80,1000)

Table 6.1 lists the functions, their arguments, and the statistical operations they perform.

Table 6.1 Statistical Functions

Function	Description
@AVG(*list*)	Calculates the arithmetic mean (average) of a list of values
@COUNT(*list*)	Counts the number of cells that contain entries
@MAX(*list*)	Returns the maximum value in a list of values
@MIN(*list*)	Returns the minimum value in a list of values
@STD(*list*)	Calculates the population standard deviation of a list of values
@SUM(*list*)	Sums a list of values
@VAR(*list*)	Calculates the population variance of a list of values

Note: The statistical functions perform differently when you specify cells as ranges instead of individually. When you specify a range of cells, 1-2-3 ignores empty cells within the specified range. When you specify cells individually, however, 1-2-3 takes empty cells into consideration for the particular functions mentioned. Also, when you specify cells, keep in mind that 1-2-3 treats cells containing labels as zeros. This is the case whether the cell is part of a range or you specify the cell individually. For this reason, don't erase cells by pressing the space bar because 1-2-3 reads the space as a label.

Computing the Arithmetic Mean with @AVG

The @AVG function is a helpful tool for calculating the commonly used arithmetic mean, or average. Use the following syntax for this function:

@AVG(*list*)

The *list* argument can contain any combination of values, cell addresses, single and multiple ranges, and range names.

Using Functions

Exercise 1.1: Using @AVG

The @AVG function can calculate the mean grade on a test and the student's grade average. The function's argument is a list of test scores. Follow these steps:

1. Create the worksheet shown in figure 6.1.

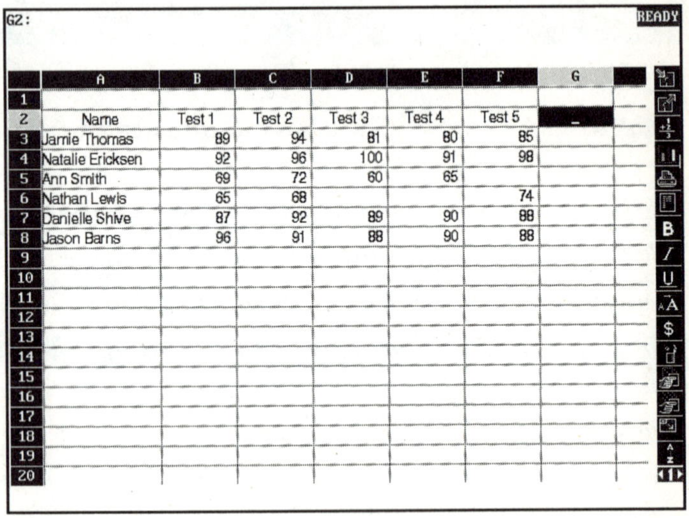

Fig. 6.1
A test score spreadsheet.

2. Move to cell G2, and label the column **Average**.
3. In cell G3, type **@AVG(B3.F3)** and press ⏎Enter.
4. Copy the formula down column G to compute all students' grade average, and format as Fixed 1 decimal place (see fig. 6.2).
5. Move to cell A11, and label the row **Mean Score**.
6. In cell B11, compute the average grade on test 1 by typing **@AVG(B3.B8)**, and then press ⏎Enter.
7. Copy the formula to the other four tests, and format for Fixed 1 decimal place (see fig. 6.3).

Counting Cell Entries with @COUNT

The @COUNT function totals the number of cells that contain entries of any kind, including labels, label-prefix characters, and the values ERR and NA.

To Learn To Use Statistical Functions

Use the following syntax for @COUNT:

@COUNT(*list*)

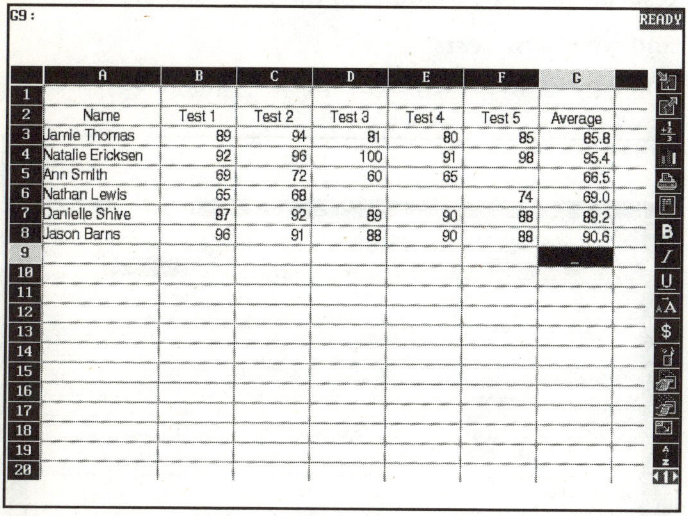

Fig. 6.2
@AVG computes the students' average grade.

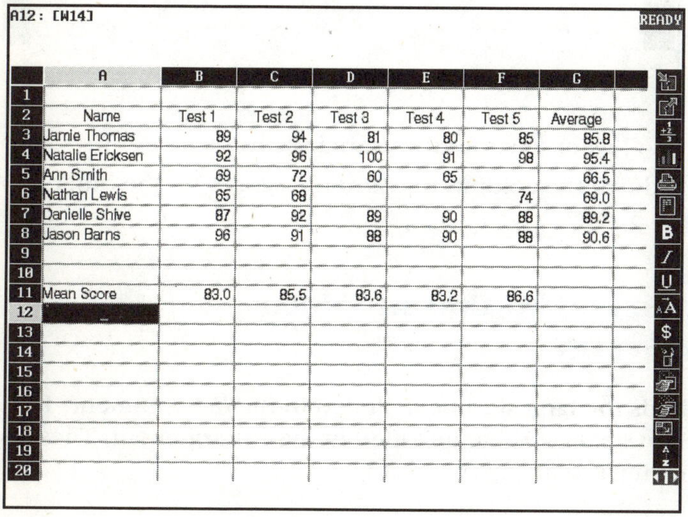

Fig. 6.3
@AVG computes the mean score on each test.

The *list* argument can contain any combination of values, cell addresses, single and multiple ranges, and range names.

Note: Be sure to include only ranges as the argument in the @COUNT function. If you specify an individual cell, 1-2-3 counts that cell as if it has an entry, even if the cell is empty.

Using Functions

Exercise 1.2: Using @COUNT

You notice that some students have missing test scores, so adding a field that counts the number of tests taken is one example of the @COUNT function:

1. Move to cell H2, and type '**# of Tests**.
2. Move to cell H3, and type **@COUNT(B3..F3)**, press ↵Enter (see fig. 6.4).

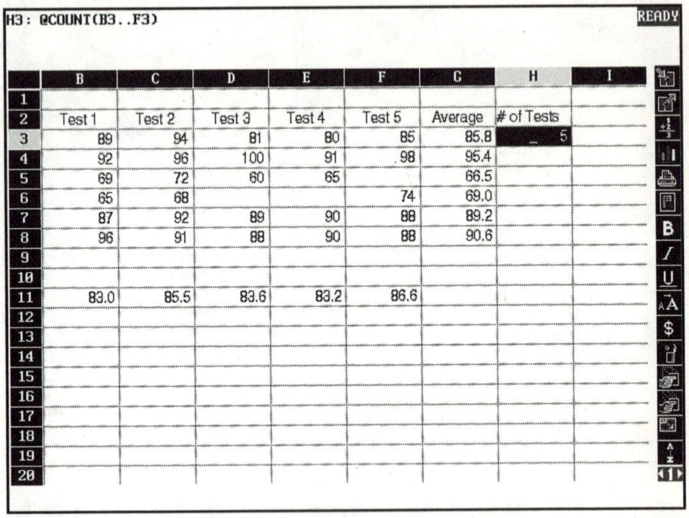

Fig. 6.4
@COUNT counts the number of tests.

Notice that you don't want to count the average score.

3. Copy the formula down the column to count the scores for the other students (see fig. 6.5).

Finding Maximum and Minimum Values with @MAX and @MIN

The @MAX function finds the largest value included in the *list* argument. The @MIN function finds the smallest value included in the *list* argument. These functions use the following syntax:

@MAX(*list*)

@MIN(*list*)

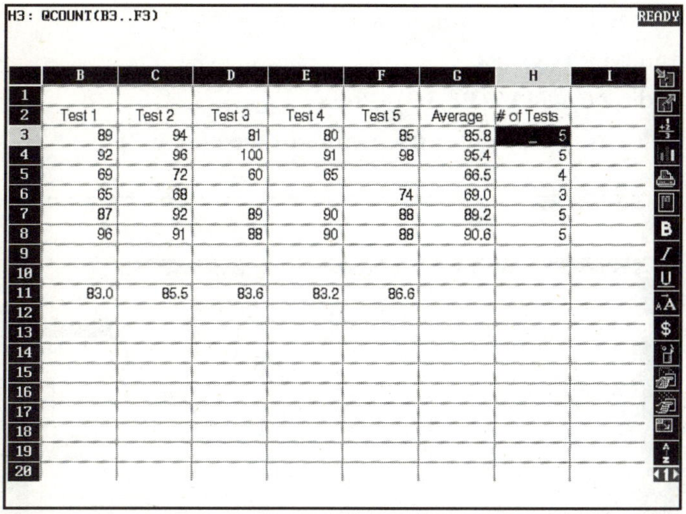

To Learn To Use Statistical Functions

Fig. 6.5
@COUNT counts the number of tests for all students.

Exercise 1.3: Using @MIN and @MAX

You can find out a student's highest and lowest grade on the five tests, and also find out the highest and lowest grade by any student on all five tests using the @MIN and @MAX functions. Follow these steps:

1. Move to cell I2, and type **Lowest**.
2. Move to cell I3, and type **@MIN(B3.F3)**. Press ⏎Enter (see fig. 6.6).

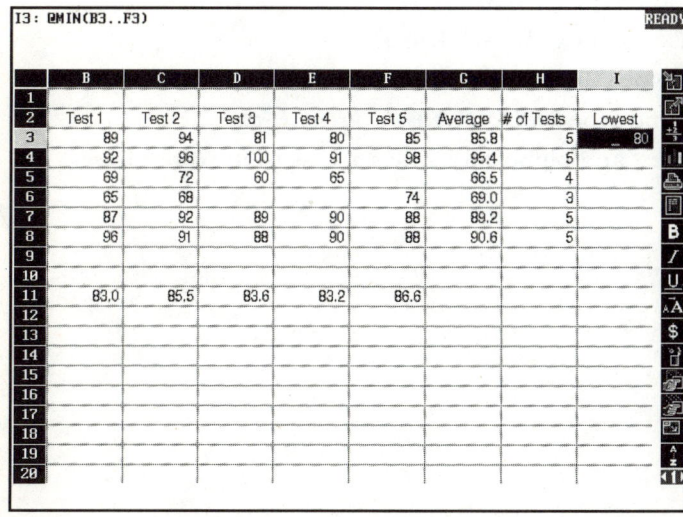

Fig. 6.6
@MIN finds the lowest score.

131

Using Functions

3. Copy the formula down column I for each student.
4. Move to cell J2, and type **Highest**.
5. Move to cell J3, and type **@MAX(B3.F3)**. Press `⏎Enter`.
6. Copy the formula down column J for each student (see fig. 6.7).

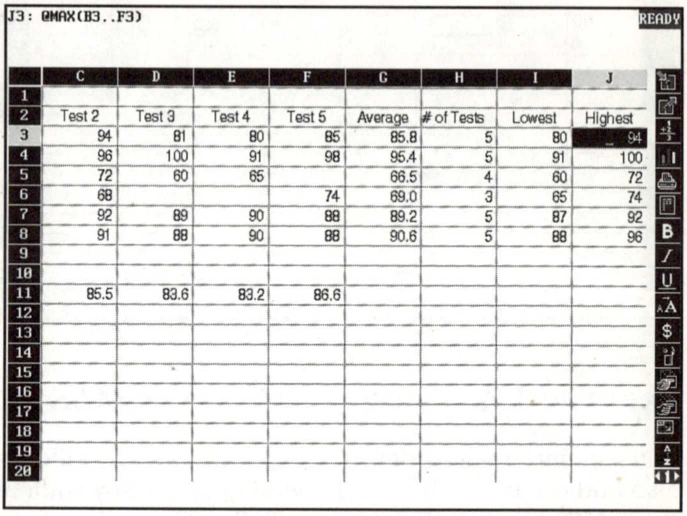

Fig. 6.7
@MAX finds the highest score, and @MIN finds the lowest.

	C	D	E	F	G	H	I	J
	Test 2	Test 3	Test 4	Test 5	Average	# of Tests	Lowest	Highest
3	94	81	80	85	85.8	5	80	94
4	96	100	91	98	95.4	5	91	100
5	72	60	65		66.5	4	60	72
6	68			74	69.0	3	65	74
7	92	89	90	88	89.2	5	87	92
8	91	88	90	88	90.6	5	88	96
11	85.5	83.6	83.2	86.6				

Notice that both the @MIN and @MAX only include the test scores—not the average or count.

7. Move to cell A12, and type **Lowest**.
8. Move to cell B12, and type **@MIN(B3.B8)**.
9. Move to A13, and type **Highest**.
10. Move to cell B13, and type **@MAX(B3.B8)**. Press `⏎Enter`.
11. Copy both the lowest and highest formulas across to the other four tests (see fig. 6.8).
12. Save as Grades.

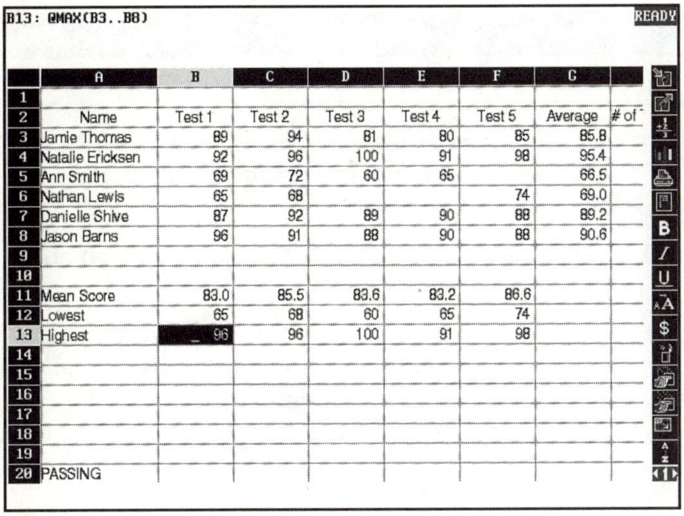

To Learn To Use Financial Functions

Fig. 6.8
@MAX finds the highest score on the tests, and @MIN finds the lowest.

Objective 2: To Learn To Use Financial Functions

The 11 financial functions enable you to perform a variety of business-related calculations. These calculations include discounting cash flows, computing loan amortization, calculating depreciation, and analyzing the return on investments. This set of functions helps you perform investment analysis and accounting, or budgeting for depreciable assets.

Table 6.2 summarizes the financial functions available in 1-2-3.

Table 6.2 Financial Functions	
Function	Description
@CTERM(*interest*, *future_value*, *present_value*)	Calculates the number of periods required for a present value amount to grow to a future value amount, given a periodic interest rate
@DDB(*cost*,*salvage*, *life*,*period*)	Calculates depreciation using the double-declining balance method

continues

Using Functions

Table 6.2 Continued	
Function	Description
@FV(*payments, interest,term*)	Calculates the future value of a series of equal payments compounded at the periodic interest rate
@IRR(*estimate,range*)	Calculates the internal rate of return on an investment
@NPV(*interest,range*)	Calculates the present value of a series of future cash flows at equal intervals when payments are discounted by the periodic interest rate
@PMT(*principal, interest,term*)	Calculates the loan payment amount
@PV(*payments, interest,term*)	Calculates the present value of a series of future cash flows of equal payments discounted by the periodic interest rate
@RATE(*future_value, present_value,term*)	Calculates the periodic rate required to increase the present value amount to the future value amount in a specified length of time
@SLN(*cost,salvage,life*)	Calculates straight-line depreciation for one period
@SYD(*cost,salvage, life,period*)	Calculates sum-of-the-years' digits depreciation for a specified period
@TERM(*payments, interest,future_value*)	Calculates the number of payment periods necessary to accumulate the future value when payments compound at the periodic interest rate

Calculating Loan Payment Amounts with @PMT

You use the @PMT function to calculate the periodic payments necessary to pay the principal on a loan with a given interest rate and time period.

To Learn To Use Financial Functions

Therefore, to use @PMT, you need to know the total loan amount (principal), periodic interest rate, and term, as shown in the following syntax:

@PMT(*principal,interest,term*)

Express the interest rate and the term in the same units of time. For example, if you make monthly payments, you should use the annual interest rate divided by 12. The term should be the number of months you will be making payments. @PMT operates on the assumption that payments are made at the end of each period.

Exercise 2.1: Using @PMT

To calculate the monthly car payment on a $10,000 car loan, you can use the @PMT function. The loan is repaid over 48 months, and the interest rate is 8 percent. With an empty spreadsheet, follow these steps:

1. Move to cell B4, and type **Principal Borrowed**.
2. In cell F4, type **10000**, and format it for Currency 0 decimal places.
3. In cell B5, type in **Term in Months**.
4. In cell F5, type **48**.
5. In cell B6, type **Interest Rate**.
6. In cell F6, type **.08**, and format the cell for Percent 2 decimal places.
7. In cell B7, type **Payment**.
8. In cell F7, type **@PMT(F4,F6/12,F5)**.
9. Format the result for Currency 2 decimal places (see fig. 6.9).

   Notice that you can save this spreadsheet and use it for any loan amount, interest rate, or term to figure the payment.

Exercise 2.2: Calculating Future Values with @FV

You can use @FV to compute your savings if you invest $100 per month in a savings account at 8 percent interest for 10 years. In an empty spreadsheet, follow these steps:

1. Move to cell B4, and type **Deposit Per Month**.
2. In cell F4, type **100**, and format for Currency 2 decimal places.
3. In cell B5, type **Years Invested**.
4. In cell F5, type **10**.
5. In cell B6, type **Interest Rate**.

135

Using Functions

6. In cell F6, type **.08** , and format for Percent 0 decimal places.
7. In cell B7, type **Total Amount** .
8. In cell F7, type **@FV(F4,F6/12,F5*12)** .
9. Format the result for Currency 2 decimal places (see fig. 6.10).

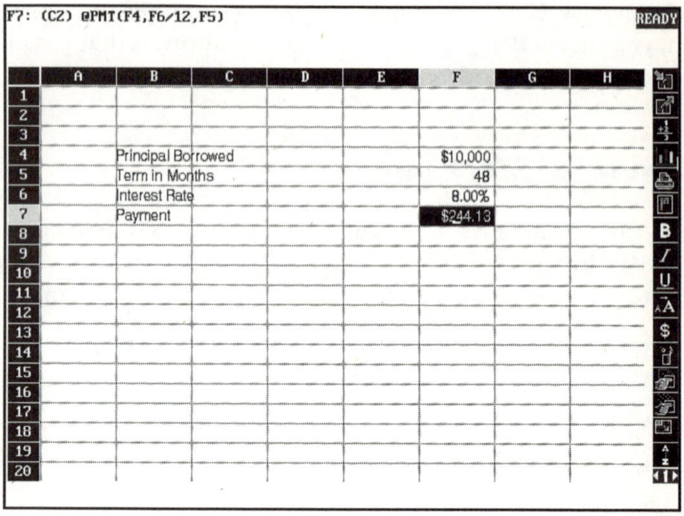

Fig. 6.9
@PMT calculates the amount of the payment.

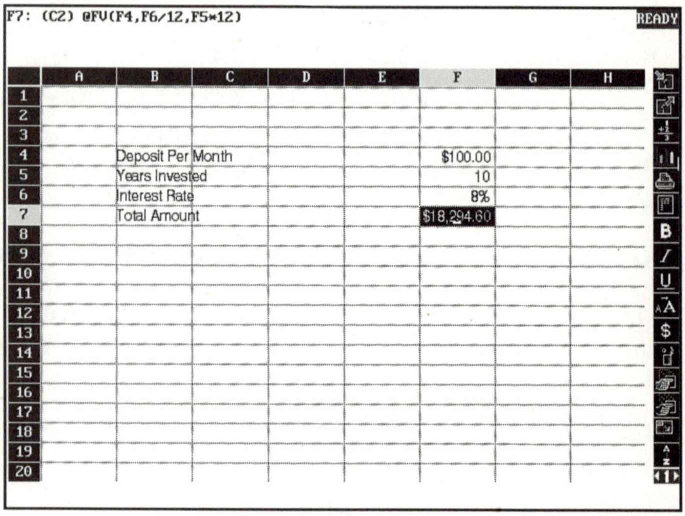

Fig. 6.10
@FV computes the amount of the savings account in 10 years.

Notice that you can save this and use it for any investment, term, or interest rate.

Objective 3: To Learn To Use Date and Time Functions

The 11 date and time functions enable you to convert dates, such as November 26, 1994, and times, such as 6:00 p.m., to serial numbers. You can then use the serial numbers to perform date and time arithmetic. These functions are valuable tools when dates and times affect calculations and logic in your worksheets.

1-2-3's internal calendar begins with the serial number 1, which represents January 1, 1900. The calendar ends with 73050, which represents December 31, 2099. 1-2-3 represents a single day with an increment of 1; therefore, 1-2-3 represents January 2, 1900, as 2. To display that serial number as a text date, format the cell with the /Range Format Date command.

Table 6.3 summarizes the date and time functions available.

Finding the Current Date and Time with @NOW

The @NOW function displays as a serial number both the current system date and the current system time. The numbers to the left of the decimal point specify the date. The numbers to the right of the decimal point define the time. This function, which requires no arguments, provides a convenient tool for adding dates to worksheets and reports.

After you enter the @NOW function, use the /Range Format Date command to display the serial date number as a text date or time.

Exercise 3.1: Using @NOW

The @NOW function, formatted as a date, inserts the current date into a worksheet. In an empty spreadsheet, follow these steps:

1. Move to cell A1, and type **@NOW**. Press ↵Enter (see fig. 6.11).
2. Use **/R**ange **F**ormat **D**ate to change the serial date to a formatted date and widen the column as necessary.

Using Functions

Table 6.3 Date and Time Functions	
Function	Description
@DATE(*year,month,day*)	Calculates the serial number of the specified date
@DATEVALUE(*date_string*)	Converts a date expressed as a string into a serial number
@DAY(*date_number*)	Extracts the day number from a serial number
@HOUR(*time_number*)	Extracts the hour number from a serial number
@MINUTE(*time_number*)	Extracts the minute number from a serial number
@MONTH(*date_number*)	Extracts the month number from a serial number
@NOW	Calculates the serial date and time from the current system date and time
@SECOND(*time_number*)	Extracts the seconds from a serial number
@TIME(*hour,minutes,seconds*)	Calculates the serial number of the specified time
@TIMEVALUE(*time_string*)	Converts a time expressed as a string into a serial number
@YEAR(*date_number*)	Extracts the year number from a serial number

Converting Date Values to Serial Numbers with @DATE

To use dates in arithmetic operations, you need to convert the dates to serial numbers. You can then use those serial numbers in arithmetic operations and sorting. The most frequently used date function is @DATE, which converts any date to a serial number. This serial number enables you to do calculations. You also can display the serial number as a date in 1-2-3. @DATE uses the following syntax:

@DATE(*year,month,day*)

To Learn To Use Date and Time Functions

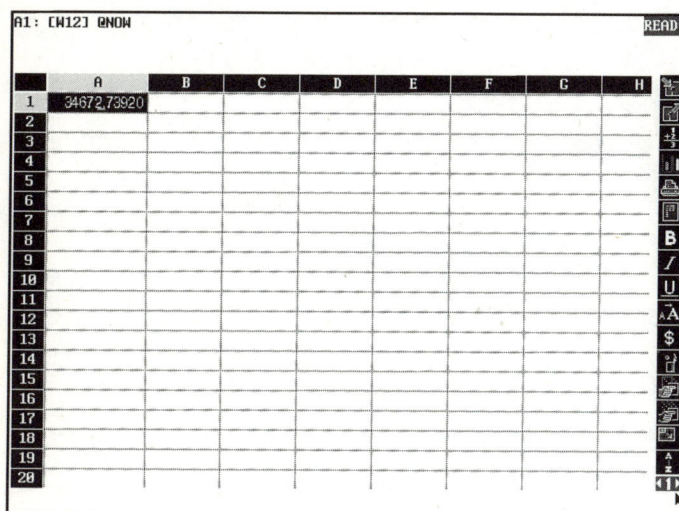

Fig. 6.11
The serial numbers representing the current date and time appear.

You use numbers to identify a year, month, and day. For example, you enter the date November 26, 1994, into the @DATE function as @DATE(94,11,26). The serial number that results is 34664.

Note: The numbers you enter to represent the year, month, and day must create a valid date. If the date is not valid, 1-2-3 returns ERR. For example, 1-2-3 allows you to specify February 29 only during leap years. You never can specify February 30.

Exercise 3.2: Using @Date

You can use the @NOW from Exercise 3.1 with @DATE to perform date calculations. To see how many days have elapsed since a given date and today's date, type the following in an empty spreadsheet:

1. Type **@NOW** in cell A1.
2. Move to cell A2, and type **@DATE(94,3,7)**. Press ⏎Enter.
3. Format cell A1 and A2 using **/R**ange **F**ormat **D**ate, and widen the column, if necessary.
4. Move to cell A3, and type **+A1-A2**. Press ⏎Enter.
5. Format the cell for Fixed 0 decimal places (see fig. 6.12).

Using Functions

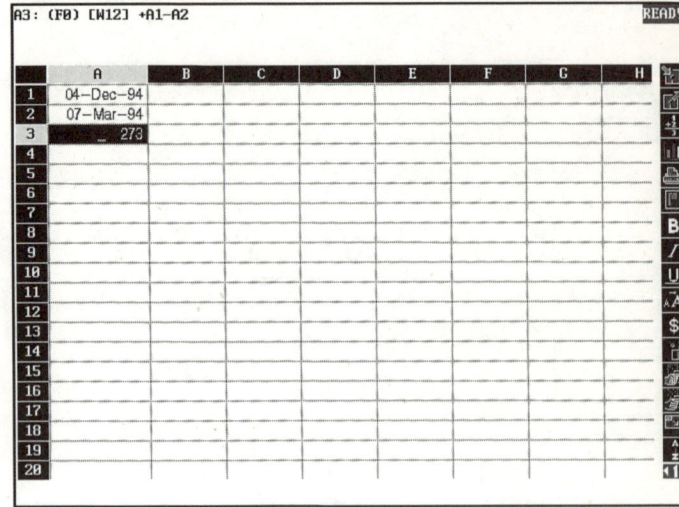

Fig. 6.12
The result of the formula is the number of days elapsed since March 7, 1994 and today.

Objective 4: To Learn To Use Logical Functions

Each of 1-2-3's nine logical functions enables you to test whether a condition is true or false. Many of these functions operate in a similar manner-by returning a 1 if the test is true or a 0 if the test is false. These logical tests are important for creating decision-making functions; the results of these functions depend on conditions elsewhere in the worksheet.

Table 6.4 summarizes the logical functions that 1-2-3 provides.

Table 6.4	Logical Functions
Function	Description
@FALSE	Returns the logical value 0, for false
@IF(*condition,true,false*)	Tests a condition and returns one result if the condition is true and another result if the condition is false
@ISAAF(*name*)	Tests for a defined add-in program
@ISAPP(*name*)	Tests for an attached add-in program
@ISERR(*cell_reference*)	Tests whether the argument results in ERR

To Learn To Use Logical Functions

Function	Description
@ISNA(*cell_reference*)	Tests whether the argument results in NA
@ISNUMBER(*cell_reference*)	Tests whether the argument is a number or blank cell
@ISSTRING(*cell_reference*)	Tests whether the argument is a string
@TRUE	Returns the logical value 1, for true

Creating Conditional Tests with @IF

The @IF function represents a powerful tool—one you can use both to manipulate text within your worksheets and to affect calculations. You can, for example, use an @IF statement to test the following condition: Is the inventory on hand below 1,000 units? You can return one value or label if the answer to the question is true, or another value or label if the answer is false. The @IF function uses the following syntax:

@IF(*condition,true,false*)

The @IF function can use six operators when testing conditions. The following list shows the operators and their corresponding descriptions.

Operator	Description
>	Greater than
<	Less than
=	Equal to
>=	Greater than or equal to
<=	Less than or equal to
<>	Not equal to

In addition, you can perform more complex conditional tests. Adding logical operators enables you to test multiple conditions in one @IF function. These operators and their descriptions are the following:

Using Functions

Operator	Description
#AND#	Tests two conditions, both of which must be true in order for the entire test to be true.
#NOT#	Tests that a condition is not true.
#OR#	Tests two conditions; if either condition is true, the entire test condition is true.

The @IF function can check whether a specified cell's content is between 4 and 10, whether a cell contains a specified text string, and whether a 1-2-3 date falls before or after the current date. The results of these tests depend on whether the condition evaluates as true or false.

In figure 6.13, examples of the @IF function test for specified values or labels.

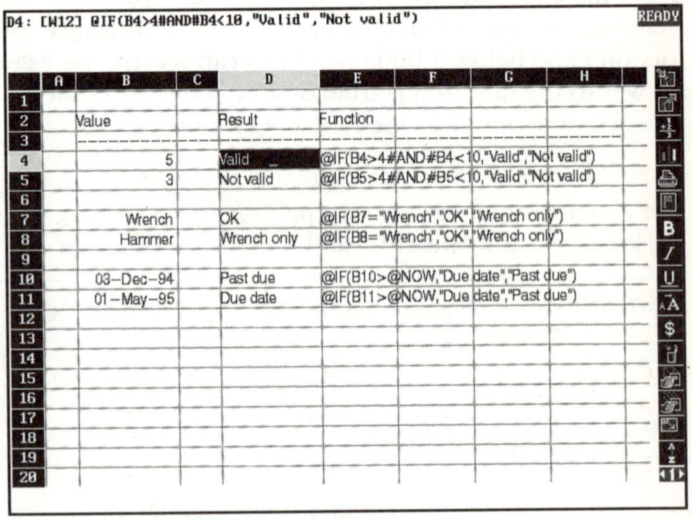

Fig. 6.13
Examples of the @IF function.

Exercise 4.1: Using @IF

You can use the @IF to determine whether a student is passing or failing the class. Follow these steps:

142

To Learn To Use Special Functions

1. If you saved the Grades spreadsheet, retrieve it.
2. Move to cell A20, and type **PASSING**.
3. Move to cell A21, and type **FAILING**.
4. Move to cell K3, and type **@IF(G3>=70,$A$20,$A$21)** (see fig. 6.14).

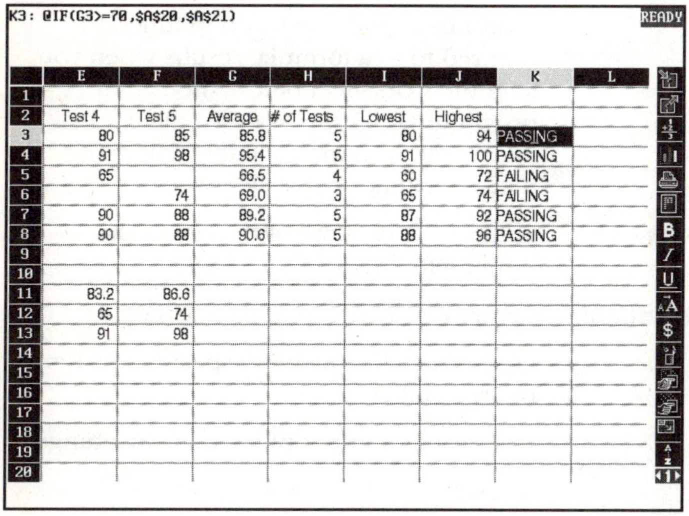

Fig. 6.14
@IF places PASSING in the cell if the score is greater than or equal to 70, but places FAILING in the cell if the score is less than 70.

5. Copy the formula down the column. Notice the need for absolute referencing in the formula.
6. Save as Grades.

Objective 5: To Learn To Use Special Functions

1-2-3 provides a set of 12 special functions. You use these special tools to perform a variety of tasks.

Table 6.5 lists 1-2-3's special functions.

Using Functions

Table 6.5 Special Functions	
Function	Description
@@(*location*)	Returns the contents of the cell referenced in the specified location
@?	Indicates an unknown add-in function referred to in a formula; results when you load the worksheet before the add-in program. (1-2-3 shows @? in the control panel and displays NA in the cell.) Note that you cannot enter @? in a cell.
@CELL(*attribute,range*)	Returns an attribute of the cell in the upper left corner of the range
@CELLPOINTER(*attribute*)	Returns an attribute of the current cell
@CHOOSE(*offset,list*)	Locates in a list the entry specified by the offset number
@COLS(*range*)	Counts the number of columns in a range
@ERR	Displays ERR in the cell
@HLOOKUP(*key,range, row_offset*)	Locates a label or number in a table and returns a label or value from that row of the range
@INDEX(*range,column_ offset, row_offset*)	Returns the contents of a cell specified by the intersection of a row and column within a range
@NA	Displays NA in the cell
@ROWS(*range*)	Counts the number of rows in a range
@VLOOKUP(*key,range, column_offset*)	Locates a label or number in a lookup table and returns a label or value from that column of the range

To Learn To Use Special Functions

Finding Table Entries with @HLOOKUP and @VLOOKUP

The @HLOOKUP and @VLOOKUP functions retrieve a string or value from a table, based on a specified key used to find the information. The operation and format of the two functions are essentially the same except that @HLOOKUP searches horizontal tables and @VLOOKUP searches vertical tables. These functions use the following syntax:

@HLOOKUP(*key,range,row_offset*)

@VLOOKUP(*key,range,column_offset*)

The *key* argument is the string or value that tells 1-2-3 which row (@HLOOKUP) or column (@VLOOKUP) to search. The key strings or values belong in the first row or column. Numeric keys must be in ascending order for the functions to work properly. The *range* argument is the area that makes up the entire lookup table. The *row_offset* or *column_offset* argument specifies from which row (@HLOOKUP) or column (@VLOOKUP) to retrieve data. The offset argument is always a number, ranging from 0 to the highest number (minus one) of columns or rows in the lookup table.

The @HLOOKUP and @VLOOKUP functions are useful for finding any type of value or label you would have to look up manually in a table. Examples include tax amounts, shipping zones, and inventory information.

Exercise 5.1: Using @VLOOKUP

You can create a table for a video store which brings up the name of the movie, its location, and the number of days it can be rented for, by matching the inventory number using @VLOOKUP:

1. In a blank worksheet, move to cell K1.
2. Create the table shown in figure 6.15. Widen columns as necessary.
3. Press (Home), move to C3, and type **Video Information**.
4. Move to cell B5, and type **Movie Number:**.
5. In cell D5, type **A102**.
6. Move to cell B6, and type **Movie Name:**.
7. Move to cell D6, and type **@VLOOKUP(D5,K1.N4,1)** (see fig. 6.16).

145

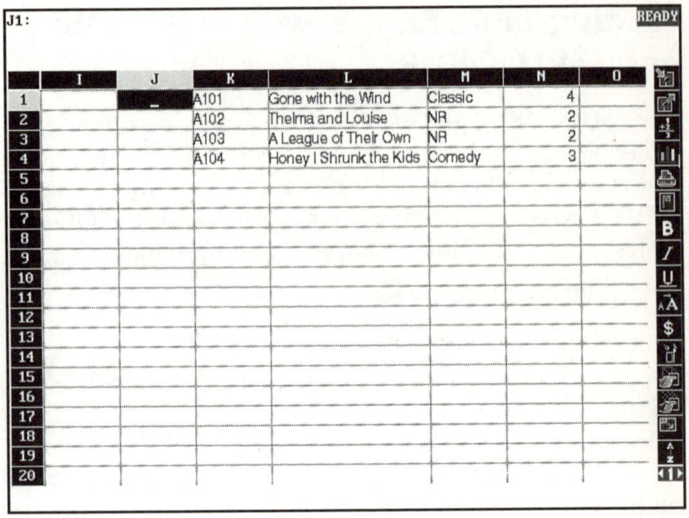

Using Functions

Fig. 6.15
Create this table, widening column L to hold the movie titles.

	I	J	K	L	M	N	O
1			A101	Gone with the Wind	Classic	4	
2			A102	Thelma and Louise	NR	2	
3			A103	A League of Their Own	NR	2	
4			A104	Honey I Shrunk the Kids	Comedy	3	

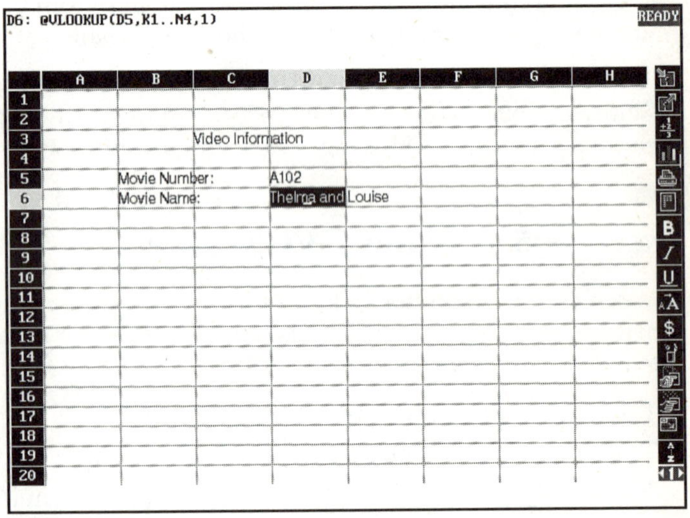

Fig. 6.16
@VLOOKUP finds the correct movie name.

D6: @VLOOKUP(D5,K1..N4,1)

	A	B	C	D	E	F	G	H
3				Video Information				
5		Movie Number:		A102				
6		Movie Name:		Thelma and Louise				

8. Move to cell B7, and type **Location:**.
9. Move to cell D7, and type **@VLOOKUP(D5,K1.N4,2)**.
10. Move to cell B8, and type **Number of Days:**.
11. Move to cell D8, and type **@VLOOKUP(D5,K1.N4,3)**.
12. Move to cell B9, and type **Date Due:**.

13. Move to cell D9, and type **@NOW+D8**.
14. Format cell D9 using **/R**ange **F**ormat **D**ate, and widen the column if necessary.
15. Save as Video.

@VLOOKUP finds all the information, and the formula in D9 uses that information to add the number of days to the current date to compute when the movie is due (see fig. 6.17).

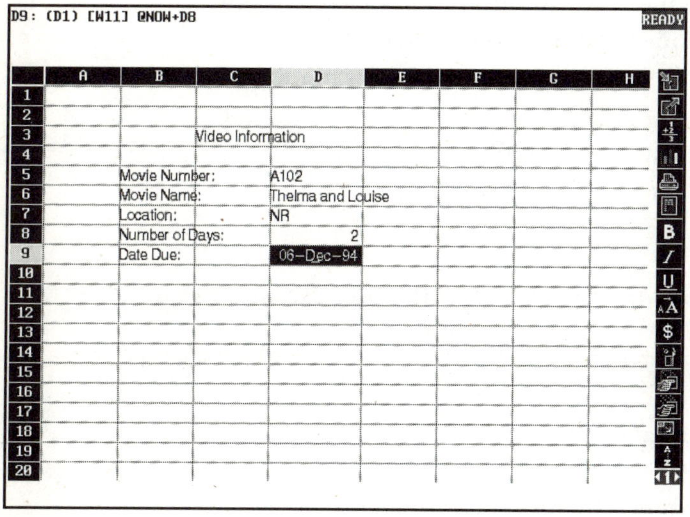

Fig. 6.17
The date the movie is due is displayed.

Substitute the other movie numbers one at a time into cell D5, that is, A101, A103, and A104. If you add more videos, you need to change the formulas to expand the table reference. This would have been a good place to make use of range names. The range K1.N4, for example, could be named Table; then the formula would read:

@VLOOKUP(D5,Table,1).

Note: You always begin counting the columns from zero.

Summary

This chapter described the functions that 1-2-3 provides to make formula and worksheet construction easier and more error-free.

147

Using Functions

Testing Your Knowledge

True/False Questions

1. Some functions require arguments to work correctly; however, some work without arguments.
2. To find the current date, you can type **@DATE** in a cell.
3. All 1-2-3's functions begin with the character @.
4. 1-2-3 converts dates to numbers called serial numbers for date calculations.
5. Day 1 for 1-2-3 is January 1, 1900.

Multiple Choice Questions

1. To change a serial date to a date that the user can understand, you must use
    - A. @CONVERT.
    - B. @DATE.
    - C. /Range Format Fixed.
    - D. /Range Format Date.

2. To enter the current date into a spreadsheet, use
    - A. @NOW.
    - B. @DATE.
    - C. @DATEVALUE.
    - D. @TIME.

3. To find the arithmetic mean of a group of cells, use
    - A. @MEAN.
    - B. @MAX.
    - C. @SUM.
    - D. @AVG.

4. To find information located in a table, use
    - A. @TABLE.
    - B. @VLOOKUP.
    - C. @DTABLE.
    - D. @DLOOKUP.

Testing Your Knowledge

5. To calculate payments on a loan, you need to use
   A. @PMT (principal, interest, term).
   B. @LOAN (principal, interest, term).
   C. @TIME (principal, interest, term).
   D. @PMT (deposit, interest, term).

Fill-in-the-Blank Questions

1. The ____statistical____ and ____logical____ functions are useful in engineering and scientific applications.
2. The ____FINANCIAL____ functions enable you to perform a variety of business-related calculations.
3. The ____Date____ and ____Time____ functions are valuable tools when dates and times affect calculations and logic in your worksheet.
4. The ____Statistical____ functions enable you to perform all the standard statistical calculations on data in your worksheet.
5. The ____Logical____ functions are important for creating decision-making functions.

Review: Short Projects

1. Using Statistical Funtions

   Retrieve the bowling worksheet created in Chapter 3 short projects or create a bowling spreadsheet. Figure each person's average, high game, and low game. Also figure the average score for each game, and the high and low score for each game.

2. Using Statistical Funtions

   Retrieve the checkbook created in Chapter 3 long projects or create a checkbook register. Calculate the average check written, average deposit, and the high and low checks written during the month.

3. Using @PMT

   Use the @PMT function to build a worksheet for a loan you have, using your term, interest rate, and principal.

149

Using Functions

Review: Long Projects

1. Using @VLOOKUP

   Using the video worksheet as an example, create a worksheet for a general rental store. Information located in the table should include item number, item description, fee, length of rental in days, and any other information you need. Use @VLOOKUP to access the information. Also use a date function to tell the customer when the item is due. Save and print the spreadsheet.

2. Using @IF

   Create the worksheet shown in figure 6.18. In cell E2, write a formula that looks at the number on-hand in column D, and if that number has fallen below five, the word REORDER should appear in column E. If the column D shows more than five on-hand, then a 0 should appear. Use zero suppression to display blanks. Save and print the spreadsheet.

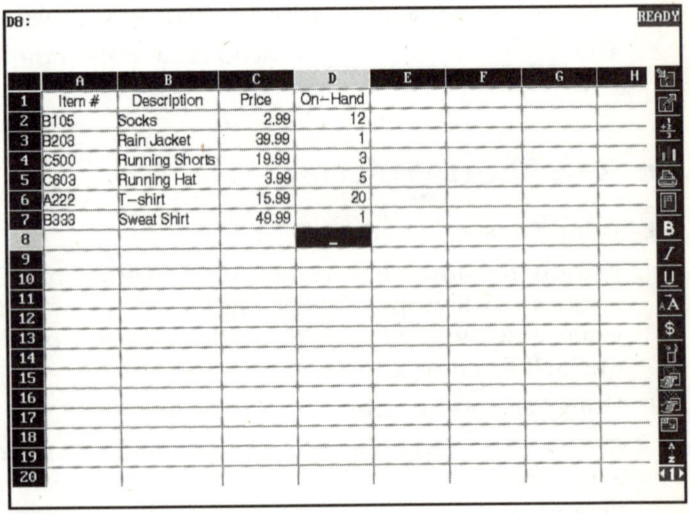

Fig. 6.18
Create this spreadsheet.

	A	B	C	D	E
1	Item #	Description	Price	On-Hand	
2	B105	Socks	2.99	12	
3	B203	Rain Jacket	39.99	1	
4	C500	Running Shorts	19.99	3	
5	C603	Running Hat	3.99	5	
6	A222	T-shirt	15.99	20	
7	B333	Sweat Shirt	49.99	1	

Printing Reports

7

1-2-3 allows you to print reports based on your spreadsheet. At times you may want to change some of the settings to produce different types of reports.

Objectives:

1. To Print Simple Spreadsheets
2. To Print Multiple Page Reports
3. To Print Excluding Segments of the Spreadsheet
4. To Learn about Other Print Options

Key Terms in This Chapter	
Print defaults	Pre-set, standard specifications for a 1-2-3 print job.
Print Settings dialog box	The dialog box that appears on-screen when you select /**P**rint **P**rinter. The dialog box shows you the current printer settings and allows you to change them on-screen.
Borders	One or more rows or columns of data or labels that 1-2-3 repeats on a multiple-page report.
Header	Information displayed on one line at the top of a page. A header may include a date and a page number.
Footer	Information displayed on one line at the bottom of a page. A footer may include a date and a page number.

Objective 1: To Print Simple Spreadsheets

Every print command in 1-2-3 starts from the /**P**rint option of the 1-2-3 main menu. After choosing /**P**rint, you must select one of the next options (see fig. 7.1).

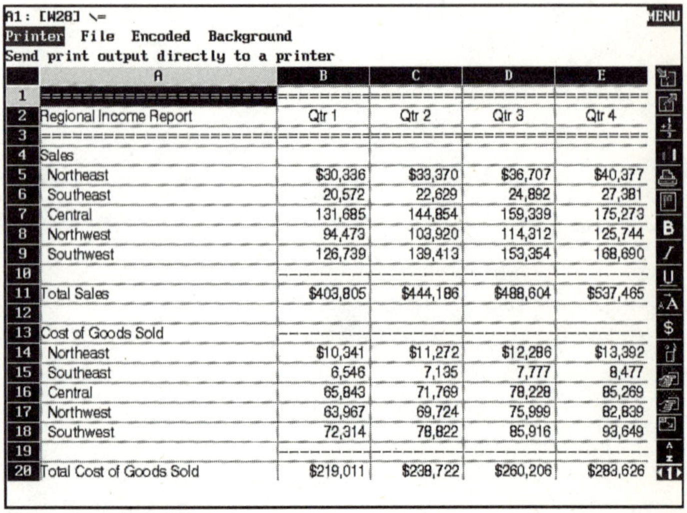

	A	B	C	D	E
1	============================	==========	==========	==========	==========
2	Regional Income Report	Qtr 1	Qtr 2	Qtr 3	Qtr 4
3	============================	==========	==========	==========	==========
4	Sales				
5	Northeast	$30,336	$33,370	$36,707	$40,377
6	Southeast	20,572	22,629	24,892	27,381
7	Central	131,685	144,854	159,339	175,273
8	Northwest	94,473	103,920	114,312	125,744
9	Southwest	126,739	139,413	153,354	168,690
10		----------	----------	----------	----------
11	Total Sales	$403,805	$444,186	$488,604	$537,465
12					
13	Cost of Goods Sold	----------	----------	----------	----------
14	Northeast	$10,341	$11,272	$12,286	$13,392
15	Southeast	6,546	7,135	7,777	8,477
16	Central	65,843	71,769	78,228	85,269
17	Northwest	63,967	69,724	75,999	82,839
18	Southwest	72,314	78,822	85,916	93,649
19		----------	----------	----------	----------
20	Total Cost of Goods Sold	$219,011	$238,722	$260,206	$283,626

Fig. 7.1
The /**P**rint command options in the control panel.

To Print Simple Spreadsheets

Select **P**rinter to send your report directly to the current printer. The other options include: File, to create a text file; Encoded, to create a disk file that includes instructions on printing; and Background, to create an encoded file that prints while you continue working in 1-2-3.

After you choose **/P**rint **P**rinter, you see the next menu, and if you are using 2.3 or 2.4 you also see the Print Settings dialog box (see fig. 7.2).

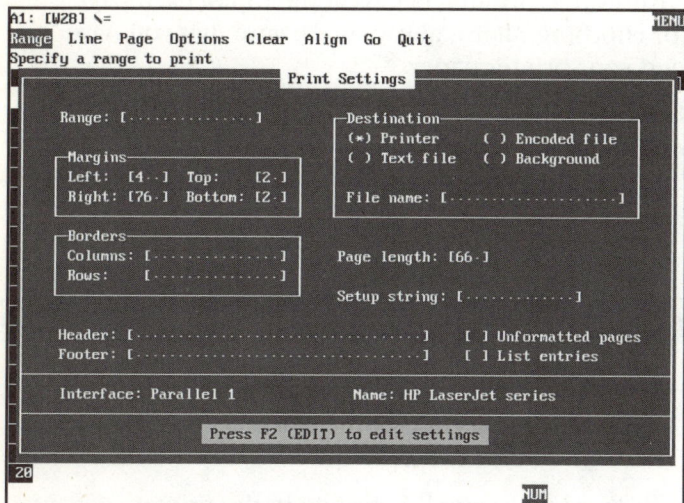

Fig. 7.2
The Print Settings dialog box in 2.3 and 2.4.

Table 7.1 outlines the various options on the /**P**rint **P**rinter menu. Regardless of which options you select in order to print, you must choose **R**ange and specify a range to print. Select **G**o and **Q**uit to return to the worksheet. All other selections are optional.

Exercise 1.1: Printing a One-Page Report

Printing a page or less with the default settings involves only a few steps:

1. Retrieve the Grades file created in Chapter 6 or create a similiar spreadsheet.
2. Check to see that your printer is on-line and that you have positioned the paper properly.
3. Select /**P**rint **P**rinter.
4. Select **R**ange.

Printing Reports

5. Press (Home), and press [↓] so that the cell pointer is on Name.
6. Press (.) to anchor the cursor and use the directional keys to highlight only columns A to G, that is, the student names, test scores, and average score (see fig. 7.3).
7. Press [↵Enter] to confirm the range.
8. After you highlight the range you want to print, select **A**lign.

    Choosing **A**lign ensures that printing begins at the top of each page. Before printing (or choosing **A**lign), always make sure that you have correctly positioned your printer paper.

9. To begin printing, select **G**o.

    The **G**o option sends your worksheet data to the printer.

10. After the printer finishes, select **P**age to advance to the top of the next page or eject the page from a laser printer.
11. Select **Q**uit to return to READY mode.

Table 7.1 Selections on the /Print Printer Menu

Selection	Description
Range	Indicates the section of the worksheet to print or save to disk as a print file
Line	Adjusts the paper line-by-line in the printer
Page	Adjusts the paper page-by-page in the printer
Options	Determines settings to enhance the appearance of the printout; you can use this menu item or the Print Settings dialog box
Clear	Erases previous settings
Align	Signals the printer position at the top of the print page
Go	Starts printing to the printer or a disk file
Quit	Exits the menu and returns 1-2-3 to READY mode

If you press **Enter** after selecting the **G**o option, the file prints a second time. If this accidentally occurs, you can stop printing by pressing **Ctrl+Break**. Even if the area of your worksheet to print is larger than one page, you can

To Print Simple Spreadsheets

use the basic steps for printing one-page reports. For information about fitting a large worksheet on to one page, see "Forcing a Range to Print on One Page" in Chapter 8.

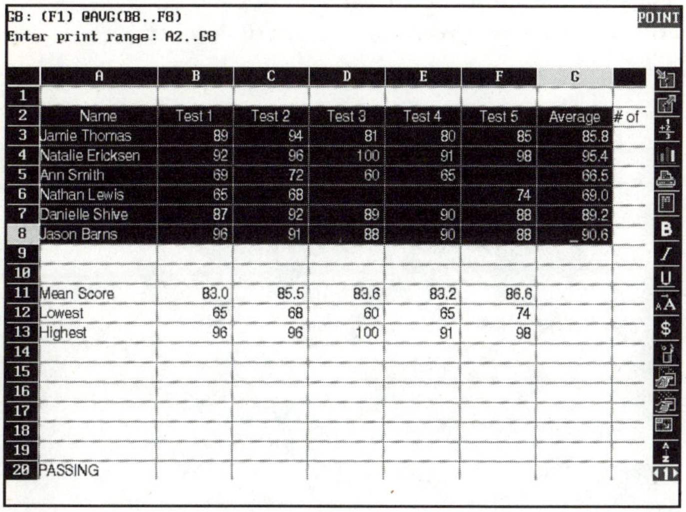

Fig. 7.3 Highlight all the names and the five test scores for printing.

Exercise 1.2: Printing with the Print Range SmartIcon in 2.4

If you don't need to adjust the paper or any print options, you can use the Print Range SmartIcon to print a range.

To use the Print Range SmartIcon to print a range, follow these steps:

1. Select the range you want to print by dragging the mouse pointer over the range. You also can press F4 (Abs), press the arrow keys to extend the highlight, and press ↵Enter.
2. Select the Print Range SmartIcon.

Exercise 1.3: Using the Print Settings Dialog Box in 2.3 and 2.4

You can use the Print Settings dialog box to view or change many print options (see fig. 7.4). The main parts of the dialog box include option buttons, check boxes, and text boxes.

Printing Reports

To use the Print Settings dialog box, follow these steps:

1. After selecting /**P**rint **P**rinter, press F2 (Edit) or click the left mouse button.

   1-2-3 highlights one letter (usually the first letter) of each option. The main Print menu disappears when you activate the dialog box.

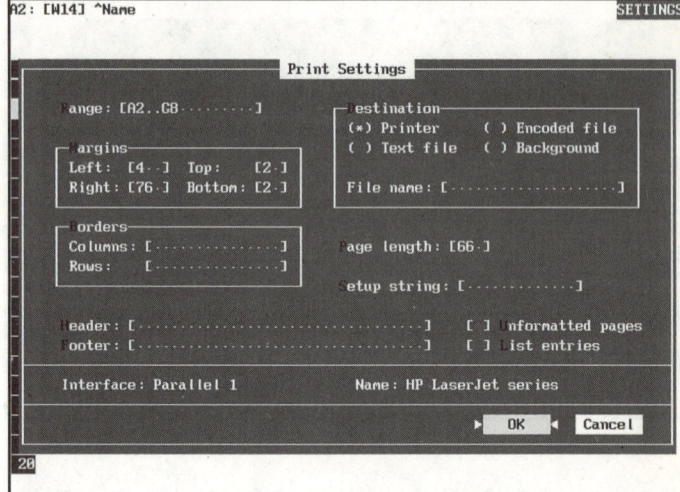

Fig. 7.4
The Print Settings dialog box.

2. To select an option button or check box, press the highlighted letter of each option until your choice is made. Or you can click the left mouse button on your choice.

   To choose **T**ext file as the destination, for example, select **D**estination **T**ext file or click the left mouse button on the **T**ext file option button. An asterisk (*) indicates your choice.

3. Press P to reset your destination to the printer.

   To choose unformatted pages, select **U**nformatted pages or click the left mouse button on the corresponding check box. An X indicates your choice.

   Note: To unmark a check box, select the check box again. The X should disappear.

4. To use a text box, press the highlighted letter of each option until the cursor is in the text box, or click the left mouse button on your choice.

5. Type the text in the box, and press Enter. Type **130**, for example, as the right margin.

To Print Multiple Page Reports

6. Where the text box calls for a range (**R**ange or **B**orders), you can select the range in one of the following ways:

    - Type the cell references for the range in the text box, and press ↵Enter.

    - Type the range name in the text box, and press ↵Enter.

    - Press F4 to go to POINT mode. Highlight the range, and press ↵Enter.

7. When you finish selecting all options in the Print Settings dialog box, press ↵Enter or click OK. The main **P**rint menu reappears.

8. To print the selected range, select **A**lign **G**o from the menu.

    Figure 7.5 shows a completed Print Settings dialog box.

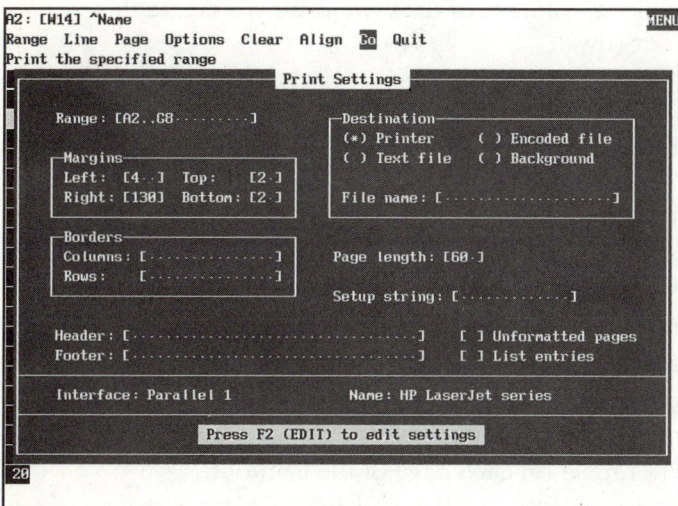

Fig. 7.5
A completed Print Settings dialog box.

9. Select **P**age to advance (or eject) the paper. Select **Q**uit to return to READY mode.

Objective 2: To Print Multiple Page Reports

When 1-2-3 encounters a print range that is wider than the margins on the Print Settings sheet, it prints this data on multiple pages. To compensate for this, 1-2-3 allows you to keep track of your data by using border columns.

157

Printing Reports

Note: To calculate whether 1-2-3 will print multiple pages of data for a wide print range, you can use this formula: Take the sum of the widths of the columns in the print range. If the sum of the widths of the columns in the print range is greater than the width of the margins, 1-2-3 will print multiple pages for your range. To find the widths of the margins, subtract the left margin from the right margin.

If you want to print information correctly when splitting data between pages, remember that 1-2-3 treats numeric and text data differently. 1-2-3 prints numbers completely because they span only one cell. However, text—such as long labels that lie across several cells—may split awkwardly from one page to the next.

Sometimes you will want to print a long list of data that covers multiple pages in the margins on the Print Settings sheet. In this case, you may want a header that lines up exactly with the columns of data you print. To create this "header," you use border rows.

Exercise 2.1: Using Border Columns on a Multiple Page Report

To repeat column borders on each page when printing, follow these steps:

1. Use the Grades worksheet created in Chapter 6.
2. Select **/P**rint **P**rinter.
3. Select **O**ptions. Or in 2.4 press `F2`. Or click the left mouse button in the dialog box to edit the settings.
4. Select **B**orders. The **B**orders option enables you to select row or column borders to repeat on each page of the printout.

   1-2-3 asks whether you want to locate the labels down one or more columns or across one or more rows.
5. Select **C**olumns (see fig. 7.6).
6. Show which column you want printed on each page by typing the cell reference, **A1**. Press `⏎Enter` (see fig. 7.7). In 2.4 choose OK and then press `⏎Enter`.
7. To return to the main **P**rint menu, choose **Q**uit.
8. To choose the range to print, select **R**ange.
9. Highlight the desired print range. For this example, highlight columns B through K and down through the bottom of the worksheet, and press `⏎Enter` (see fig. 7.8).

   Note: Do not include in your print range the borders you want

To Print Multiple Page Reports

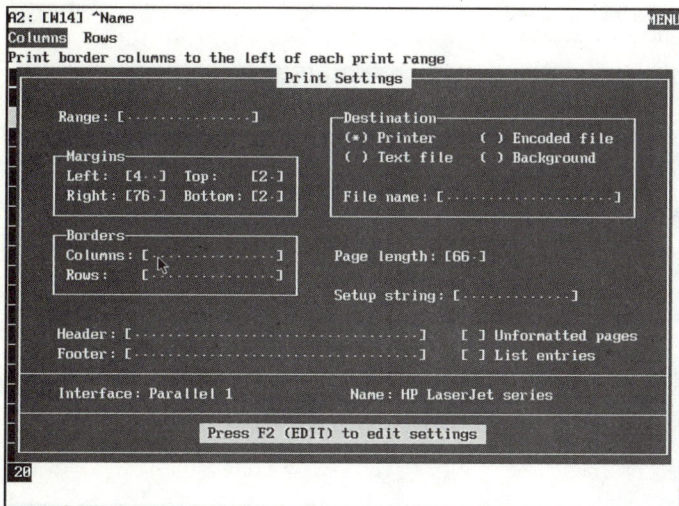

Fig. 7.6
In this example, select **Columns**.

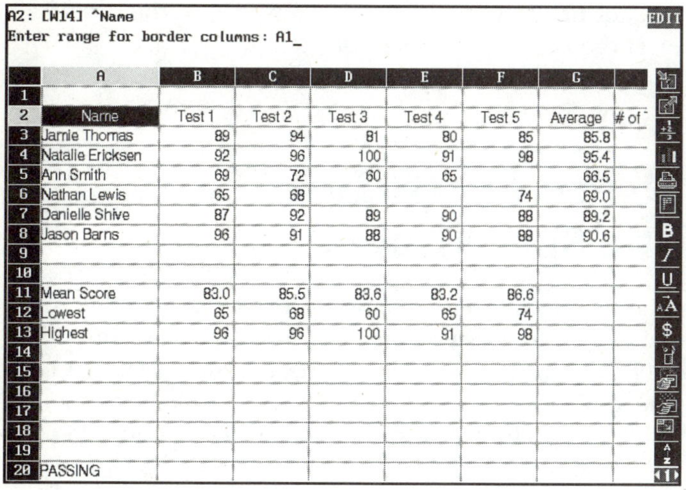

Fig. 7.7
To have column A become a repeating border, you make use of the Border command.

repeated on each page. 1-2-3 automatically prints the borders on every page of the printout. If you include the borders in the print range, 1-2-3 prints them twice on each page.

10. Select **A**lign **G**o.

159

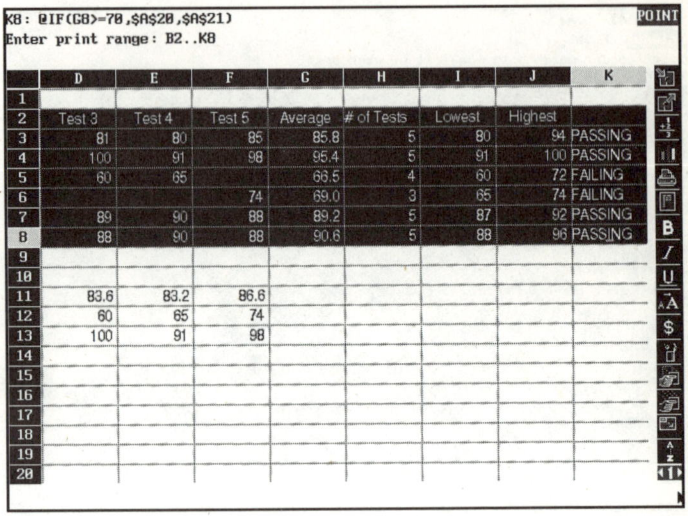

Printing Reports

Fig. 7.8
Do not include column A in the print range.

11. After the printer finishes printing, select **P**age to advance to the top of the next page or eject the page from a laser printer.
12. Select **Q**uit.

Objective 3: To Print Excluding Segments of the Spreadsheet

Because the /Print commands require that you specify a range to print, you can print only rectangular blocks from the worksheet. You can, however, suppress the display of cell contents in the range. You can hide entire rows or columns, or you can remove from view a segment that spans only part of a row or a column. You can hide a column (or range) of sensitive financial information.

Exercise 3.1: Excluding Columns

To print a worksheet range and exclude one or more columns in that range, follow these steps:

1. Use the Grades worksheet created in Chapter 6.
2. Move the cell pointer to cell B2.

To Print Excluding Segments of the Spreadsheet

3. Select **/W**orksheet **C**olumn **H**ide.
4. When the `Specify column to hide:` prompt appears, highlight columns B through F (see fig. 7.9). Press `⏎Enter`, and the columns disappear from view (see fig. 7.10).

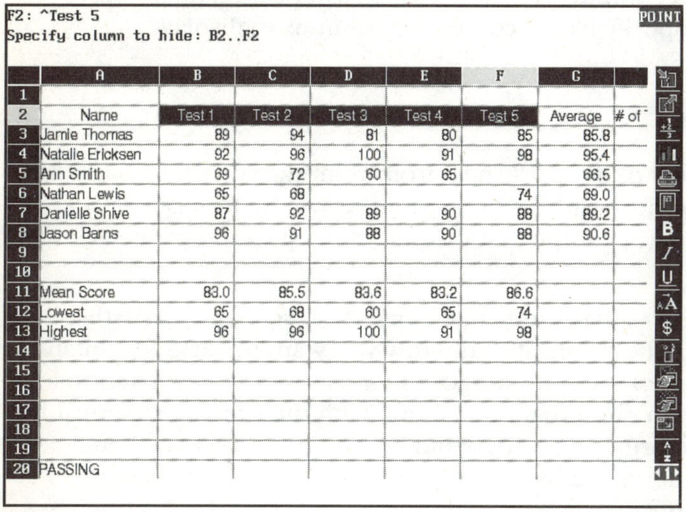

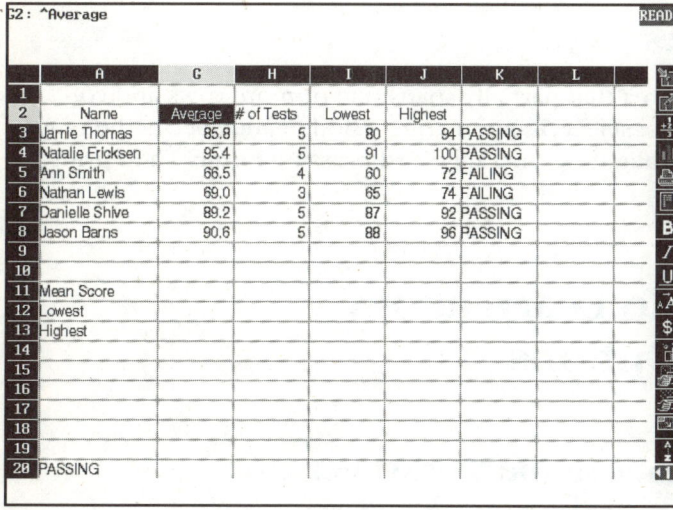

Fig. 7.9
Highlight the columns to Hide.

Fig. 7.10
The columns disappear from the screen.

161

Printing Reports

5. Select **/P**rint **P**rinter **R**ange.
6. Highlight all of the worksheet data, and press ⏎Enter.
7. Select **A**lign **G**o **P**age **Q**uit.

   Note: To restore hidden columns, select **/W**orksheet **C**olumn **D**isplay. When the hidden columns (marked with an asterisk) reappear on-screen, you can specify which column or columns to display.

Excluding Rows

To prevent specific rows of the worksheet from printing, you must mark these rows with a symbol for nonprinting. You enter the symbol for nonprinting by typing two vertical bars (||) in the first column of the print range in each row you want to exclude.

After you type both vertical bars, only one appears on-screen, and neither vertical bar appears on the printout. If the row you want to exclude contains data in the first column of the print range, you must insert a new column for the vertical bars. Keep in mind that the column with the vertical bars must be the first column of the print range. To avoid alignment problems when inserting this new column, use **/W**orksheet **C**olumn **H**ide to suppress the printing of the column.

Excluding Ranges

If you want to hide an area that partially spans one or more rows and columns, follow these steps: select **/R**ange **F**ormat **H**idden and specify the range you want to hide by highlighting the range and pressing **Enter**. Then print normally.

Objective 4: To Learn about Other Print Options

Setting Page Breaks in the Worksheet

You can insert page breaks in the worksheet by using the command **/W**orksheet **P**age. Execute this command with the cell pointer at the first

To Learn about Other Print Options

column of the range to print. The cell pointer also should be in the row that should begin the new page. The command automatically inserts a new blank row containing a page-break symbol (|::) in the cell at the cell pointer.

Adding Headers and Footers

If you prepare a report for distribution, you can add some simple enhancements. 1-2-3 reserves three lines in a document for a header and an additional three lines for a footer. If specified, headers and footers appear at the top and bottom of each page of your printout. You can keep the six lines reserved for these options (regardless of whether you use them). Or you can drop all six lines by selecting the /**P**rint **P**rinter **O**ptions **O**ther **U**nformatted command, or by modifying the Print Settings dialog box.

The **H**eader and **F**ooter options are located in the Print Settings dialog box or on the Print Printer Options menu. The header or footer can be up to 240 characters of text in one line of your printed output. You also can position the header and footer at the left, right, or center of the page. The size of both the paper and the printed characters, however, limits the size of the header and footer lines. When printing on 8 1/2-by-11-inch paper with 1/2-inch margins and 10-characters-per-inch type, for example, you can print only 75 characters in the header and footer.

1-2-3 prints the header text on the first line after any blank top margin lines. 1-2-3 follows the header by two blank header lines for spacing. The footer text line is printed above any blank bottom margin lines and below two blank footer lines (for spacing).

You can enter all features of the text manually. 1-2-3 provides special characters for controlling page numbers, however, adding the current date, and positioning text in a header or footer. The following list shows the characters that you use to place page numbers and dates in headers, and to set the alignment of the header:

Character	*Function*
#	Automatically prints consecutive page numbers, starting with 1.
@	Automatically prints the current date.

continues

Printing Reports

Character	Function
|	Automatically separates text (absence of a | symbol left-justifies all text); the first | symbol centers the text that follows, and the second | symbol right-justifies remaining text.
\\	When followed by a cell address or range name, left-aligns and fills the header or footer with the contents of the indicated cell.

Exercise 4.1: Adding Headers and Footers

To add a header or footer, follow these steps:

1. Use the Income worksheet created in Chapter 5.
2. Select /Print Printer.
3. Range; type or highlight the desired print range, and press ⏎Enter.

   Note: When using 2.3 or 2.4's dialog box to highlight the range, you must first press F4 to clear the dialog box. For example, press F4, highlight the range A1..E13, and press ⏎Enter.

4. Select Options Header or Footer. Or select Header or Footer in the dialog box. Select Header, for example, to add a header to the report.
5. In the text box, type the header text and codes for date and page number, and press ⏎Enter. Type @|NATIONAL MICRO|#, for example, and press ⏎Enter.
6. To return to the Printer menu, press ⏎Enter or click OK, and then select Quit.
7. Select Align Go Page Quit. The header appears at the top of the printed report (see fig. 7.11).

1-2-3, to a limited extent, can insert the contents of a cell into a header or footer. When the prompt to enter a header or footer appears, use the backslash character (\\) followed by a cell address or existing range name. Your printed output contains that cell's contents in the header or footer. You cannot, however, use this capability effectively when you want to segment a header or footer into left, center, and right portions. Note the effect of using an address in the following header lines. Each entry would be typed in the Header text box.

To Learn about Other Print Options

```
28-Nov-94              NATIONAL MICRO                          1
================================================================
 INCOME REPORT         January    February    March   1st Quarter
================================================================
Sales
Northeast              $30,336     $33,370   $36,707    $100,413
Southeast               20,572      22,629    24,892      68,093
Central                131,685     144,854   159,339     435,878
Northwest               94,473     103,920   114,312     312,705
Southwest              126,739     139,413   153,354     419,506
                       -------     -------   -------     -------
Total Sales           $403,805    $444,186  $488,604  $1,336,595

Percent of 1st Quarter   30.21%      33.23%    36.56%     100.00%
```

Fig. 7.11
The header appears at the top of the report.

Entry	Result
\A1	Prints the contents of cell A1 left-justified.
|\A1	Prints the string \A1 (not the contents of cell A1) centered in the header.
@|\A1	Prints the date left-justified and the string \A1 (not the contents of cell A1) centered.
\A3..A6	Prints the contents of cell A3 only, not the range A3..A6.
\SALES	Prints the contents of the range named SALES, if it

165

Printing Reports

exists; otherwise, prints nothing in the header.

Whenever the print range exceeds one single page, 1-2-3 repeats the header on each succeeding page, and the page number increases by one. If you have used the special page-number character (#) and want to print your report a second time before you leave the main **Print** menu, reset the page counter and set the top of the form by selecting **Align** before you choose **G**o.

If the centered or right-justified text in your header or footer doesn't print, look at the right-margin setting. Make sure that the right margin is appropriate for the current type size and paper width. To change the header, repeat the sequence to establish the text, pressing **Esc** to remove the existing header from the control panel or dialog box. (You can delete a header or footer without removing other specified options.)

To print a footer on the last page of a report (or on a single-page report), you must use the **Page** command. If you select the **Quit** command from the main **Print** menu without issuing the **Page** command, this final footer does not print. You can, however, reissue the **/Print Printer** command and select **Page**. In this case, the footer prints.

Changing the Page Layout

Before you change the page layout defaults, be aware of the current settings. 1-2-3 initially assumes 8 1/2-by-11-inch paper, a printer output of 6 lines per inch, and the default page length of 66 lines. 1-2-3 reserves 2 lines at the top and bottom of each page for the top and bottom margins. Also, 1-2-3 automatically reserves 3 lines at the top and 3 lines at the bottom for headers and footers. The header or footer takes 1 line, and 2 lines are for spacing before or after the main text. Therefore, on a default page length of 66 lines, only 56 lines are available for other text (see fig. 7.12).

If you want to check the default settings for margins and page length, select **/W**orksheet **G**lobal **D**efault **P**rinter.

The Default Printer Settings dialog box appears on-screen, showing the current margins and page length (see fig. 7.13).

Exercise 4.2: Changing Margins

To change the page layout of the current worksheet, follow these steps:

To Learn about Other Print Options

1. Select /Print Printer.
2. Choose Options Margins. Or in 2.3 or 2.4 press F2. Or click the left mouse button in the dialog box to edit the settings. Select Margins in the Print Settings dialog box.

   The Margins option allows you to change the size of the margins in the printed report.
3. Select Left, Right, Top, or Bottom.

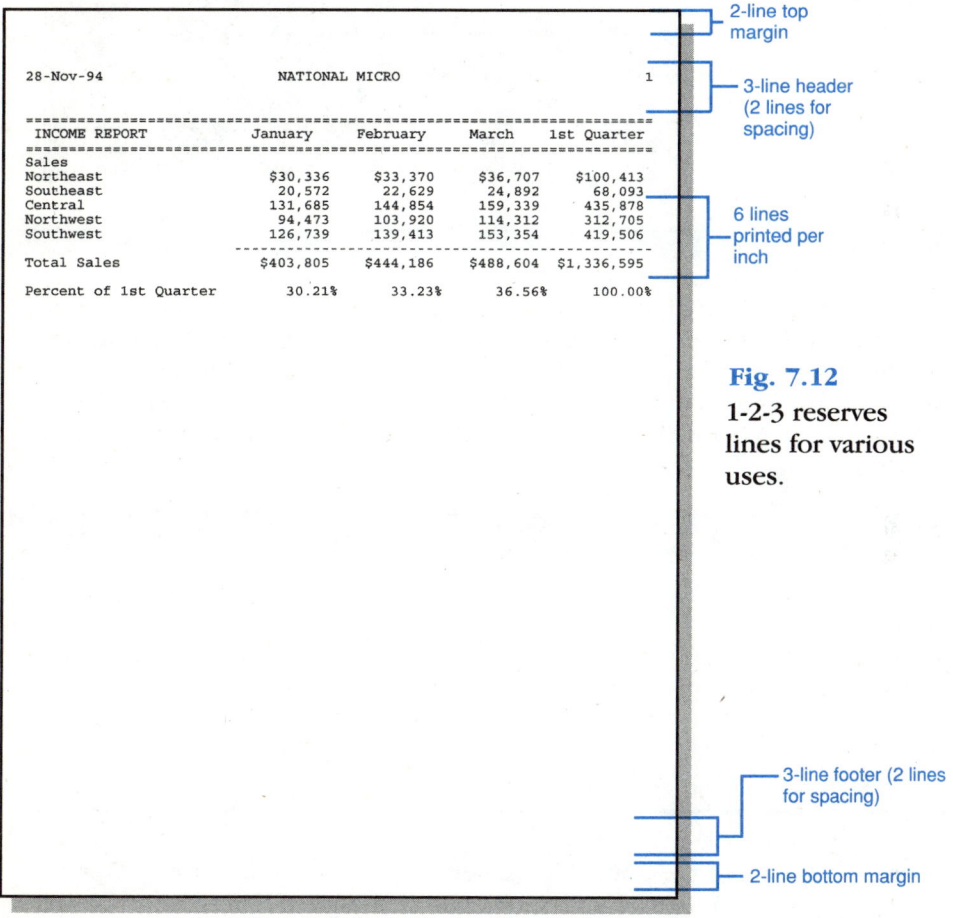

Fig. 7.12
1-2-3 reserves lines for various uses.

4. Type a value in the text box, and press Enter.
5. To return to the Print Printer menu, press Enter or click OK, and then select Quit.

Printing Reports

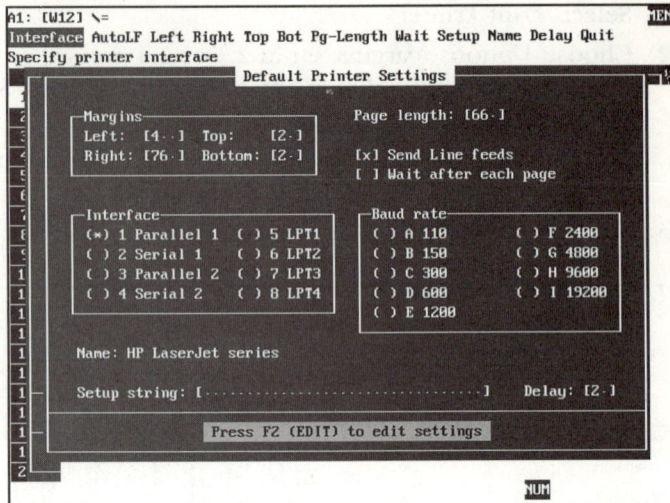

Fig. 7.13
The Default Printer Settings dialog box.

Be sure that you set left and right margins consistent with the width of your paper and the printer's pitch (characters per inch). The right margin must be greater than the left margin. And make sure that settings for the top and bottom margins are consistent with the paper's length and the established number of lines per inch. 1-2-3 shows the options listed in table 7.2 when you change margin settings.

Table 7.2	Selections for Changing Margin Settings	
Selection	*Setting Range*	*Minimum Option*
Left	0..240	0
Right	0..240	240
Top	0..32	0
Bottom	0..32	0

Note: In addition to the options in the dialog box, the /**Print Printer Options Margins None** command sets all options to the minimum amount.

Printing a Listing of Cell Contents

You can spend hours developing and debugging a model worksheet and additional time entering and verifying data. You should safeguard your work

To Learn about Other Print Options

by making backup copies of your important files on disk. You also can print a listing of the cell contents of important worksheets. Be aware, however, that this print job can eat up lots of time (and paper) if you have a large worksheet (in which case, you may want to use /Print File).

You can produce printed documentation of cell contents by selecting **/Print Printer Options Other Cell-Formulas** or selecting the **List entries** option in the Print Settings dialog box. Choosing **List entries** produces a list with one cell per line showing the Wysiwyg format, cell format, the width of the cell (if different from the default), the cell-protection status, and the contents of cells (including any formulas) in the print range. With **List** not checked, the data prints as it is on-screen.

Exercise 4.3: Listing the Cell Contents

To print a cell-by-cell listing of the contents of a particular range, follow these steps:

1. Select **/P**rint **P**rinter.
2. Choose **O**ptions **O**ther **C**ell-Formulas. Or in 2.3 or 2.4 press [F2]. Or click the left mouse button in the dialog box to edit the settings. Select the **L**ist entries option in the Print Settings dialog box. An X in the check box indicates that your output will show cell contents, one line at a time. An empty check box indicates that the range will print as it appears on-screen.

   In this example, select **L**ist entries (see fig. 7.14).

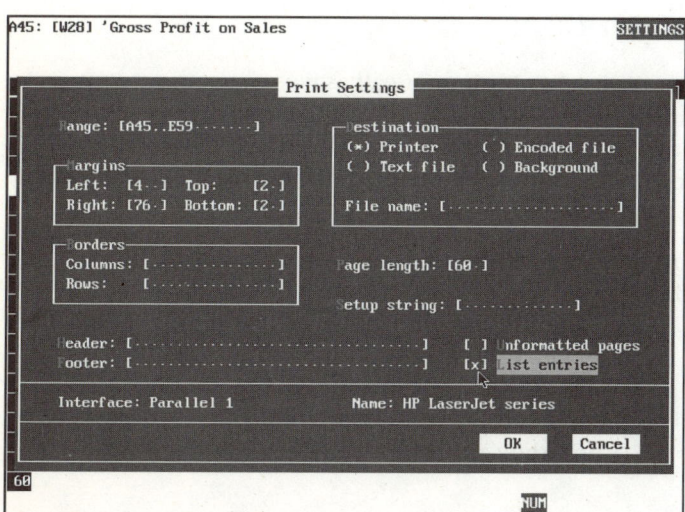

Fig. 7.14
Select **List** entries.

Printing Reports

3. Select **R**ange, type or highlight the range of cells you want printed, and press ⏎Enter.
4. Return to the **P**rinter menu by pressing ⏎Enter or clicking OK, and then select **Q**uit.
5. Select **A**lign **G**o **P**age **Q**uit.

   1-2-3 lists each entry in the resulting printout just as you would see it in the control panel if you moved your cell pointer to each location. Each entry is printed in the following format:

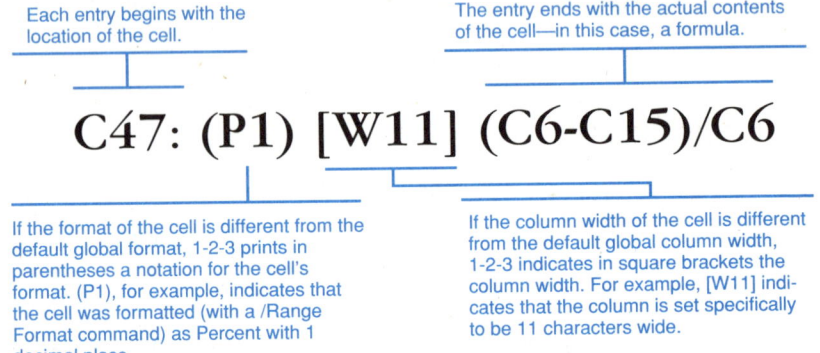

Each entry begins with the location of the cell.

The entry ends with the actual contents of the cell—in this case, a formula.

If the format of the cell is different from the default global format, 1-2-3 prints in parentheses a notation for the cell's format. (P1), for example, indicates that the cell was formatted (with a /Range Format command) as Percent with 1 decimal place.

If the column width of the cell is different from the default global column width, 1-2-3 indicates in square brackets the column width. For example, [W11] indicates that the column is set specifically to be 11 characters wide.

1-2-3 prints the contents of each cell, moving horizontally across each row of the print range (see fig. 7.15).

Clearing the Print Options

When you select **P**rint options, 1-2-3 automatically saves the settings you specify with the worksheet when you select /File **S**ave. Saving the settings with the worksheet for a future print job is a good practice, rather than clearing them after each printing. You can quickly make minor changes to the existing settings.

At times, however, you benefit by clearing all or some of the print settings. You can do this with the /Print Printer Clear command. For example, you may want to print a report in the same worksheet from which you printed earlier, but specify a different print range. You can use /Print Printer Clear **R**ange to eliminate only the range setting. All other print settings remain intact. The /Print Printer Clear **A**ll command can prove to be helpful when a report isn't printing properly. Table 7.3 lists the options on the Print Printer Clear menu.

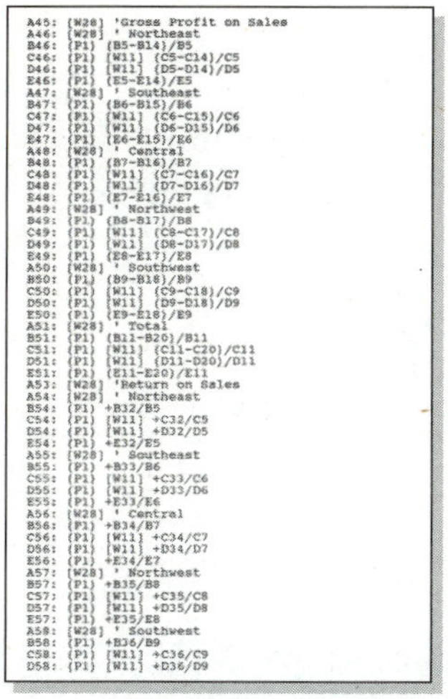

```
A45: [W28] 'Gross Profit on Sales
A46: [W28] ' Northeast
B46: (P1) (B5-B14)/B5
C46: (P1) [W11] (C5-C14)/C5
D46: (P1) [W11] (D5-D14)/D5
E46: (P1) (E5-E14)/E5
A47: [W28] ' Southeast
B47: (P1) (B6-B15)/B6
C47: (P1) [W11] (C6-C15)/C6
D47: (P1) [W11] (D6-D15)/D6
E47: (P1) (E6-E15)/E6
A48: [W28] ' Central
B48: (P1) (B7-B16)/B7
C48: (P1) [W11] (C7-C16)/C7
D48: (P1) [W11] (D7-D16)/D7
E48: (P1) (E7-E16)/E7
A49: [W28] ' Northwest
B49: (P1) (B8-B17)/B8
C49: (P1) [W11] (C8-C17)/C8
D49: (P1) [W11] (D8-D17)/D8
E49: (P1) (E8-E17)/E8
A50: [W28] ' Southwest
B50: (P1) (B9-B18)/B9
C50: (P1) [W11] (C9-C18)/C9
D50: (P1) [W11] (D9-D18)/D9
E50: (P1) (E9-E18)/E9
A51: [W28] ' Total
B51: (P1) (B11-B20)/B11
C51: (P1) [W11] (C11-C20)/C11
D51: (P1) [W11] (D11-D20)/D11
E51: (P1) (E11-E20)/E11
A53: [W28] 'Return on Sales
A54: [W28] ' Northeast
B54: (P1) +B32/B5
C54: (P1) [W11] +C32/C5
D54: (P1) [W11] +D32/D5
E54: (P1) +E32/E5
A55: [W28] ' Southeast
B55: (P1) +B33/B6
C55: (P1) [W11] +C33/C6
D55: (P1) [W11] +D33/D6
E55: (P1) +E33/E6
A56: [W28] ' Central
B56: (P1) +B34/B7
C56: (P1) [W11] +C34/C7
D56: (P1) [W11] +D34/D7
E56: (P1) +E34/E7
A57: [W28] ' Northwest
B57: (P1) +B35/B8
C57: (P1) [W11] +C35/C8
D57: (P1) [W11] +D35/D8
E57: (P1) +E35/E8
A58: [W28] ' Southwest
B58: (P1) +B36/B9
C58: (P1) [W11] +C36/C9
D58: (P1) [W11] +D36/D9
```

Fig. 7.15
The contents of each cell are printed.

7

Table 7.3 Selections on the Print Printer Clear Menu

Selection	*Description*
All	Clears every print option, including the print range
Range	Removes only the previous print-range specification
Borders	Cancels only columns and rows specified as borders
Format	Returns **M**argins, **P**g-Length, and **S**etup string settings to the default settings displayed in the /**W**orksheet **G**lobal **D**efault **P**rinter screen

Preparing Output for Other Programs

Many word processing and other software packages import ASCII text files. To prepare output for other programs, follow these steps:

1. Select /**P**rint **F**ile and name the text file.
2. Select the range of the worksheet as usual, and from the menu select **O**ption **O**ther **U**nformatted. Or select **U**nformatted from the dialog box.
3. To return to the Print File menu, press ↵Enter or click OK, then select **Q**uit.
4. There is no need to align paper, so simply select **G**o and **Q**uit. This file appears on your disk with a PRN three letter extension.

Printing Reports

Summary

In this chapter you learned to create one-page or multiple-page print outs with enhancements, such as headers and border columns.

Testing Your Knowledge

True/False Questions

1. Borders are one or more rows or columns of data that 1-2-3 repeats on a multiple-page report.
2. The **A**lign command starts printing to the printer.
3. You can exclude from printing columns, rows, and ranges that appear on the screen.
4. The default page setting is set at 66 lines per page.
5. A PRN file is a normal file created by 1-2-3 for use in 1-2-3.

Multiple Choice Questions

1. Which character automatically prints the current date in a header?
    - A. \.
    - B. /.
    - C. @.
    - D. #.
2. If you want to clear only the print range, you would choose
    - A. **/P**rint **P**rinter **C**lear **F**ormat.
    - B. **/P**rint **P**rinter **C**lear **B**orders.
    - C. **/P**rint **P**rinter **C**lear **A**ll.
    - D. **/P**rint **P**rinter **C**lear **R**ange.
3. When setting the left and right margins, you must enter numbers between
    - A. 0 and 240.
    - B. 5 and 240.
    - C. 0 and 32.
    - D. 0 and 120.

Testing Your Knowledge

4. To print the contents of cell A1 left-justified in a header, you must type
   A. **\A1**.
   B. **/A1**.
   C. **|\A1**.
   D. **@|A1**.
5. To advance to the top of the next page or eject the page from a laser printer, you must choose one of the following commands
   A. **Align**.
   B. **Quit**.
   C. **Go**.
   D. **Page**.

Fill-in-the-Blank Questions

1. _____ are preset, standard specifications for a 1-2-3 print job.
2. _____ is information displayed on one line at the bottom of a page.
3. Choose **/P**rint _____ to create a text file.
4. To exclude one or more columns from printing, choose **/W**orksheet **C**olumn _____, and designate the columns.
5. To insert a page break into the worksheet, use the **/W**orksheet _____ command.

Review: Short Projects

1. **Printing Formulas**

   Using the savings analysis created in the short projects of Chapter 6, create a formula listing.

2. **Hiding Columns**

   Using the inventory created in the long projects of Chapter 6, print only the Item Number and Reorder columns.

3. **Listing Formulas**

   Retrieve the checkbook register created in Chapter 3. Create a formula listing.

Printing Reports

Review: Long Projects

1. Printing Borders, Headers, and Footers

   Using the 12-month budget created in the long projects of Chapter 3, print the entire spreadsheet using column A as repeating borders on each page. Also include a header on each page that inserts the current date and numbers the pages, and a footer that includes your name centered on the bottom of each page.

2. Hiding Columns

   Using the 12-month budget created in the long projects of Chapter 3, print only column A and the Total's column.

Printing with Wysiwyg

8

In Releases 2.3 and 2.4, 1-2-3 includes a spreadsheet publishing add-in program. Lotus calls this option Wysiwyg, an acronym for "what you see is what you get." This add-in offers many features for enhancing a spreadsheet both on-screen and in print.

Objectives

1. To Become Familiar with Wysiwyg
2. To Change Fonts
3. To Enhance Cells with Shading, Lines, Bold, and Grid Lines
4. To Manage Formats
5. To Print in Wysiwyg

Printing with Wysiwyg

Key Terms in This Chapter	
Typeface	The design of a character set, such as Swiss or Dutch.
Font	A character set displaying a particular size and style of typeface, such as 12-point Swiss.
Point size	The size of a particular font. One point is equal to 1/72 of an inch; therefore, 12-point Swiss is about 1/6 of an inch high.
Soft fonts	Fonts provided with Wysiwyg. These include various sizes and styles of Swiss, Dutch, Courier, and a symbol font set.
Wysiwyg	An acronym for "What you see is what you get." This spreadsheet publishing add-in allows you to see graphical changes (fonts outlining, bold) on-screen as you make them on the worksheet.

8

Objective 1: To Become Familiar with Wysiwyg

Comparing Reports Printed with 1-2-3 and Wysiwyg

If you compare a worksheet printed with 1-2-3's /Print commands and one printed with Wysiwyg's :Print commands, you see a dramatic difference (see figs. 8.1 and 8.2).

To Become Familiar with Wysiwyg

```
TERMS OF LOAN

        First Payment Date          31-Jul-93
        Principal Borrowed          $10,000
        Term in Months              48
        Beginning Interest Rate     10.50%
        Payment                     $256.03

AMORTIZATION SCHEDULE

Payment  Payment    Current                Interest  Principal  Principal
Number   Date       Rate      Payment      Portion   Portion    Balance
   1     31-Jul-93  10.50%    $256.03      $87.50    $168.53    $9,831.47
   2     31-Aug-93  10.50%    $256.03      $86.03    $170.01    $9,661.46
   3     30-Sep-93  10.50%    $256.03      $84.54    $171.50    $9,489.96
   4     31-Oct-93  10.50%    $256.03      $83.04    $173.00    $9,316.97
   5     30-Nov-93  10.50%    $256.03      $81.52    $174.51    $9,142.45
   6     31-Dec-93  10.50%    $256.03      $80.00    $176.04    $8,966.42
   7     31-Jan-94  10.50%    $256.03      $78.46    $177.58    $8,788.84
   8     28-Feb-94  10.50%    $256.03      $76.90    $179.13    $8,609.71
   9     31-Mar-94  10.50%    $256.03      $75.33    $180.70    $8,429.01
  10     30-Apr-94  10.50%    $256.03      $73.75    $182.28    $8,246.73
  11     31-May-94  10.50%    $256.03      $72.16    $183.87    $8,062.85
  12     30-Jun-94  10.50%    $256.03      $70.55    $185.48    $7,877.37
  13     31-Jul-94  10.50%    $256.03      $68.93    $187.11    $7,690.26
  14     31-Aug-94  10.50%    $256.03      $67.29    $188.74    $7,501.52
  15     30-Sep-94  10.50%    $256.03      $65.64    $190.40    $7,311.12
  16     31-Oct-94  10.50%    $256.03      $63.97    $192.06    $7,119.06
  17     30-Nov-94  10.50%    $256.03      $62.29    $193.74    $6,925.32
  18     31-Dec-94  10.50%    $256.03      $60.60    $195.44    $6,729.88
  19     31-Jan-95  10.50%    $256.03      $58.89    $197.15    $6,532.74
  20     28-Feb-95  10.50%    $256.03      $57.16    $198.87    $6,333.86
  21     31-Mar-95  10.50%    $256.03      $55.42    $200.61    $6,133.25
```

Fig. 8.1
This report was created using 1-2-3's /Print commands.

TERMS OF LOAN

First Payment Date	31-Jul-93
Principal Borrowed	$10,000
Term in Months	48
Beginning Interest Rate	10.50%
Payment	$256.03

AMORTIZATION SCHEDULE

Payment Number	Payment Date	Current Rate	Payment	Interest Portion	Principal Portion	Principal Balance
1	31-Jul-93	10.50%	$256.03	$87.50	$168.53	$9,831.47
2	31-Aug-93	10.50%	$256.03	$86.03	$170.01	$9,661.46
3	30-Sep-93	10.50%	$256.03	$84.54	$171.50	$9,489.96
4	31-Oct-93	10.50%	$256.03	$83.04	$173.00	$9,316.97
5	30-Nov-93	10.50%	$256.03	$81.52	$174.51	$9,142.45
6	31-Dec-93	10.50%	$256.03	$80.00	$176.04	$8,966.42
7	31-Jan-94	10.50%	$256.03	$78.46	$177.58	$8,788.84
8	28-Feb-94	10.50%	$256.03	$76.90	$179.13	$8,609.71
9	31-Mar-94	10.50%	$256.03	$75.33	$180.70	$8,429.01
10	30-Apr-94	10.50%	$256.03	$73.75	$182.28	$8,246.73
11	31-May-94	10.50%	$256.03	$72.16	$183.87	$8,062.85
12	30-Jun-94	10.50%	$256.03	$70.55	$185.48	$7,877.37
13	31-Jul-94	10.50%	$256.03	$68.93	$187.11	$7,690.26
14	31-Aug-94	10.50%	$256.03	$67.29	$188.74	$7,501.52
15	30-Sep-94	10.50%	$256.03	$65.64	$190.40	$7,311.12
16	31-Oct-94	10.50%	$256.03	$63.97	$192.06	$7,119.06
17	30-Nov-94	10.50%	$256.03	$62.29	$193.74	$6,925.32
18	31-Dec-94	10.50%	$256.03	$60.60	$195.44	$6,729.88
19	31-Jan-95	10.50%	$256.03	$58.89	$197.15	$6,532.74
20	28-Feb-95	10.50%	$256.03	$57.16	$198.87	$6,333.86
21	31-Mar-95	10.50%	$256.03	$55.42	$200.61	$6,133.25

Fig. 8.2
This report was created using Wysiwyg's :Print commands.

Printing with Wysiwyg

Understanding How 1-2-3 and Wysiwyg Work Together

1-2-3 Releases 2.3 and 2.4 integrate closely with Wysiwyg—much better than Allways integrates with Release 2.2. You don't need to switch between the graphical and the standard interface because there is now only one interface: graphical.

In Wysiwyg, two menus are available; the slash key displays the standard 1-2-3 menu. The MENU mode indicator appears and, for color monitors, the default highlighted menu choice is cyan. To display the Wysiwyg menu, press the colon (:) (see fig. 8.3). The WYSIWYG mode indicator appears and, for color monitors, the highlighted menu choice is magenta. Press **Esc** to back out of any displayed menu.

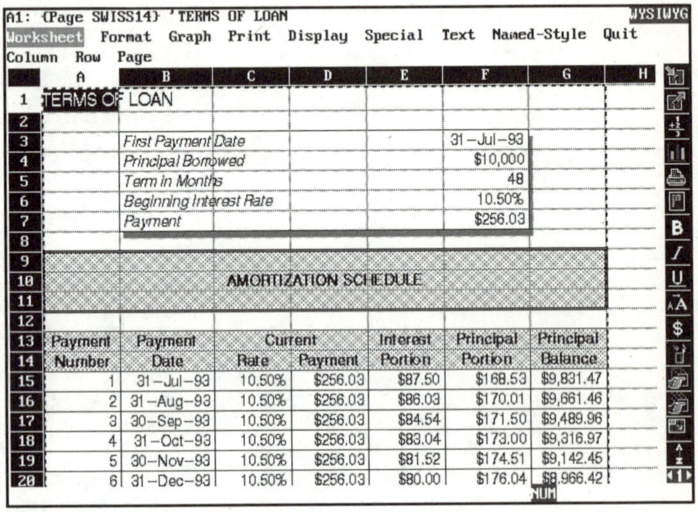

Fig. 8.3
The Wysiwyg menu is displayed.

You also can use the mouse to display the menus. A menu automatically appears when you place the mouse pointer in the control panel. The menu that displays depends on which menu you used last; to switch to the other menu, press the right mouse button. The right mouse button switches you back and forth between the two menus.

Wysiwyg menus work the same way as 1-2-3 menus: select a command by typing the first letter, pointing to the command and clicking the left mouse button, or highlighting the command and pressing **Enter**. Wysiwyg options are explained throughout this chapter.

Saving Your Wysiwyg Formatting

Wysiwyg stores the enhanced formatting information in its own file, separate from the worksheet file. The Wysiwyg file has the same first name as your 1-2-3 file, but with an FMT extension. For example, if you save a worksheet file called BUDGET.WK1 with Wysiwyg attached, Wysiwyg saves an associated BUDGET.FMT file. This file contains all the formatting enhancements selected with Wysiwyg.

Wysiwyg saves enhanced formatting only when you use the 1-2-3 /**File Save** command to save the current 1-2-3 worksheet. If you press **Alt+F10** (or /**Add-In**) **Detach**, you erase Wysiwyg from memory and therefore can no longer save enhanced formatting. If you detach Wysiwyg before you save the worksheet, the program does not update your FMT file and you may lose much of your special formatting. When you retrieve a file with Wysiwyg attached, 1-2-3 automatically retrieves the file's associated FMT file, if there is one.

Do not modify the structure of a Wysiwyg-formatted worksheet without attaching Wysiwyg. If you delete, insert, or move anything, the formatting will not match the same cells the next time you attach Wysiwyg.

Learning To Format with Wysiwyg

The heart of Wysiwyg's power is its capability to add professional formatting touches. The 1-2-3 formats—numeric display and label alignment—carry through automatically to Wysiwyg. Wysiwyg's formats determine the printed typeface, character size, boldface, and other stylistic features, such as lines and shading.

Wysiwyg's additional formats provide many ways to enhance the appearance of printed text. To assign a Wysiwyg format to a cell or range, use the Wysiwyg **:Format** command. To determine the format of a cell, move the cell pointer to the cell. The format displays at the top of the screen, next to the current cell address. If you use Wysiwyg in graphics mode (the default), you actually see the formatting on-screen.

Exercise 1.1: Using SmartIcons with Wysiwyg

Release 2.4 includes several SmartIcons that make using Wysiwyg easier. Follow these steps:

Printing with Wysiwyg

1. Select the range that you want to format. You can select the range by either dragging the mouse pointer over the range or by pressing [Ins], using the arrow keys, and pressing [↵Enter].
2. Select one of the icons in table 8.1 by clicking the arrows on the bottom of the SmartIcon palettes or pressing the icon add-in key that you assigned SmartIcons to when you attached SmartIcons (such as [Alt]+[F7]). Then use [←] and [→] to move to different icons palettes and use [↑] and [↓] to move to the icon that you want.

Table 8.1	Wysiwyg SmartIcons
SmartIcon	Function
U	Underlines the range
U	Double underlines the range
A	Increases to next font size
AA	Scrolls through available colors for the range
AA	Scrolls through available background colors for the range
◻	Adds an outline and drop shadow to the range
◻	Adds an outline to the range
▦	Scrolls through available shading for the range
🖨	Prints the defined range
📄	Previews the range
	Copies the Wysiwyg formats of preselected range to another range

SmartIcon	Function
B	Applies boldface to the range
I	Applies italic to the range
N	Clears all Wysiwyg formatting
	Aligns text across the preselected range
	Adds a Wysiwyg page break to a row
	Adds a Wysiwyg page break to a column
	Puts a dark blue circle in the selected range
	Zooms in and out
	Enables you to edit text in the preselected range

Objective 2: To Change Fonts

One of the highlights of Wysiwyg is its capability to use different fonts. A *font* consists of a typeface (for example, Times Roman) and a point size. A *point* is a unit of measurement used in publishing, equal to 1/72 inch. The larger the point size, the larger the type. Your choice of fonts depends on your printer; Wysiwyg can use any font that your printer can print.

Wysiwyg comes with four soft fonts: Swiss, Dutch, Courier, and XSymbol. A *soft font* is a file on disk that specifies to a printer how to make a font. Your program sends soft fonts to the printer's memory before it prints the document so that the printer can use the information to print the document. If you have a dot-matrix printer, Wysiwyg uses its graphics mode to produce these fonts. If you have a laser printer, Wysiwyg downloads these four fonts automatically to your printer when you use them. Your printer, however, may not have enough memory for many different fonts or larger point sizes.

Printing with Wysiwyg

If your printer provides additional fonts, these fonts also are available to Wysiwyg. The HP LaserJet comes with built-in fonts, and you can purchase dozens of cartridges to access additional fonts.

Each worksheet can use up to eight different fonts. Wysiwyg stores these eight fonts in a *font set*. The default fonts are Swiss, Dutch, and XSymbol. If you want to change the sizes of these fonts or change to Courier, you can replace any of the default fonts.

With Wysiwyg, you can format each cell or range of cells with a different font, and you can use up to eight fonts for a single worksheet. By default, however, Wysiwyg assigns all cells to font 1. Examples of Wysiwyg's default fonts are shown in figure 8.4.

Fig. 8.4
Examples of Wysiwyg default fonts.

Exercise 2.1: Changing the Font for a Range of the Worksheet

You assign a font to a cell or range with the Wysiwyg **:F**ormat Font command. Follow these steps:

1. Select **:F**ormat. The Wysiwyg Format menu appears.
2. Select **F**ont. The Font menu lists the eight default fonts by typeface and point size (see fig. 8.5).
3. Choose the font you want by typing the number of the font or clicking the choice in the dialog box.
4. Indicate the range where you want the font by highlighting the range (as you would in 1-2-3). Press ⏎Enter.

If necessary, Wysiwyg adjusts the height of the row to conform to the tallest point size present.

Note: You also can select the Font Size SmartIcon, which increases the font size to the next available size.

182

To Change Fonts

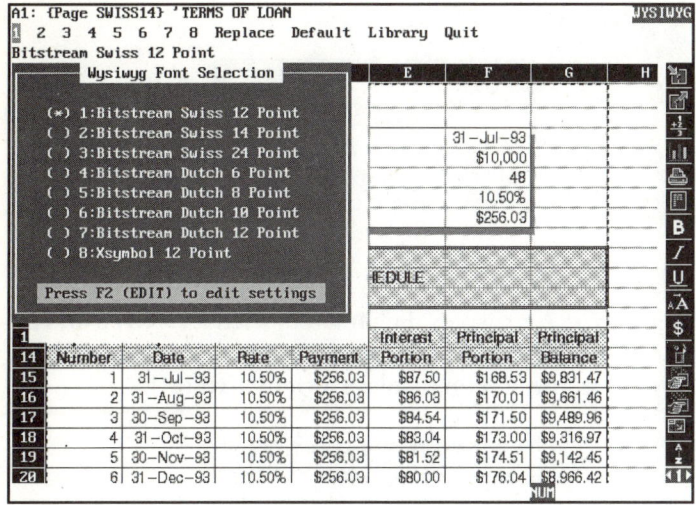

Fig. 8.5
The default fonts.

Exercise 2.2: Choosing Alternative Fonts for the Entire Worksheet

If you want to replace all occurrences of one font with another, regardless of where they occur in the worksheet, use the command sequence :**F**ormat **F**ont **R**eplace. This command lists the different fonts that you can select.

To change one font used throughout the worksheet, follow these steps:

1. Select :**F**ormat **F**ont **R**eplace.
2. Type the number of the font to change.
3. Select the new typeface. You can select from **S**wiss, **D**utch, **C**ourier, **X**Symbol, or **O**ther.
4. Type the new point size, and press ⏎Enter.
5. Select **Q**uit to return to READY mode.

Two factors determine the available typeface and point sizes. First, typeface and point size depend on which fonts you generated when you installed 1-2-3. Second, they depend on which fonts your printer supports (including soft fonts and cartridges) (see fig. 8.6). If you select a font that your printer cannot use, Wysiwyg substitutes a similar typeface.

183

Printing with Wysiwyg

Fig. 8.6
This range of fonts includes point sizes from 3 to 72, font cartridges, and downloadable fonts.

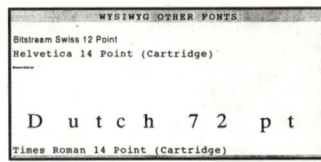

The XSymbol font contains *dingbats*, special characters such as arrows and circled numbers (see fig. 8.7). If, for example you enter a lowercase *a* in a cell and format it to XSymbol font, the screen displays a right arrow.

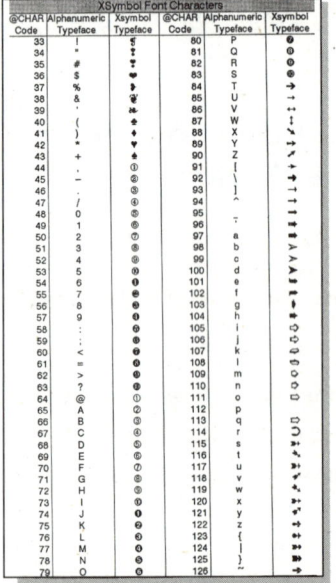

Fig. 8.7
Letters and numbers, as well as characters (dingbats) formatted with the XSymbol font are shown in this figure.

All cells automatically display font 1. Thus, when you replace font 1 with a different font, all cells not assigned to other font numbers change to the new font.

After experimenting with Wysiwyg, you may decide that a particular group of fonts is the one you normally want to use. Wysiwyg lets you store font selections in a file so that you can access those fonts later.

To Enhance Cells with Shading, Lines, Bold, and Grid Lines

To store a set of fonts in a file, follow these steps:

1. Select **:Format Font Library Save**.
2. Type the name of the file, and press ⏎Enter. Wysiwyg saves your file with an AFS extension.

To recall these groups of fonts, use the **:Format Font Library Retrieve** command.

If you find that you frequently retrieve the same font library, make it the default font set. To do this, retrieve the font library you want as the default and select **:Format Font Default Update**.

Objective 3: To Enhance Cells with Shading, Lines, Bold, and Grid Lines

The **:Format Shade** command and SmartIcon enable you to highlight important areas on the printed worksheet. The net income row and heading in figure 8.8 stand out because of the background shading.

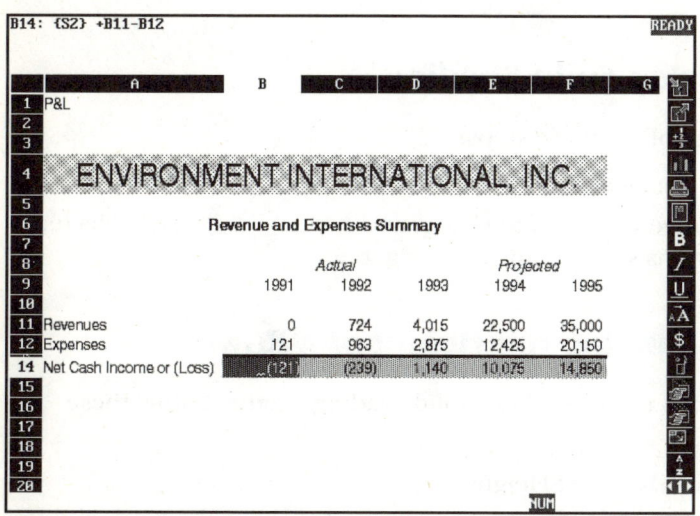

Fig. 8.8
Headings and important values are emphasized with light and dark shades.

Using Light and Dark Shading

If you use light or dark shading on cells with data, the contents will remain visible through the shading. To shade a range with light or dark shading, use

Printing with Wysiwyg

the **:Format Shade Light** or **:Format Shade Dark** command. You also can use the Light Shading SmartIcon to cycle through shading from light to dark to solid to none.

Exercise 3.1: Shading Cells

To highlight or accent portions of a worksheet with light or dark shading, follow these steps:

1. Select **:Format Shade**. The Wysiwyg shading options appear on-screen.
2. Select **Light** to apply light shading or **Dark** to apply dark shading.
3. Highlight the range you want to shade, and press ⏎Enter.

Using Solid Shading

Use the **S**olid shade only on blank cells to create solid lines. You cannot see the cell contents if you assign **S**olid to cells containing data. When you want to create a thick, dark line, select **:Format Shade Solid**. Then use **:Worksheet Row Set-Height** to shrink the height of the row to the desired line thickness.

Exercise 3.2: Using Solid Shading

To add solid shading, follow these steps:

1. Select **:Format Shade Solid**.
2. Highlight the range you want to shade, and press ⏎Enter. The selected range now contains solid shading (see fig. 8.9).

Exercise 3.3: Changing the Height of a Row

To change the height of the row where solid shading occurs, follow these steps:

1. Select **:Worksheet Row Set-Height**.
2. At the prompt `Select the rows to set height to:`, highlight one cell from each row for which you want to change the height.

   For this example, because you are only changing the height of one row, you can highlight any cell in row 13.

To Enhance Cells with Shading, Lines, Bold, and Grid Lines

3. At the prompt Enter new row height in points (1..255):, use ↑ or ↓ to decrease or increase the height of the row; the adjusted row height appears on-screen.

4. Press ←Enter to accept the adjusted height. In figure 8.10, the row height is 2 points. (The default is 14.)

Note: You can also adjust the row height by dragging the line below the row's number in the worksheet frame.

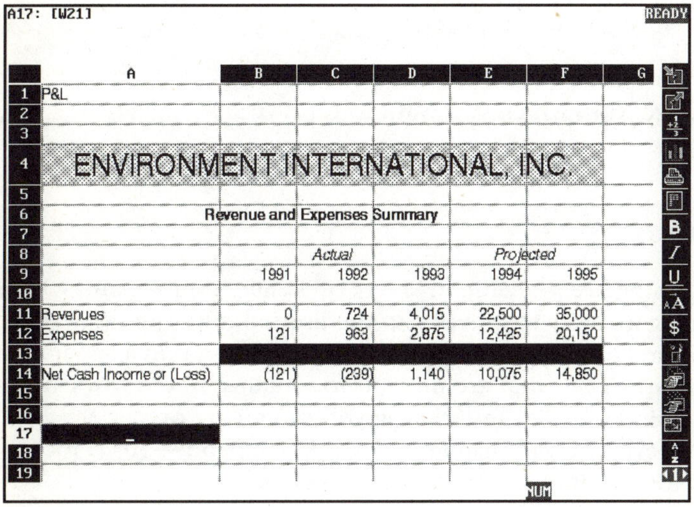

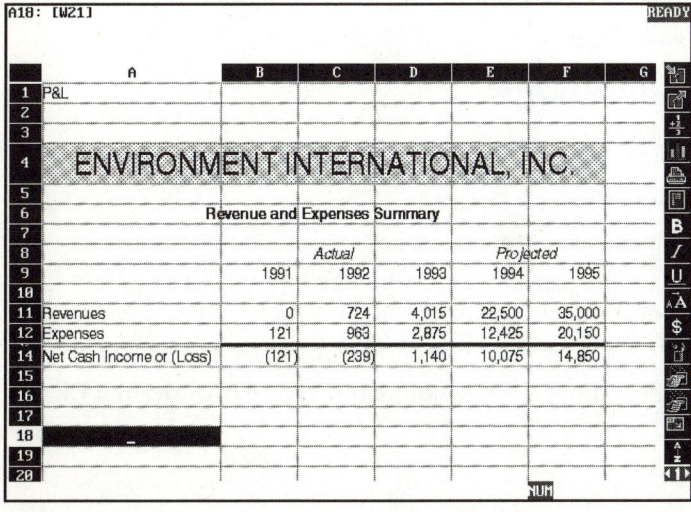

Fig. 8.9
The range is filled with solid shading.

Fig. 8.10
The row height is 2 points.

Removing Existing Shading

You remove existing shading by using the command **:Format Shade Clear** and indicating the desired range.

Exercise 3.4: Removing Shading

To remove existing shading, follow these steps:

1. Select **:Format Shade Clear**.
2. Highlight the range from which you want to remove shading, and press [↵Enter].

Using Underlining

Three styles of underlining are available in Wysiwyg: single, double, and wide. Wysiwyg's underlining capability is superior to the limited underlining available in 1-2-3, which merely repeats the minus sign or equal sign in a separate cell or uses printer setup strings that are difficult to visualize in the worksheet. Wysiwyg provides the kind of solid underlining you can create on paper with a pencil and ruler. Underlining will display in the control panel—{U1}, for example—but not in the cell if that cell contains no data.

Note: You also can use the Underline and Double-underline SmartIcons to add or remove single and double underlining to a highlighted range.

Exercise 3.5: Underlining

To underline a range, follow these steps:

1. Select **:Format Underline**.
2. Select **Single**, **Double**, or **Wide**.
3. Highlight or type the range(s) or individual cell addresses separated by commas to underline, and press [↵Enter].

    The specified cells are formatted with underlining (see fig. 8.11).

To remove existing underlining, use the command **:Format Underline Clear**.

To Enhance Cells with Shading, Lines, Bold, and Grid Lines

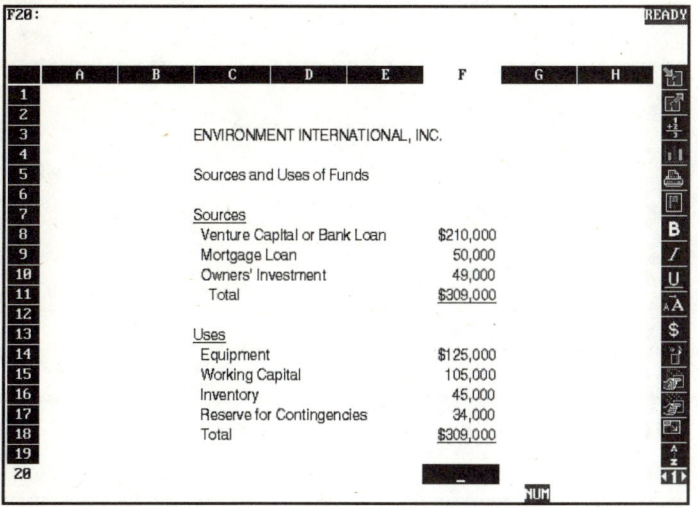

Fig. 8.11
The specified cells are underlined.

Using Boldface

For emphasis, you may want to make the contents of some cells darker than other cells. Wysiwyg lets you choose any cell or range of cells that you want to appear darker. When you use light or dark shading in cells that contain data, you can see the contents more clearly if the characters are bold. Use the :Format Bold command or the Bold SmartIcon to select boldface formatting. Then highlight the range of cells to appear in bold type at the prompt.

Exercise 3.6: Using Bold

To create boldface characters, follow these steps:

1. Select :Format Bold Set.
2. Highlight or type the range(s) or individual cell addresses separated by commas where you want boldface to appear, and press ↵Enter.

    The result of selecting boldface appears on-screen (see fig. 8.12).

To remove existing boldface, use the command :Format Bold Clear and specify the range for which you want to remove boldface.

189

Printing with Wysiwyg

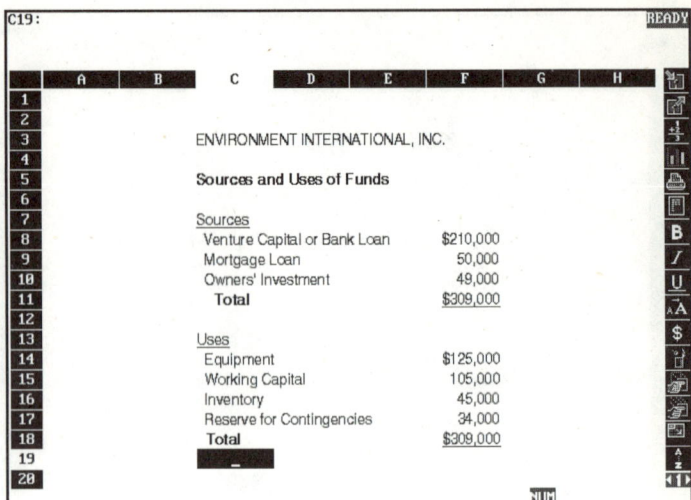

Fig. 8.12
Specified cells boldfaced.

Outlining Cells

Wysiwyg provides a variety of ways to use lines to enclose or separate parts of the worksheet. Access the options for outlining particular cells with the **:Format Lines** command. If you want to show the boundaries of all cells in the worksheet, you can print grid lines by choosing the **Grid** option on the Wysiwyg Print Settings dialog box (or by selecting **:Print Settings Grid Yes Quit Quit**). If you want grid lines displayed on-screen, select **:Display Options Grid Yes Quit Quit**. You also can use the Outline or Outline and Shadow SmartIcons to add or remove outlines and shadows from a range.

When you select **:Format Lines**, you see the options **Outline**, **Left**, **Right**, **Top**, **Bottom**, **All**, **Double**, **Wide**, **Clear**, and **Shadow**. Usually, you surround all cells in a given range by selecting **All** or draw lines around the perimeter of a range by choosing **Outline**. To create a three-dimensional appearance, choose **Shadow**. If you want to draw a box around a single cell, you can use either **:Format Lines Outline** or **:Format Lines All**. A shaded range will be more clearly defined if you surround it by using **:Format Lines Outline**. Remove existing lines with **:Format Lines Clear**. The control panel prompts you for the kinds of lines you want cleared.

To Enhance Cells with Shading, Lines, Bold, and Grid Lines

Exercise 3.7: Outlining Cells

To draw lines on all sides of the cells in a range, follow these steps:

1. Select **:Format Lines All**.
2. Highlight the range of cells where you want to show lines around each cell, and press ⏎Enter.

To draw lines on the perimeter (outline) of the cells in a range, follow these steps:

1. Select **:Format Lines Outline**.
2. Highlight the range of cells to outline, and press ⏎Enter. The information is outlined in a block (see fig. 8.13).

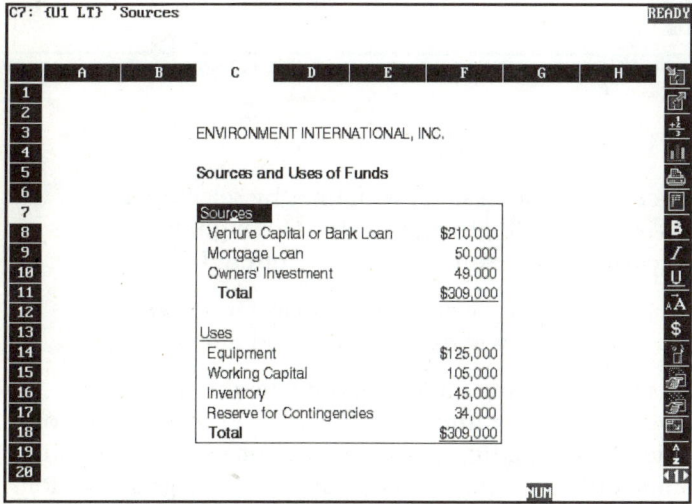

Fig. 8.13
The range is outlined.

Exercise 3.8: Using Shadow

To draw a shadow around a range and create a three-dimensional appearance, follow these steps:

1. Select **:Format Lines Shadow Set**.
2. Highlight the range of cells to shadow, and press ⏎Enter. A shadow appears around the block of information (see fig. 8.14).

To clear the shadow, use the **:Format Lines Shadow Clear** command and specify the range from which you want to remove the shadow.

191

Printing with Wysiwyg

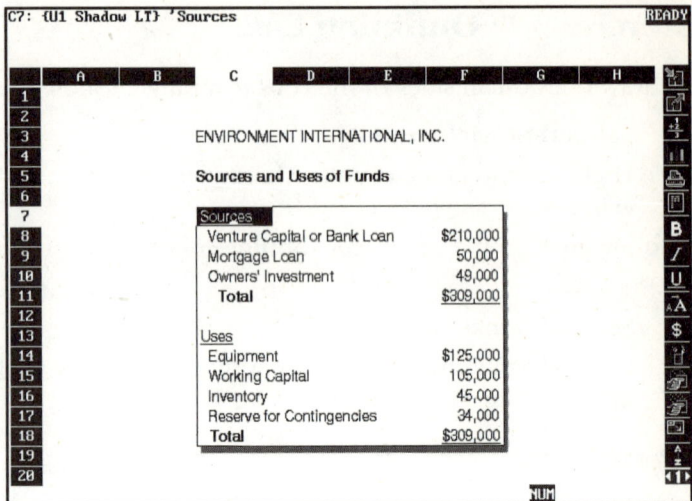

Fig. 8.14
A shadow appears around the block of information.

Creating Grid Lines

You can surround every cell in the worksheet with lines by selecting the command **:Format Lines All** and highlighting all cells. Although this process displays cell boundaries clearly, the result can appear cluttered.

You can display grid lines on-screen by using the **:Display Options Grid Yes** command. This command, however, will not print the grid lines.

To print cell boundaries without letting the lines dominate the text, select **:Print**, and select the **Grid** check box in the Wysiwyg Print Settings dialog box. Alternatively, you can select **:Print Settings Grid**. This command draws lightly dotted lines for all column and row separations. You cannot use grid lines for a selected range of cells; the **Grid** option affects the entire worksheet.

Exercise 3.9: Creating Grid Lines

To create grid lines throughout the worksheet, follow these steps:

1. Select **:P**rint. The Wysiwyg Print Settings dialog box appears.
2. Select **S**ettings **G**rid **Y**es **Q**uit **Q**uit. Alternatively, you can access the dialog box by pressing F2; then select **S**ettings **G**rid.

An X in the check box indicates that grid lines will appear in your printed report; if the box is empty, grid lines will not appear.

Grid lines surround all cells in the worksheet, including labels that cross cell boundaries and graphs added to the worksheet.

Objective 4: To Manage Formats

Because formatting is the heart of Wysiwyg, the program offers several commands for dealing with the formats assigned to your cells. You can copy and move formats—not the cell contents, but the formats associated with the cell. You can assign a name to the set of formatting instructions in a cell, and apply this format to any range. You can save *all* the formats associated with the file and apply this format to another file.

Copying Formats

If you want to format one cell or range with the same highlighting features as another formatted cell or range, you can use the **:**S**pecial C**opy command and SmartIcon to copy the formatting instructions. If, for example you have formatted a range as 14-point Swiss bold with shading and an outline, you can save a lot of time by copying the format to another range rather than using four separate **:**Format commands. The command copies formats only, not cell contents. 1-2-3's /Copy command copies cell contents and formats (with Wysiwyg attached). **:**S**pecial C**opy copies the following formats: font, boldface, italic, underline, shade, color, and lines.

Exercise 4.1: Copying a Format

To copy a format from one range to another range of cells, follow these steps:

1. Select **:**S**pecial C**opy.
2. Highlight the range of cells you want to copy from, and press ⏎Enter.
3. Highlight the range of cells you want to copy to, and press ⏎Enter.

Note: The Copy Format SmartIcon will copy the format of a highlighted range to another range.

Using Named-Styles

Another way to apply a format from one cell to another is by creating and using named-styles. You should create named-styles for the formats you use

Printing with Wysiwyg

frequently. Suppose, for example, that your worksheet contains 10 subheadings and you want them to be in 14-point Swiss bold with heavy shading. To ease formatting and ensure consistency, you can name this particular formatting style HEAD, and apply the style to all headings.

Another advantage to using named-styles is that you can make format changes rapidly. If you decide that you want your headings to have a light shade instead of a heavy one, you need to change the format of only one cell.

Exercise 4.2: Defining a Style

To define a style, first format a cell with the desired attributes. Then follow these steps:

1. Select :Named-Style Define.
2. Choose any style number from 1 to 8 that does not already have a style attached to it. In this example, type **1** to choose the first style to define (see fig. 8.15).

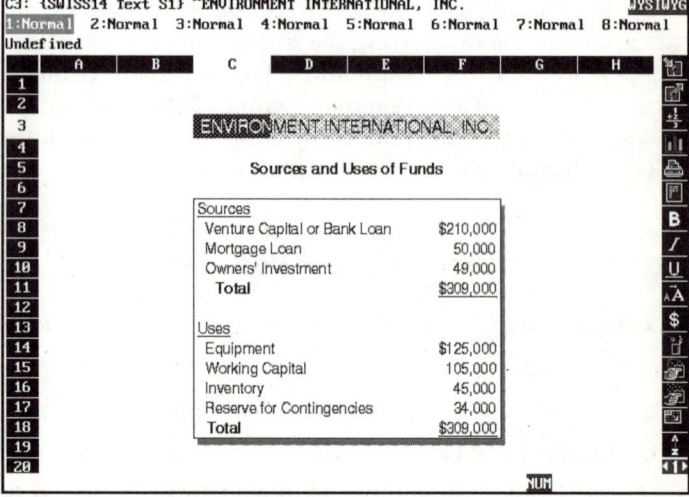

Fig. 8.15
Type **1** to choose the first style to define.

3. Highlight the cell you want as the defined style, and press ⏎Enter.
4. Press Backspace to remove the existing style name (if any).
5. Type the name of the style, and press ⏎Enter.
6. Type a description for the style, and press ⏎Enter.

The description appears on the third line of the display panel when you select the named-style.

Exercise 4.3: Applying the Named Style

To apply a named-style to a cell or range, follow these steps:

1. Select **:N**amed-Style.
2. Choose the style you want from the menu that appears.
3. Highlight the range of cells to receive the style, and press `Enter`.

Objective 5: To Print in Wysiwyg

After you finish formatting a report with Wysiwyg, you can easily print it with the **:P**rint **G**o command. Before you print, you must specify a print range with the **:P**rint **R**ange command; then select **G**o from the Wysiwyg Print menu to begin printing. If you choose to print your report at a later time, you can instead select **:P**rint **F**ile, which creates an encoded file on disk with the ENC extension. Print the file using the DOS COPY command (for example, **COPY REVENUE/B LPT1**). You also can print to the background—allowing you to work in 1-2-3 while Wysiwyg prints the worksheet. Load BPrint, and select **:P**rint **B**ackground to print to the background.

Exercise 5.1: Printing a Report in Wysiwyg

To print a report created with Wysiwyg, follow these steps:

1. Select **:P**rint **R**ange.
2. Select **S**et and highlight the range you want to print. (If necessary, select **C**lear to clear the current print range.) Alternatively, you can press `F2` to activate the Wysiwyg Print Settings dialog box; then select **R**ange and specify the print range.

    Make sure that you are configured for the right printer and the right interface by looking at the Wysiwyg Print Settings dialog box.
3. Press `Enter`. (Press `Enter` twice if you used the dialog box.)
4. Select **G**o to begin printing.

    If you select **:P**rint **R**ange **S**et and specify a print range, Wysiwyg displays the print range boundaries and page breaks as dashed lines on-screen.

Printing with Wysiwyg

Note: You also can use the Print Range or Preview Range SmartIcons to print or preview a selected range.

Preview Printing to the Screen

The **:P**rint **P**review command lets you see on-screen how your worksheet looks before you print it on paper. This option displays your print range one page at a time. Press any key to display subsequent pages and to return to the Print menu.

Exercise 5.2: Previewing the Document

To preview your document, follow these steps:

1. Select the print range and layout settings you want.
2. Select **:P**rint **P**review.

   You can press F6 and the + and - keys to zoom in and back out of a previewed page and view different parts of the page. Use the arrow keys to scroll around the page.
3. If multiple pages exist, press any key to view the next page(s) until you return to the Print menu.

Printing Across the Length of the Page

The command **:P**rint **C**onfig **O**rientation **L**andscape allows you to print text along the length of the page instead of across the width. Release 2.4 also enables you to print in landscape mode, even if you have a dot-matrix printer.

Exercise 5.3: Printing in Landscape Mode

To print in landscape mode, follow these steps:

1. Select **:P**rint.
2. On the Wysiwyg Print Settings dialog box, press F2, and select **C**onfiguration **L**andscape orientation (see fig. 8.16).

   Fill in the rest of the dialog box with **M**argins; **S**ettings, such as page numbers to print, number of copies, starting page number, and show grid and frame; and **L**ayout options, such as paper size, borders, headers, footers, and compression.

To Print in Wysiwyg

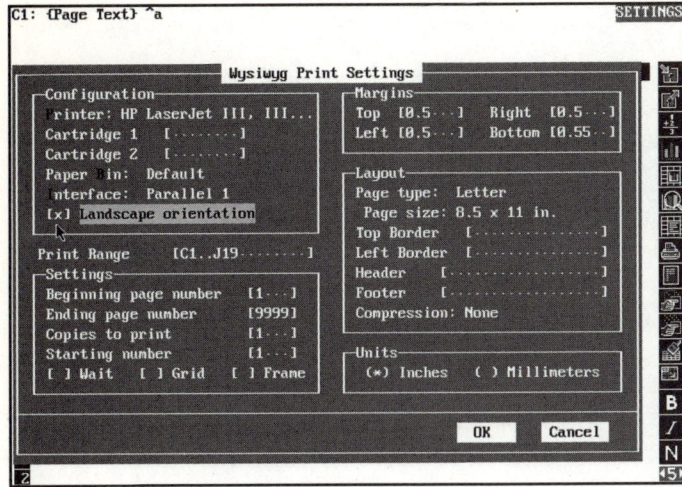

Fig. 8.16
Click the Landscape orientation check box in the Configuration area of the Wysiwyg Print Settings dialog box.

Forcing a Range To Print on One Page

The **:P**rint **L**ayout **C**ompression **A**utomatic command offers an ideal way to fit a large worksheet onto one page. Rather than guess at the font size needed to print a report on a single page, you can use this option. Wysiwyg will then determine by how much it needs to reduce the font size.

Exercise 5.4: Compressing the Print Range

To compress the print range to fit on one page, follow these steps:

1. Select **:P**rint.
2. On the Wysiwyg Print Settings dialog box, press F2, and select **L**ayout **C**ompression.
3. From the pop-up dialog box that appears, select **A**utomatic to fit the range onto one page (see fig. 8.17).

You can use additional Wysiwyg **:P**rint **L**ayout options to choose the paper size, change margins, add headers and footers, and add borders to the printout.

The Wysiwyg **:P**rint **C**onfig options enable you to change the current printer and interface. Depending on your selected printer, other **C**onfig options may be available. These options enable you to select the orientation (**P**ortrait or **L**andscape) of your printout, the font cartridges you use, and the paper-feed option.

197

Printing with Wysiwyg

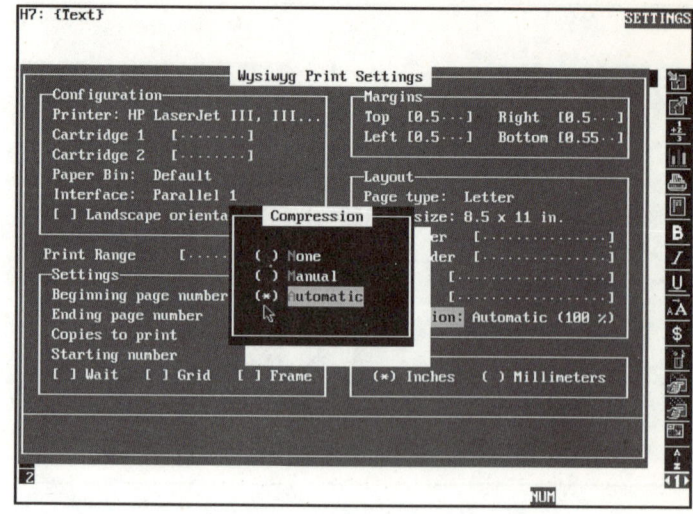

Fig. 8.17
The Wysiwyg Print Settings dialog box with Automatic print compression selected.

Use the **:Print Settings** options to select which pages of a multipage report to print, the page number of the first page, the number of copies to print, whether to print the worksheet grid and frame, and whether to pause the printer for a paper change before printing pages.

Summary

In this chapter, you learned how to use Wysiwyg to enhance 1-2-3 worksheets on the screen or in printouts.

Testing Your Knowledge

True/False Questions

1. Wysiwyg is an acronym for "What you see is what you get."
2. Wysiwyg comes with only Releases 2.3 and 2.4 of Lotus 1-2-3.
3. You display the Wysiwyg menu with the 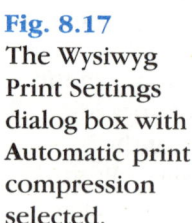 key.

Testing Your Knowledge

4. Wysiwyg stores the enhanced formatting in its own file separate from the worksheet file.
5. A soft font is a file on disk that specifies to a printer how to make a font.

Multiple Choice Questions

1. The Wysiwyg file has the same first name as your 1-2-3 file, but with an extension of
   - A. WK1.
   - B. PIC.
   - C. FMT.
   - D. WK?.
2. The XSymbol font contains
   - A. cartridges.
   - B. dingbats.
   - C. downloadable fonts.
   - D. SmartIcons.
3. If you want to format one cell or range with the same highlighting features as another formatted cell or range, you can use
   - A. /Copy.
   - B. /Move.
   - C. :Special Copy.
   - D. :Display.
4. To access the Wysiwyg menu, you can
   - A. use the slash key.
   - B. use the colon key.
   - C. move the mouse to the control panel.
   - D. both B and C.
5. In Wysiwyg you can
   - A. preview your document on-screen to see how your worksheet looks before printing on paper.
   - B. print in landscape mode even on a dot-matrix printer.
   - C. force 1-2-3 to print a worksheet on one page, having 1-2-3 compress the print.
   - D. all the above.

Printing with Wysiwyg

Fill-in-the-Blank Questions

1. A _____ is the design of a character set.
2. Just like 1-2-3, in Wysiwyg you press the _____ key to back out of any menu.
3. Release 2.4 includes several _____ that make using Wysiwyg easier.
4. The size of a particular font is called its _____ size.
5. A _____ is a character set displaying a particular size and style of typeface.

Review: Short Projects

1. Printing with Wysiwyg

    Retrieve the budget worksheet created in Chapter 3 and enhance it with Wysiwyg features. Save and print it.

2. Printing with Wysiwyg

    Retrieve the loan analysis created in Chapter 6 and enhance it with Wysiwyg features. Save and print it.

3. Printing with Wysiwyg

    Retrieve the Bowling worksheet you created in Chapter 3, and enhance it with Wysiwyg features. Save and print the enhanced worksheet.

Review: Long Projects

1. Creating Professional Output

    Retrieve the Video Store table created in Chapter 6. Give the store a name and center it on the screen. Use lines, shading, and any other features to enhance the table Save and print it.

2. Printing with Wysiwyg

    Retrieve the checkbook register created in Chapter 3. Enhance it with Wysiwyg features. Save and print it.

    Notice that, for each file you enhance and resave using Wysiwyg, there is a second file on your disk with the same name but with an FMT three-letter extension.

Creating and Printing Graphs

9

This chapter looks at 1-2-3's graphic capabilities, which help make a spreadsheet of data more easily understood.

Objectives

1. To Create a Simple Graph
2. To Become Familiar with Graph Types
3. To Specify Data Ranges
4. To Enhance the Appearance of a Graph
5. To Save a Graph
6. To Print a Graph

Creating and Printing Graphs

Key Terms in This Chapter	
Graph type	The manner in which data is represented graphically.
X-axis	The horizontal bottom edge of a graph (also called the *categories axis*).
Y-axis	The vertical left edge of a graph (also called the *values axis*).
Origin	The intersection of the x- and y-axes.
Legend	The description of the shading, color, or symbols assigned to data ranges in line or bar graphs. The legend appears across the bottom of the graph.
Tick marks	The small marks on the axes of a graph, which indicate the increments between the minimum and maximum graph values.
Scale Indicator	An automatic label that 1-2-3 provides on the x-axis and y-axis showing the scaling factor of the data. For example, (Thousands) or (Millions).
Zero line	The line that extends through zero on the y-axis or the x-axis. Negative values are below or to the left of the zero line. Positive values are above or to the right of the zero line. You choose whether or not to display the zero lines.
Frame	A set of four lines creating a box that surrounds the graph. You can remove any or all of the lines.
Data labels	Text or values that you can add to data points on the graph.

To Create a Simple Graph

The following SmartIcons are used in Release 2.4 in creating graphs:

Wysiwyg	Non-Wysiwyg	Function
		Displays the QuickGraph Settings dialog box, which allows you to choose a graph type; select whether data will be interpreted by rows or columns; select vertical or horizontal orientation and 3-D effect; and turn colors on or off. Selecting OK from this dialog box will graph the data in your predefined range.
		Enables you to add the current graph to your redefined range.
	VIEW GRPH	Operates like pressing F10 while you are in READY mode; displays the current graph.

Hardware Requirements

To view a graph on-screen, you need a graphics monitor or a monitor with a graphics-display adapter. Without this monitor, you can construct and save a 1-2-3 graph, but you must print the graph to view it. To print a graph, you need a graphics printer supported by 1-2-3.

Objective 1: To Create a Simple Graph

To create a 1-2-3 graph, begin by selecting the /Graph command while the worksheet containing the data you want to graph is displayed.

Table 9.1 describes each option on the Graph menu, as well as the options that are common to the Graph Settings dialog box.

203

Creating and Printing Graphs

Table 9.1 Selections on the /Graph Menu	
Selection	*Description*
Type	Provides options for creating seven types of graphs: line, bar, XY, stacked bar, pie, HLCO, or mixed; you can use the dialog box or the menu to choose this option.
X	Specifies the range to be used as x-axis labels or values, or labels of pie slices; you can use the dialog box or the menu to choose this option.
A through F	Specifies the ranges containing the numeric data to graph; you can use the dialog box or the menu to choose these options.
Reset	Clears the current graph settings.
View	Displays a full-screen view of the current graph.
Save	Saves a graph in the file format needed for using the graph with other programs and for printing without Wysiwyg.
Options	Provides choices for labeling, enhancing, or customizing a graph; you can use the menu or dialog box to choose graph options.
Name	Lets you assign a name to one or more graphs and store the graph settings so that you can redisplay the graph(s) whenever you retrieve the worksheet file.
Group	Lets you define a range of contiguous cells to be the X and A through F ranges.
Quit	Quits the Graph menu and returns the worksheet to READY mode.

Exercise 1.1: Creating a Graph

You must have a worksheet created that holds the data you want to graph. To produce a simple graph, follow these steps:

1. Create the worksheet shown in figure 9.1.

To Create a Simple Graph

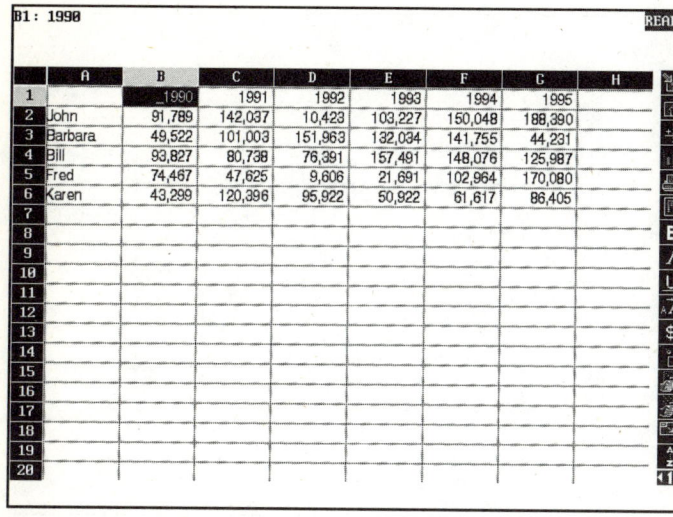

Fig. 9.1
A sales worksheet.

2. Select **/G**raph.
3. Select **T**ype **B**ar.
4. Select **X** (for x-axis labels).

   Next, you need to indicate the data values to be represented by each bar.

5. Move to cell B1, press `.`, highlight through cell G1, and press `↵Enter`.
6. Select **A**, and move to cell B2. Press `.`, highlight through cell G2, and press `↵Enter`.
7. Select **B**, and move to cell B3. Press `.`, highlight through cell G3, and press `↵Enter`.
8. Select **C**, and move to cell B4. Press `.`, highlight through cell G4, and press `↵Enter`.
9. Select **D**, and move to cell B5. Press `.`, highlight through cell G5, and press `↵Enter`.
10. Select **E**, and move to cell B6. Press `.`, highlight through cell G6, and press `↵Enter`.
11. Select **V**iew to see your graph (see fig. 9.2).
12. Press `↵Enter` to remove the graph from the screen, and select **Q**uit.

Creating and Printing Graphs

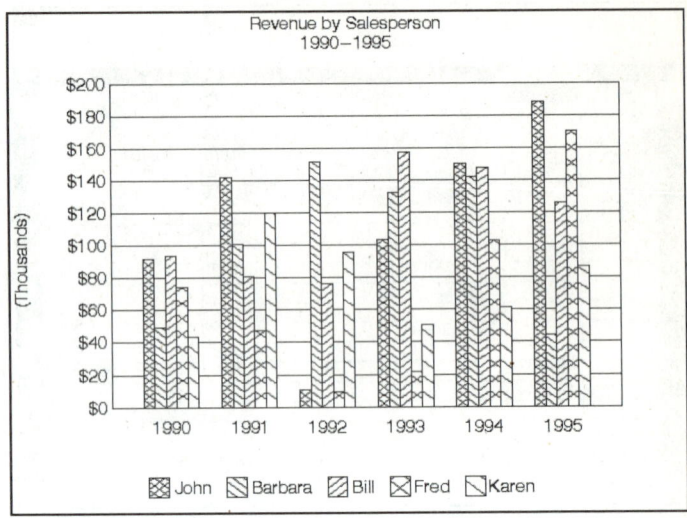

Fig. 9.2
This graph has been enhanced in several ways, which you will learn about in this chapter.

Using the Graph Settings Dialog Box

In addition to the Graph menu, the Graph Settings dialog box appears when you choose /**G**raph in Release 2.3 or 2.4. You can use this dialog box to change graph options.

Exercise 1.2: Using the Dialog Box

The three main ways to change an option on the dialog box involve option buttons, check boxes, and text boxes. To use the dialog box, follow these steps:

1. After selecting /**G**raph, press F2 (Edit), or click the left mouse button in the dialog box.

   1-2-3 highlights a character from each option (usually the first letter). Also, the Graph menu disappears when you activate the dialog box (see fig. 9.3).

2. To select an option button or check box, press the highlighted letter of each option, or click the left mouse button on your choice.

3. To use a text box, press the highlighted letter of each option until the pointer is positioned in that text box, or click the left mouse button on your choice.

To Become Familiar with Graph Types

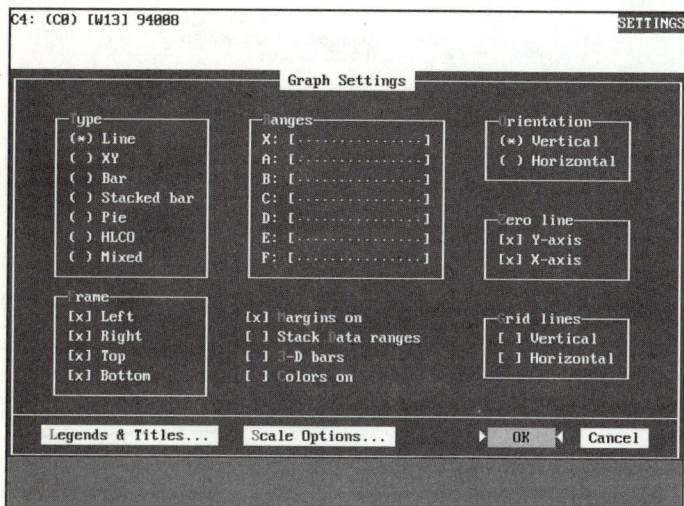

Fig. 9.3
The Graph Settings dialog box.

Objective 2: To Become Familiar with Graph Types

1-2-3's graphic capabilities increase the program's power by giving you a way to represent your data visually. Do you want to see whether a trend exists in the latest sales increase of a particular product? A 1-2-3 graph can show you the answer quickly, when deciphering that type of information from columns of numbers would be difficult. 1-2-3 offers seven basic graph types: line, bar, XY, stacked bar, pie, HLCO (high-low-close-open), and mixed. Selecting one of the seven available graph types is easy.

A line graph is best used for showing numeric data across time. You can, for example, show temperature at different stations with a line graph (see fig. 9.4).

An XY graph compares one numeric data series to another across time, to determine whether one set of values (the dependent variable) depends on the other (the independent variable). Use an XY graph, for example, to plot total sales and temperature to determine whether sales data appears to depend on temperature (see fig. 9.5).

Creating and Printing Graphs

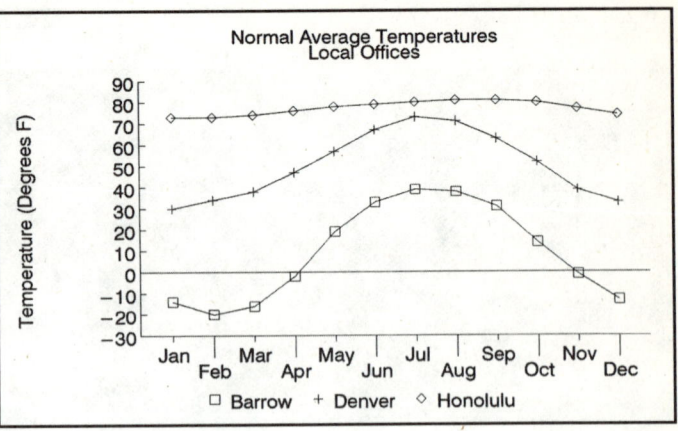

Fig. 9.4
A line graph.

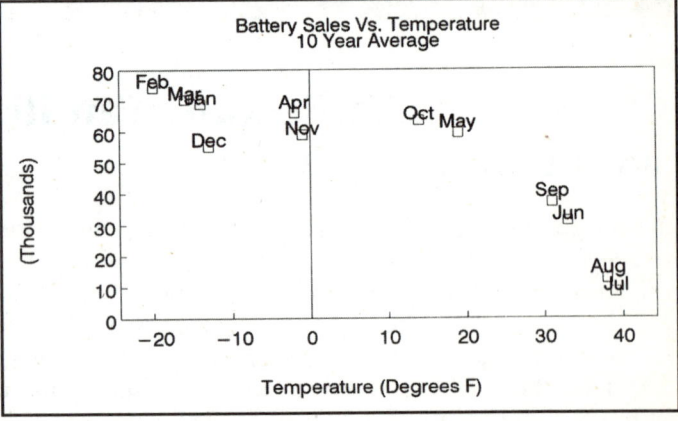

Fig. 9.5
An XY graph.

A bar graph shows the trend of numeric data across time. You can, for example, track the progress of company profits with a bar graph (see fig. 9.6).

A stacked-bar graph shows two or more data series that total 100 percent of a specific numeric category. (Do not use this type of graph if your data contains negative numbers.) Use a stacked-bar graph, for example, to graph data series for three company divisions (displayed one above the other) to depict the proportion each represents of total revenue for each quarter (see fig. 9.7). The graph shown in figure 9.7 also shows the effect of the 3-D option.

To Become Familiar with Graph Types

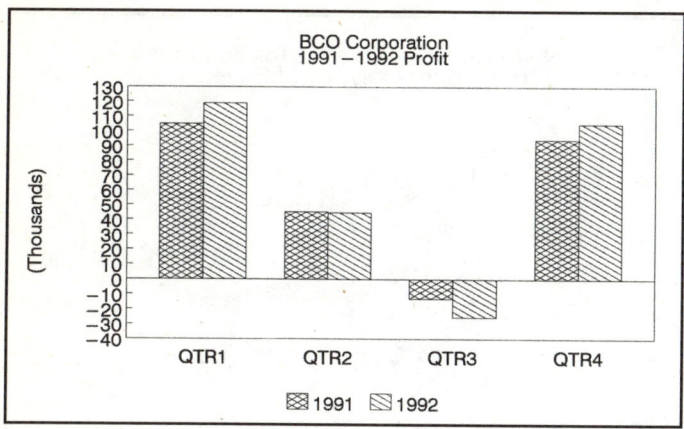

Fig. 9.6
A bar graph.

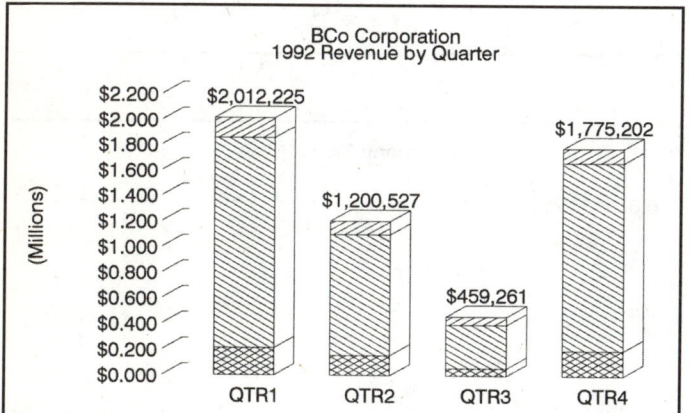

Fig. 9.7
A stacked-bar graph.

A pie graph is used to graph only one data series in which the components total 100 percent of a specific numeric category. (Do not use this type of graph if your data contains negative numbers.) Use a pie graph, for example, to graph the percentage of total sales by quarter (see fig. 9.8).

An HLCO (high-low-close-open) graph can be used to graph stock trends—showing changes in the high, low, closing, and opening prices over time. HLCO graphs can be used for tracking other data trends as well, such as sales information. In HLCO graphs, the top of the line represents the high value, and the bottom represents the low value. The left tick mark represents the opening value, and the right tick mark represents the closing value. Use an HLCO graph, for example, to show the high, low, closing, and opening prices of a particular stock (see fig. 9.9).

Creating and Printing Graphs

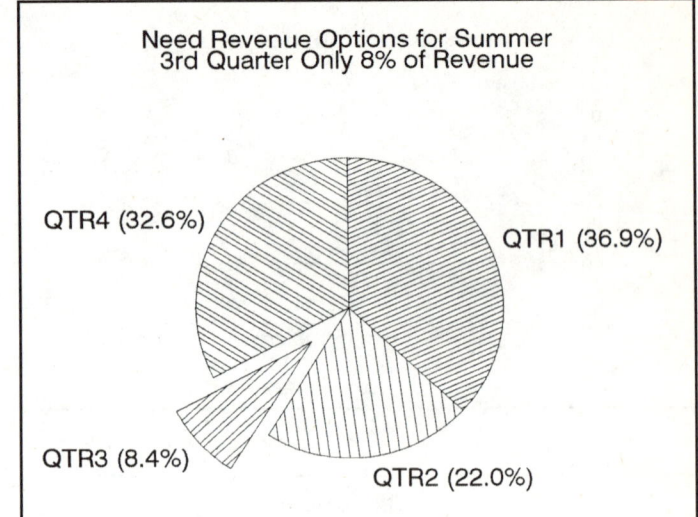

Fig. 9.8
A pie graph.

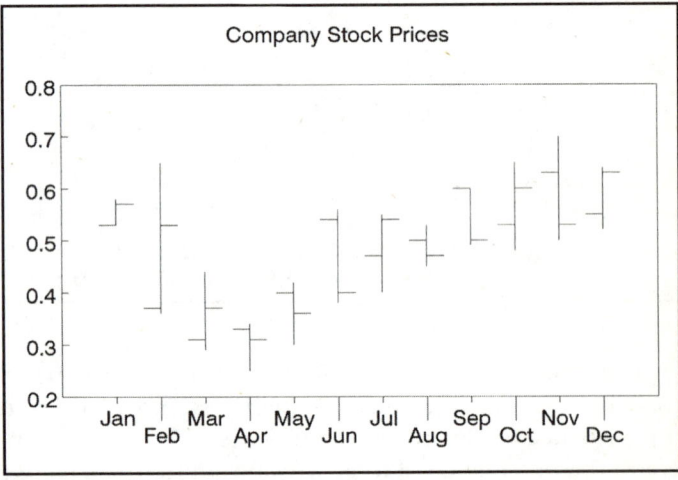

Fig. 9.9
An HLCO graph.

A mixed graph combines a bar graph and a line graph to display two types of data. Use the bars of a mixed graph, for example, to show profits by division. Use a line to show the total company profit (see fig. 9.10).

To understand which type will best display specific numeric data, you must know something about plotting points on a graph. All graphs (except pie graphs) have two axes: the *x-axis* (the horizontal bottom edge or categories axis) and the *y-axis* (the vertical left edge or values axis). 1-2-3 automatically provides tick marks for the axes. The program also scales the adjacent numbers on the y-axis, based on the minimum and maximum figures included in the plotted data range(s).

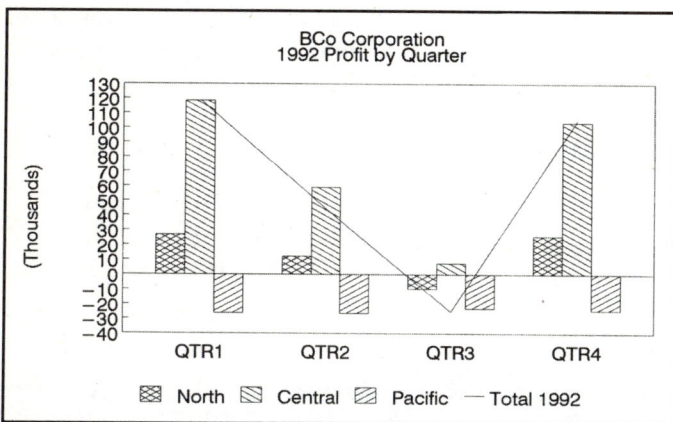

Fig. 9.10
A mixed graph.

Every point plotted on a graph has a unique location (x,y): *x* represents the time period or the amount measured along the horizontal axis; *y* measures the corresponding amount along the vertical axis. The intersection of the x-axis and the y-axis is called the *origin*. To avoid the misinterpretation of graph results and to make graphs easier to compare, use a zero origin in your graphs. Later in this chapter, you learn how to manually change the upper or lower limits of the scale; 1-2-3 initially sets these limits automatically.

Of the seven 1-2-3 graph types, all but the pie graph display both x- and y-axes. Line, bar, stacked-bar, HLCO, and mixed graphs display values (centered on the tick marks) along the y-axis only. The XY graph displays values on both axes.

Objective 3: To Specify Data Ranges

Because more than one type of graph can accomplish the desired presentation, you need to consider what data ranges you want to graph and the relationships among data you want to show. To create a graph, you must specify the range(s) of cells from the current worksheet to be used as data series.

211

Creating and Printing Graphs

You have the option of defining each data range on the worksheet separately or defining all the data ranges you want to plot at one time. To define one data range at a time, you fill in the Ranges section of the dialog box or choose each one individually, as you did in Exercise 1.1. If all the ranges you want to plot are contiguous (next to each other without any intervening rows or columns), select **G**roup from the Graph menu to define all the ranges at once. You also can use the Graph Range SmartIcon to define all the ranges at once.

Defining One Data Range at a Time

If the ranges you want to plot are located in various parts of the worksheet—that is, the ranges are not all contiguous—you must define one range at a time, as you did in Exercise 1.1. You can do so by choosing from the options **X** and **A** to **F**.

Table 9.2 shows ranges that appear in graphs broken down into graph types.

Table 9.2   Graph Types

Range	Line, Bar Stacked-Bar	XY	Pie	HLCO	Mixed
X	X-axis labels	Independent variable (x-axis)	Slice labels	X-axis labels	X-axis labels
A	1st data range	Dependent variable (y-axis)	Slice values	High	1st bar
B	2nd data range		Shading, color, and explosion	Low	2nd bar
C	3rd data range			Close	3rd bar
D	4th data range			Open	1st line
E	5th data range				2nd line
F	6th data range				3rd line

To Enhance the Appearance of a Graph

Every data series displayed in monochrome (one color) has unique shading. Data series displayed in color are assigned up to six different colors. Refer to table 9.3 for assignments of the colors used in bar, stacked-bar, and mixed graphs. Note that the colors listed in the table are those displayed on a VGA monitor with Wysiwyg attached. (Other monitors may display different results.)

Table 9.3	Data Range Colors for Bar Graphs
Data Range	*Wysiwyg Bar Graph Color*
A	Dark Blue
B	Green
C	Cyan
D	Red
E	Magenta
F	Yellow

With pie graphs, choose **X** to identify each piece of the pie. Then enter only one data series by selecting **A** from the Graph Settings dialog box or the menu.

Objective 4: To Enhance the Appearance of a Graph

After you have created a basic graph, you can improve the appearance of your graph and produce final-quality output suitable for business presentations. By selecting choices from the Graph Settings dialog box or from the /Graph Options menu, you can enhance a graph by adding descriptive labels and numbers, and by changing the default graph display items.

The \Graph Options menu has the following options:

Legend Format Titles Grid Scale Color B&W Data-Labels Quit

Table 9.4 describes Graph Settings dialog box options that enable you to enhance the graph.

Creating and Printing Graphs

Table 9.4 Selections in the Graph Settings Dialog Box

Selection	Description
Frame	Check boxes that enable you to define a border line around all, part, or none of the graph
Orientation	Option buttons that give you the choice of producing the graph vertically or horizontally
Zero line	A check box that allows you to add or remove the origin or zero line from the x- or y-axis
Grid lines	A check box that produces spaced vertical or horizontal lines in the graph to orient bars or lines
Margins on	A check box that leaves space between the y-axis and the first and last data points; if this check box is empty, the first and last data points plot against the graph frame
Stack Data ranges	A check box that stacks lines and bars on top of each other
3-D bars	A check box that produces three-dimensional bars
Colors on	A check box that displays and prints a graph in color, if the proper equipment is available
Legends & Titles	A command button that displays a dialog box in which you specify additional options
Scale Options	A command button that displays a dialog box in which you control the division and format of values along the x-axis or y-axis

Changing Axis Scale Settings

You can use the **Scale Options** command button in the Graph Settings dialog box or the \Graph Options Scale menu to alter three distinct default settings associated with the values displayed along a graph's x- and y-axes. These settings let you change the upper and lower limits of the x- and y-axis scale, change the format of y-axis values, and suppress the x- and y-axis scale indicator(s). In addition, you can use the Graph Scale settings dialog box to change the number of labels displayed along the x-axis and whether to display labels in the left and right sides of the graph.

214

To Enhance the Appearance of a Graph

Creating a 3-D Bar Graph

Three dimensional bar graphs can highlight and add variety to your presentations. In Releases 2.3 and 2.4, you can create 3-D bar graphs by selecting the **3-D bars** check box in the Graph Settings dialog box.

Displaying a Graph in Color

If you have a monitor or output device that displays color, you can turn on color by selecting the **Colors on** check box in the Graph Settings dialog box or selecting **/Graph Options Color**. To display the graph in monochrome (black and white), unmark the **Colors** check box or choose **/Graph Options B&W**.

If you intend to print the graph on a black-and-white printer, even if you have a color monitor, choose **B&W** from the Graph Options menu, or leave the **Color** option unmarked in the dialog box before saving the graph. A graph saved under the **Color** option will print all ranges on a black-and-white printer as solid blocks of black when you use the PrintGraph program. However, this is not true in Wysiwyg.

Adding Legends

In most cases, like the graph you created in Exercise 1.1, a graph without explanations is incomplete. To add text and symbols to various parts of the graph, you use the **Legends & Titles** command button to display another dialog box or the **/Options Titles** and **/Options Legend** menus.

Exercise 4.1: Adding Legends

To enhance the graph created in Exercise 1.1, follow these steps:

1. Select **/G**raph.
2. Press [F2] (Edit) or click the left mouse button somewhere in the dialog box to display the options in the Graph Settings dialog box.

   Or, select **O**ptions **L**egend. Select **A**, and type **John**. Select **L**egend **B**, and type **Barbara**. Select **L**egend **C**, and type **Bill**. Select **L**egend **D**, and type **Fred**. Select **L**egend **E**, and type **Karen**.

   Or select the **L**egends & Titles command button. The Graph Legends & Titles dialog box appears. Type the names in the **L**egends text boxes. (see fig. 9.11).

Creating and Printing Graphs

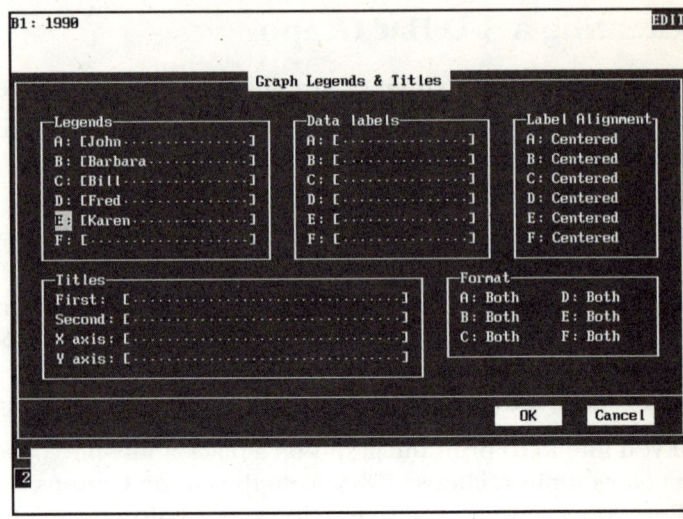

Fig. 9.11
The Graph
Legends & Titles
dialog box.

Table 9.5 describes each item in the Graph Legends & Titles dialog box.

Table 9.5 Selections in the Graph Legends & Titles Dialog Box

Selection	Description
Legends	Adds descriptions below the x-axis that link symbols, shadings, or colors to depict the data ranges
Titles	Includes graph titles and axis titles
Data labels	Adds labels that identify different data points in the graph
Label Alignment	Determines the position of data labels relative to data points
Format	Adds the lines or symbols that connect or represent data points

Exercise 4.2: Adding a Title

You can enter one or two centered titles at the top of the graph, a title below the x-axis, and a title to the left of the y-axis. You can enter titles by typing a new description, by specifying a range name, or by referencing the cell location of a label or a number that is already in the worksheet.

To Enhance the Appearance of a Graph

To add titles to a graph (after you have chosen the graph type and entered data ranges), complete the following steps:

1. In the **T**itles area of the Graph Legends & Titles dialog box, choose from the following selections:

Selection	Description
First	Displays a title on the top line of a graph
Second	Displays a title on the second line of a graph
X-Axis	Displays a title below the x-axis
Y-Axis	Displays a title to the left of the y-axis

    Note: The **X**-Axis and **Y**-Axis titles do not apply when you construct a pie graph.

2. To enter a title, type the text, and press ⏎Enter, or type a \ (backslash) followed by the cell reference or range name containing the title.

3. Repeat steps 1 and 2 for each title desired.

    Or, select **O**ption **T**itle **F**irst and type **Revenue by Salesperson**. Select **O**ption **T**itle **S**econd, and type **1990-1995**. Quit the Options menu. Select **V**iew or press F10.

4. Press ⏎Enter to clear the graph.

Setting a Background Grid

Ordinarily, you use the default background (clear, without a grid) for your graphs. You may, however, want to impose a grid on a graph so that the data-point amounts are easier to read.

Exercise 4.3: Adding a Grid

To add a grid to your graph, follow these steps:

1. Select /**G**raph.
2. Press F2 (Edit), or click the left mouse button somewhere in the dialog box to display the options in the Graph Settings dialog box.

217

Creating and Printing Graphs

3. Select **G**rid lines, and then select **V**ertical or **H**orizontal. An x indicates that lines will be present; an empty check box indicates that the lines will be absent.

   Or, select **O**ptions **G**rid **B**oth.

4. View the graph by selecting **V**iew from the /Graph menu or by pressing [F10].

5. Press [↵Enter] to clear the graph.

Objective 5: To Save a Graph

To create a disk file of a graph to be used with other programs, use the /Graph Save command. This command creates a file with the extension PIC. To save the graph specifications along with the underlying worksheet, first use the /Graph Name Create command to name the graph, and then use /File Save to save the worksheet to retain the graph settings.

Suppose that you have constructed a graph that you want to store for subsequent printing or importing to another program, such as a word processing program. After you verify that the graph type chosen is appropriate for your presentation needs, that the graph data ranges have been specified accurately, and that all desired enhancements have been added, use /Graph Save to create a PIC file on disk.

Exercise 5.1: Saving the Sales Graph

To save a graph as a PIC file so that it can be used with other programs, follow these steps:

1. Select /**G**raph **S**ave.

   1-2-3 prompts you for a file name and displays (across the top of the screen) a list of the PIC files in the current directory.

2. Type **Sales**, and press [↵Enter].

Saving Graph Settings

If you want to view on-screen a graph that you created in an earlier graphing session, you must have given the graph a name when you originally constructed the graph. You also must have saved the worksheet, unless the same worksheet is still active. To name a graph, you issue the /Graph Name Create command. Use the /Graph Name options to save the graph along with the

To Save a Graph

underlying worksheet or to retrieve or delete a named graph you have saved.

Only one graph at a time can be the current graph. If you want to save a graph that you have just completed (for subsequent recall to the screen) as well as build a new graph, you must first issue the **/Graph Name Create** command. The only way to store a graph for later screen display is to issue this command, which instructs 1-2-3 to remember the specifications used to define the current graph. If you do not name a graph and subsequently either reset the graph or change the specifications, you cannot restore the original graph without having to rebuild it.

Exercise 5.2: Saving the Graph Settings

To use the graph name settings, follow these steps:

1. Select **/G**raph **N**ame **C**reate.
2. Type **Sales1** and Press ⏎Enter.

The options listed in table 9.6 are available when you select **/Graph Name**.

Table 9.6 /Graph Name Options

Selection	Description
Use	Displays a graph whose settings have already been saved with /Graph Name Create; this option allows you to recall any named graph from within the active worksheet
Create	Creates a name for the currently defined graph so that you can later access and modify the graph
Delete	Erases an individual graph name and the settings associated with that graph
Reset	Erases all graph names
Table	Produces a listing directly in the worksheet of all graph names, their types (pie, bar, and so on), and titles (the top line of the graph); use caution to avoid writing over existing data

Note: If you want graph names to be stored with their worksheet, remember to save the worksheet file by using **/F**ile **S**ave after creating the names.

Creating and Printing Graphs

Objective 6: To Print a Graph

The first part of this chapter showed you how to create 1-2-3 graphs that are displayed on-screen. The remainder of this chapter shows you how to create printed copies of your graphs.

Accessing PrintGraph

After you create a graph within 1-2-3 and save it as a PIC file with /**Graph S**ave, you need to access the PrintGraph program to print the graph. You can access the PrintGraph program either directly from DOS or through the Lotus 1-2-3 Access menu.

Accessing the PrintGraph Program

To access PrintGraph directly from DOS, type **pgraph** at the DOS prompt, and press **Enter**. The PrintGraph program must be in the current directory. If you use a printer driver other than the default 1-2-3 driver, you must type the name of that driver set (**pgraph hp**, for example) to reach the PrintGraph main menu. You are more likely, however, to use PrintGraph immediately after you have created a graph.

If you originally accessed 1-2-3 by typing **lotus**, select /**Q**uit, and select **Y**es. You return to the Lotus 1-2-3 Access menu. From the Lotus 1-2-3 Access menu, select **P**rintGraph (see fig. 9.12).

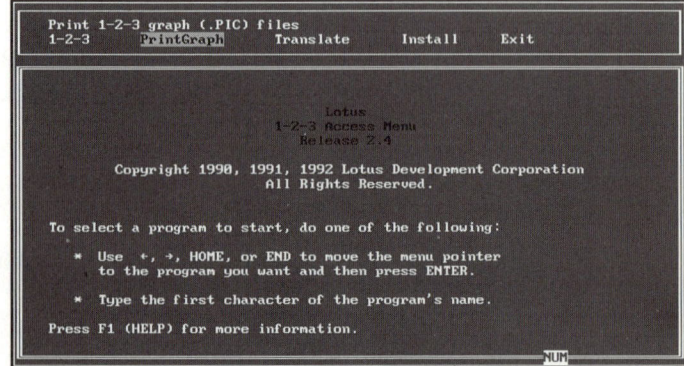

Fig. 9.12
Select PrintGraph from the Lotus 1-2-3 Access menu.

When the opening screen of the PrintGraph program is displayed, you can choose the options you want to set and print your graph (see fig. 9.13).

To Print a Graph

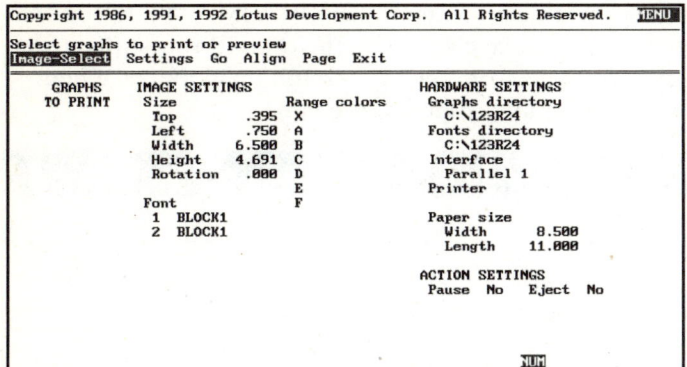

Fig. 9.13
The opening PrintGraph screen.

Understanding the PrintGraph Menu

Like 1-2-3, the PrintGraph program is menu-driven. The menu screens not only provide instructions for printing graph (PIC) files, but also information about current print conditions.

The first three text lines—which display a copyright message, a description of menu items, and current menu options—always remain on-screen. In the settings sheet area, below the double line, selections are continually updated (see fig. 9.14).

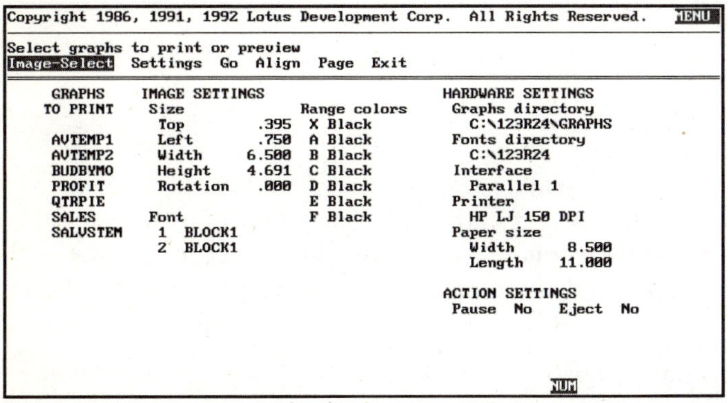

Fig. 9.14
The PrintGraph menu.

Before you begin printing a graph, make sure that you check the settings sheet. The settings displayed in the settings sheet are organized into four areas that are related to either the **Image-Select** or **Settings** options of the PrintGraph menu.

Creating and Printing Graphs

A list of graphs selected for printing appears under GRAPHS TO PRINT on the left side of the settings sheet. To make changes in the other three settings sheet areas, you first select Settings from the PrintGraph main menu. When you select Settings, a menu of options appears (see table 9.7).

Table 9.7	Selections on the PrintGraph Settings Menu
Selection	*Description*
Image	Changes the size, font, and color of the graph; the updated revisions are displayed in the IMAGE SETTINGS area of the settings sheet
Hardware	Alters the paper size, printer, or disk-drive specifications displayed in the HARDWARE SETTINGS area
Action	Moves to a new page and pauses while you change specifications for the next graph
Save	Allows you to save the current settings in a configuration file, to be used when starting PrintGraph
Reset	Restores the settings to those saved in the configuration file
Quit	Returns you to the PrintGraph main menu

Printing a Basic Graph

Printing a graph can be simple if you accept PrintGraph's default print settings. If you have specified the correct hardware configuration, you can produce a half-size, block-style typeface, black-and-white graph on 8 1/2-by-11-inch continuous-feed paper simply by marking a graph for printing and then printing it.

Suppose, for example, that you want to print a bar graph with the file name SALES.PIC. Before you begin the printing procedure, make sure that the current printer and interface specifications accurately reflect your hardware, that you're using continuous-feed paper, and that the printer is on-line and the print head is positioned at the page's top. Then use the following steps to print the graph with the default settings.

To Print a Graph

Exercise 6.1: Printing a Graph

To print a graph using PrintGraph's default settings, follow these steps:

1. Access PrintGraph using one of the methods described earlier in the chapter.
2. From the PrintGraph main menu, select **I**mage-Select.
3. Move the pointer to the name of the graph(s) you want to print (SALES), and press the [Spacebar]. A # appears next to the selected graph.
4. Press [↵Enter] to select the graph and return to the PrintGraph menu.
5. Select **A**lign to let PrintGraph know that the paper is correctly aligned at the top of the page.
6. Select **G**o to print the graph.

The printed graph is centered upright (zero degrees rotation) on the paper and fills the top half of an 8 1/2-by-11-inch page. The titles are printed in the default BLOCK1 font.

Note: A printed graph looks different from its on-screen display. The two titles at the top of the graph in the on-screen version appear to be the same size, but the first title automatically appears larger in a printed graph. Another variation can occur within the y-axis-the tick marks in the on-screen version are occasionally scaled in increments different from that of the printed graph. A third potential difference between an on-screen display and the printed graph is in the legends. In versions of 1-2-3 prior to Release 2.2, legends may spread out so that the first and last items in the legends are not printed. You can solve the problem by reducing the amount of text in each legend.

If you want to enhance this default graph, you can do so by using any or all of PrintGraph's many special features. These special capabilities (which are not available in the main 1-2-3 program) include the enlargement, reduction, and rotation of graph printouts and the use of different colors and fonts.

Changing the Appearance of the Printed Graph

You can enhance a basic graph you have created with PrintGraph's default settings in a number of ways. You can change the appearance of the printed graph by adjusting its size and orientation, by selecting different fonts, and by choosing alternate colors. When you select **S**ettings **I**mage from the PrintGraph menu, 1-2-3 provides the options **S**ize, **F**ont, and **R**ange-Colors (as well as **Q**uit). Use these options, respectively, to change the size of a graph, to

223

Creating and Printing Graphs

specify one or two print typefaces on a single graph, and to select colors for the different data ranges. The settings for these options are displayed in the middle of the PrintGraph settings sheet under IMAGE SETTINGS. Refer to your Lotus documentation for more information on these options.

Setting Up Your Hardware for Printing

Printing involves more than just inserting a sheet of paper into a printer, and pressing a key. Although the printing process is governed to some extent by your hardware and software, most of the initial decisions are up to you. You need to make decisions about the disk drives containing the print files, the printer type and name, and the size of the paper. The hardware settings are displayed in the far right column of the settings sheet.

When you select **Settings Hardware**, you see the menu shown in figure 9.15.

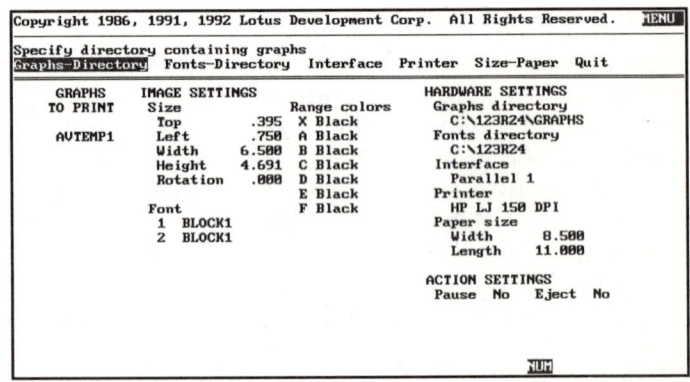

Fig. 9.15
The Settings Hardware menu.

The **Graphs-Directory** and **Fonts-Directory** options pertain to disk-drive specifications; **Interface** and **Printer** determine the current printer name and type; and **Size-Paper** permits you to specify the paper width and length in inches.

Controlling Printing Actions

In addition to specifying hardware settings, you can control printing actions by indicating certain settings before you start the printing process. In particular, you can make the printer pause between graphs, and you can decide whether you want the paper ejected after each graph. These ACTION SETTINGS are displayed in the far right column of the settings screen.

Completing the Print Cycle

After you create a graph and specify which options you want to use when printing, you can save the PrintGraph settings (if you want to use them again later), preview the graph on-screen (optional), and print the graph.

Saving PrintGraph Settings

After you establish the current Image, Hardware, and Action settings, you can select Settings Save if you want to use these settings in a later PrintGraph session.

To save the current PrintGraph settings for use in a later session, select Settings Save from the PrintGraph main menu.

The current settings are stored in a file named PGRAPH.CNF and are used whenever PrintGraph is loaded (until you modify and save the settings again) (see fig. 9.16).

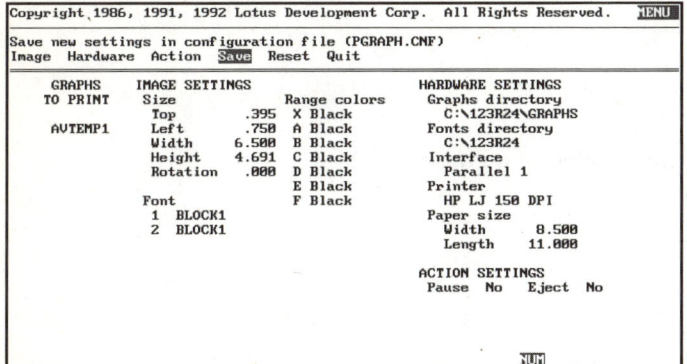

Fig. 9.16
The current settings are saved.

Select Settings Reset to restore all Image, Hardware, and Action settings to PrintGraph's default settings or to the options most recently saved. Note, however, that graphs selected to print with the Image-Select command are not reset when you issue Settings Reset.

Summary

Graphs of spreadsheets are easily created, and they help your audience understand the data.

225

Creating and Printing Graphs

Testing Your Knowledge

True/False Questions

1. The origin is small marks on the axes of a graph.
2. The X range specifies the range to be used as labels.
3. A pie graph is used to graph only one data series in which the components total 100 percent of a specific numeric category.
4. Legends add descriptions below the x-axis to explain the data ranges' colors or shading.
5. To print a graph, you must use the Translate program.

Multiple Choice Questions

1. When you save a graph, it is saved with the three letter extension
    A. WK1.
    B. PIC.
    C. WK?.
    D. GRA.
2. The horizontal bottom edge of a graph is the
    A. y-axis.
    B. legend.
    C. frame.
    D. x-axis.
3. 1-2-3 provides options to
    A. put a grid in one or both directions on the graph.
    B. place titles at the top of the screen.
    C. place legends at the bottom of the screen to explain the shading or coloring of the data.
    D. all the above.
4. To show the trend of numeric data across time, you should use
    A. a line graph.
    B. a bar graph.
    C. a pie graph.
    D. either a line or a bar graph.

5. To graph only one data series in which the components total 100 percent of a specific category, you should use

   A. a line graph.
   B. a bar graph.
   C. a pie graph.
   D. either a line or bar graph.

Fill-in-the-Blank Questions

1. _____ _____ are small marks on the axes of a graph, which indicate the increments between the minimum and maximum graph values.
2. The vertical left edge of a graph is the _____.
3. The intersection of the x- and y-axes is the _____.
4. To print a graph, you must access the _____ program.
5. To print a graph, you must first _____ the graph and exit 1-2-3.

Review: Short Projects

1. Changing Graph Types

   Use the sales graph created in this chapter. Select /Graph Type and view the graph as every possible graph type. Notice the differences in the way the data is presented.

2. Creating a Graph

   Using the bowling worksheet created in Chapter 3, graph the scores for three games for each player. Create a bar graph using titles, grid, and legend to enhance it. Save the graph and print it.

3. Creating a Pie Graph

   Using the bowling worksheet created in Chapter 3, graph the average for each person. Create a pie graph and include a title. Save the graph and print it.

Review: Long Projects

1. Creating a Graph

   Using the 12-month budget created in Chapter 3 long projects, create a line graph of the 12 months for 6 of the data items. Enhance it so

Creating and Printing Graphs

that it has titles and legends. Save it. Change some of the data in the worksheet, such as the rent and entertainment. Create a second line graph, and save it under a different name. Print both line graphs.

2. Changing Graph Types

    Using the 12-month budget created in Chapter 3 long projects, create a bar graph of the 12 months for 6 of the data items. Enhance it so that it has titles, legends, and a grid. Save it. Change some of the data in the worksheet, such as car and utilities. Create a second bar graph, and save it under a different name. Print both bar graphs.

Managing Data

10

In addition to the electronic spreadsheet and business graphics, 1-2-3 provides a third element: data management. 1-2-3's database feature is fast, easy to access, and relatively simple to use.

Objectives

1. To Become Familiar with Databases
2. To Become Familiar with /Data Menu
3. To Plan and Build a Database
4. To Sort Database Records
5. To Search for Records

Managing Data

Key Terms in This Chapter	
Database	A collection of data organized so that you can list, sort, or search its contents.
Field	One information item, such as an address or a name. The 1-2-3 documentation defines a field as one column of information; this book, however, uses the more common computer use of the word: one item of information.
Field name	The label in the first row of a database that identifies the contents of the field or column.
Record	A collection of associated fields. In 1-2-3, a record is a row of cells in a database.
Primary key	A column (or field) that determines the sorting order for rows in a database.
Input range	The range of the database on which 1-2-3 performs database operations.
Output range	The range to which 1-2-3 copies data when extracted from the database.
Criteria range	The range of the database in which you enter range search criteria.

Objective 1: To Become Familiar with Databases

A *database* is a collection of data organized so that you can list, sort, or search its contents. The list of data can contain any kind of information, from addresses to tax-deductible payments. A Rolodex is one form of a database. Other examples of databases include address books and a file cabinet of employee records (see fig. 10.1).

In 1-2-3, the word *database* means a range of cells that spans at least one column and more than one row. This definition, however, does not distinguish between a database and any other range of cells in a worksheet. Because a database is actually a list, its manner of organization distinguishes it from an ordinary range. Just as a list must be organized to be useful, you also must arrange a database so that the information is easy to access.

To Become Familiar with the /Data Menu

Fig. 10.1
Examples of databases.

The smallest unit in a database is a *field*, or single data item. If, for example, you were to develop an information database of customer accounts that are overdue, you might include the following fields of information:

Customer Last Name	Area Code
Customer First Name	Telephone Number
Street Address	Account Number
City	Payment Due Date
State	Date Paid
ZIP Code	Amount Due

A *database record* is a collection of associated fields. The accumulation of all data about one customer, for example, forms one record. In 1-2-3, a record is a row of cells in a database, and a field is one type of information, such as City.

You must set up a database so that you can access the information it contains. Retrieval of information usually involves relying on field names. A *database field* is any item in the first row of a database that describes the rest of the column below it. Field names are the basis for list or search operations. You could, for example, use *State* as a field name for a column of state abbreviations in an address database. Then you could extract all customers by state. Figure 10.2 shows the parts of a database.

Objective 2: To Become Familiar with the /Data Menu

You use the Data menu for many of 1-2-3's data management tasks. All other options from the 1-2-3 main menu work as well on databases as they do on worksheets. When you select **Data** from the 1-2-3 main menu, the control panel displays the following options:

   Fill Table Sort Query Distribution Matrix Regression Parse

Managing Data

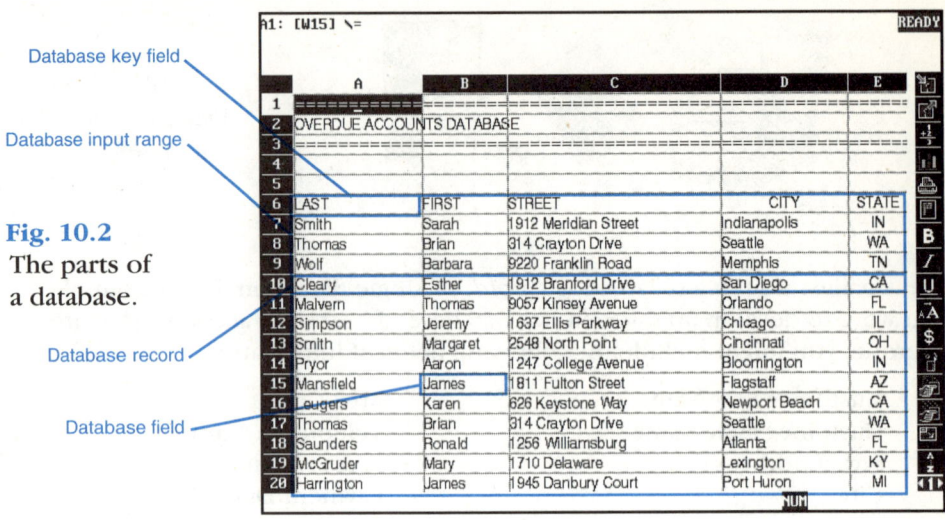

Fig. 10.2
The parts of a database.

Table 10.1 describes each of these options.

	Table 10.1 Selections on the /Data Menu
Selection	*Description*
Fill	Fills a specified range with values; you can choose the increment by which 1-2-3 increases or decreases successive numbers.
Table	Substitutes different values for a variable used in a formula; often used for "what-if" analyses.
Sort	Organizes the database in ascending or descending order based on one or two specified key fields.
Query	Offers different options for performing search operations and manipulating the found data items.
Distribution	Reports how often specific data occurs in a database.
Matrix	Enables you to solve systems of simultaneous linear equations and manipulate the resulting solutions.
Regression	Performs multiple regression analysis on X and Y values.
Parse	Separates long labels resulting from /File Import into discrete text and numeric cell entries.

Objective 3: To Plan and Build a Database

Before you begin to create a database in 1-2-3, you should determine the categories (fields) of information you want to include. You can determine these fields by planning what kind of output you expect to produce from your data. Next, decide which area of the worksheet to use. Then create a database by specifying field names across a row. Finally, enter data into cells beneath these names, as you would for any other 1-2-3 application. Entering database contents is simple. The most critical step in creating a database is choosing your fields accurately.

Determining Required Output

1-2-3's data-retrieval techniques rely on finding data by field names. Before you begin typing the kinds of data items you think you may need, write down the output you expect from the database. You also need to consider any source documents already in use that can provide input to the file.

Before you set up the items in your database, be sure to consider how you may look for data in each field. Consider, for example, how you will look for a particular information item. Will you search by date? By last name? Knowing beforehand how you will use your database will prevent you having to redesign the database.

After you decide on the fields, select the appropriate column width (which you can later modify) and determine whether you will enter the data as a number, label, or date, as shown in figure 10.3.

Overdue Accounts Database

Item	Column Width	Type of Entry
1. Customer Last Name	15	Label
2. Customer First Name	10	Label
3. Street Address	25	Label
4. City	15	Label
5. State	7	Label
6. ZIP Code	6	Label
7. Area Code	6	Number
8. Telephone Number	11	Label
9. Account Number	10	Number
10. Payment Due Date	11	Date
11. Date Paid	11	Date
12. Amount Due	12	Number

Fig. 10.3
Choose the column width and data type.

Managing Data

Here are some tips for planning various types of fields (columns) in your database:

- For ease in sorting, put last and first names in separate columns. Or you can put both names in the same cell and separate the last and first names with a comma.
- Some ZIP codes begin with 0, which will not appear in the cell if you enter the ZIP code as a value. Enter ZIP codes as labels by preceding them with a label prefix.
- Set up an area code field that is separate from the telephone number field. This configuration helps if you want to search, sort, or extract records by area code.
- Enter a telephone number as a label. This number must be a label because of the hyphen between the first three and last four digits of a telephone number. A hyphen signifies subtraction in a number entered as a value.

Be sure to plan your database carefully before you type field names, set column widths and range formats, and enter data. Although you can make changes after you set up your database, planning helps to reduce the time required for making those changes.

Positioning the Database

You can create a database as a new database file or as part of an existing worksheet. If you decide to build a database as part of an existing worksheet, choose an area where inserting or deleting lines will not affect the worksheet or another database.

Entering Data

After you plan your database and decide which area of the worksheet to use, you can start entering data. Build a database by specifying field names as labels across a row. Make sure that each field name is unique and in a separate column.

You can use one or more rows for field names, but 1-2-3 processes only the bottom row. Therefore, each field name in the bottom row must be unique.

To Sort Database Records

After you enter the field names, enter data in cells as you would for any other 1-2-3 application. Change the column width to fit the information you enter by using the /Worksheet Column Set-Width command.

Exercise 3.1: Building a Database

To build a 1-2-3 database, follow these steps:

1. Enter the field names shown in figure 10.4 across a single row, starting at cell A1.

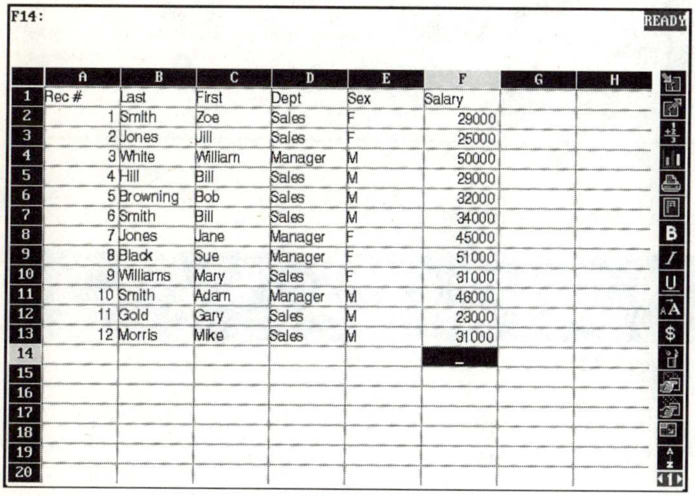

Fig. 10.4
Database labels.

	A	B	C	D	E	F
1	Rec #	Last	First	Dept	Sex	Salary
2	1	Smith	Zoe	Sales	F	29000
3	2	Jones	Jill	Sales	F	25000
4	3	White	William	Manager	M	50000
5	4	Hill	Bill	Sales	M	29000
6	5	Browning	Bob	Sales	M	32000
7	6	Smith	Bill	Sales	M	34000
8	7	Jones	Jane	Manager	F	45000
9	8	Black	Sue	Manager	F	51000
10	9	Williams	Mary	Sales	F	31000
11	10	Smith	Adam	Manager	M	46000
12	11	Gold	Gary	Sales	M	23000
13	12	Morris	Mike	Sales	M	31000

2. Enter all the records shown in figure 10.4. Notice the record numbers in column A.

Objective 4: To Sort Database Records

Storing data in a database would be meaningless if you were unable to alphabetize the data or sort it numerically. Sorting is an important function of any database. 1-2-3's data management capability enables you to change the order of records by sorting them according to the contents of the fields. Figure 10.5 shows the Data Sort menu and the Sort Settings dialog box.

Managing Data

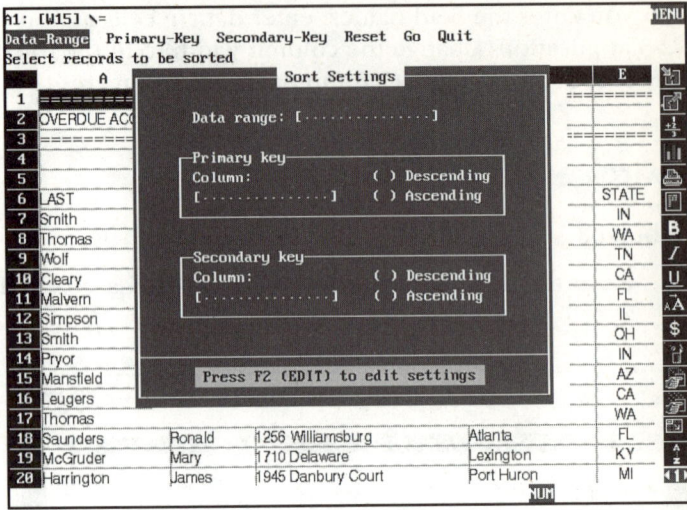

Fig. 10.5
The Data Sort menu and the Sort Settings dialog box.

Table 10.2 describes each of these options.

Table 10.2 Selections on the Data Sort Menu and Sort Settings Dialog Box	
Selection	*Description*
Data-Range	Allows you to specify the range on which the sort operation occurs.
Primary-Key	Lets you specify the first column to organize the sort.
Secondary-Key	Lets you specify the second column to organize the sort.
Reset	Resets the sort options.
Go	Starts the sort.
Quit	Exits the Data Sort menu.

To sort the records, you must tell 1-2-3 what area to sort; this is the Data-Range. You must also tell 1-2-3 at least one field to sort by; this is the Primary-Key. If there is a tie in the primary key field, such as more than one Smith in the name field, the tie is broken by the Secondary-Key (if it is defined).

To Sort Database Records

One note of caution before you issue a /Data Sort command: save the database to disk. That way, if the sort does not produce the results you expected, you can restore the file to its original order by retrieving it.

Exercise 4.1: Sorting the Database Using the Sort Menu

To sort a database, follow these steps:

1. Select /Data Sort.
2. Select Data-Range from the menu or dialog box and define the range you want to sort. This range must be long enough to include all the records and wide enough to include all the fields in each record (see fig. 10.6).

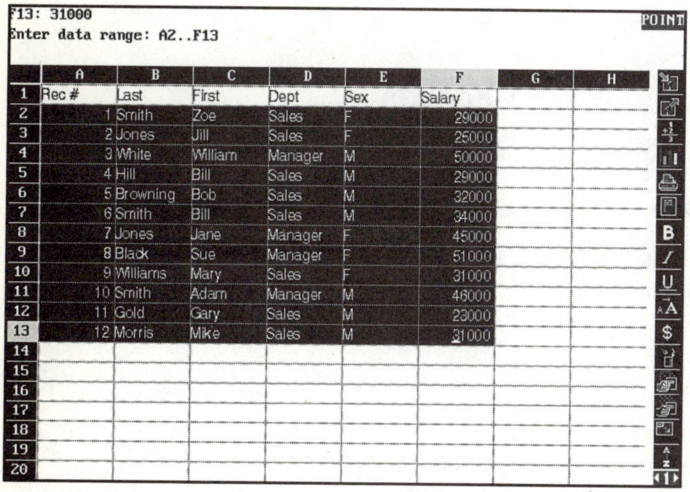

Fig. 10.6
The data range.

Note: Do not include the field names row or they will be sorted with the rest of the database.

3. Specify the key field(s) for the sort from the menu or dialog box by choosing Primary-Key, moving your cursor to cell B2, and pressing ⏎Enter. Type A for ascending, and press ⏎Enter.
4. Select Secondary-Key, move your cursor to cell C2, and press ⏎Enter. Type A for ascending, and press ⏎Enter.
5. Select Go to perform the sort. The database is sorted (see fig. 10.7).

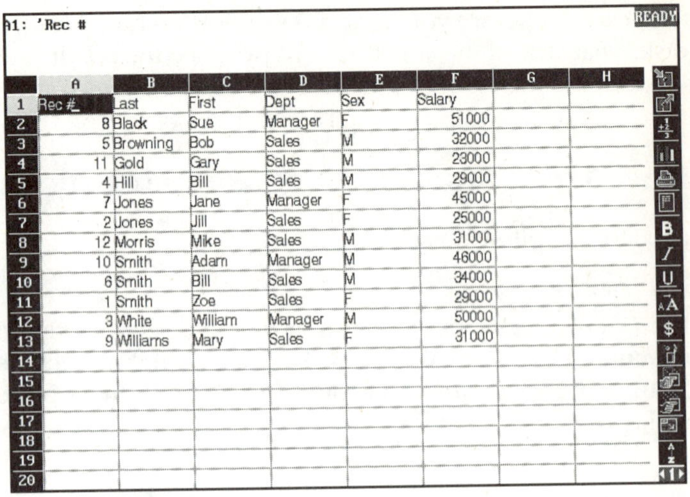
A1: 'Rec # READY

	A	B	C	D	E	F	G	H
1	Rec #	Last	First	Dept	Sex	Salary		
2	8	Black	Sue	Manager	F	51000		
3	5	Browning	Bob	Sales	M	32000		
4	11	Gold	Gary	Sales	M	23000		
5	4	Hill	Bill	Sales	M	29000		
6	7	Jones	Jane	Manager	F	45000		
7	2	Jones	Jill	Sales	F	25000		
8	12	Morris	Mike	Sales	M	31000		
9	10	Smith	Adam	Manager	M	46000		
10	6	Smith	Bill	Sales	M	34000		
11	1	Smith	Zoe	Sales	F	29000		
12	3	White	William	Manager	M	50000		
13	9	Williams	Mary	Sales	F	31000		
14								
15								
16								
17								
18								
19								
20								

Fig. 10.7
The sorted database.

Tips for Sorting Database Records

Here are a few tips to help you sort database records more successfully.

Tip 1: Don't include blank rows in your data range.

If you accidentally include one or more blank rows in your data range, the blank rows appear at the top of your data range. Therefore, remember to include only rows that contain data when you specify the data range.

Tip 2: After you sort the original contents of the database on any field, you cannot restore the records to their original order. To avoid mistakes and restore the records to the original order, add a counter column to the database before any sort, (column A in fig. 10.6). Include the counter column in the sort range. You can restore the original order by re-sorting on the counter field.

Tip 3: You can add a record to an alphabetized name-and-address database without having to insert the record in the correct position manually. Simply add the record to the bottom of the current database, expand the sort data range, and then sort again by last name.

Objective 5: To Search for Records

Looking for records that meet one condition is the simplest form of searching a 1-2-3 database. In an inventory database, for example, you can determine when to reorder items. Use a search operation to find any records with an on-hand quantity of fewer than four units. After you find the information you want, you can extract or copy the found records from the database to another empty section of the worksheet. You can, for example, extract all records with a future purchase order date and print the newly extracted area as a record of pending purchases.

Minimum Search Requirements

The /Data Query command lets you search for and extract data that meets specific criteria. After you choose /Data Query, 1-2-3 displays a menu of nine options and a Query Settings dialog box for performing search and extract operations (see fig. 10.8).

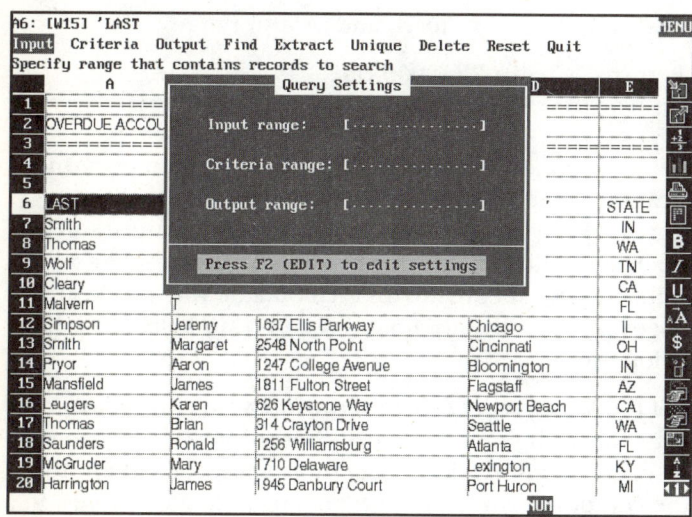

Fig. 10.8
The Data Query menu and the Query Settings dialog box.

Table 10.3 describes these options.

Managing Data

Table 10.3 Selections on the Data Query Menu	
Selection	*Description*
Input	Allows you to define the database to be searched.
Criteria	Lets you specify the conditions for searching the database.
Output	Allows you to specify the range where you want to locate the records extracted from the database.
Find	Finds records based on the specified criteria.
Extract	Copies from the database the records matching the specified criteria and places them in the Output range.
Unique	Eliminates duplicate records in the Output range.
Delete	Removes from the Input range records that match the specified criteria.
Reset	Resets the input, criteria, and output ranges.
Quit	Returns 1-2-3 to READY mode.

The first three options specify ranges applicable to the search operation. **Input** and **Criteria** give the locations of the search area and the search conditions. You must specify both in all Query operations. You specify the Output range with the Output option. The Output range is necessary when you select a /Data Query command that copies records to an area outside the database. You can enter these ranges through the command menu or in Releases 2.3 and 2.4 through the dialog box.

The next four options of the Data Query menu perform a variety of search functions. Find moves down through a database and positions the cell pointer on records that match the given criteria. You can enter or change data in the records as you move the cell pointer through them. Extract creates copies, in a specified area of the worksheet, of all or some of the fields in certain records that match the given criteria. Unique is similar to Extract, but ignores duplicate records as 1-2-3 copies entries to the Output range. Delete erases from a database all the records that match the given criteria and closes the remaining gaps.

To Search for Records

The last two options of the Data Query menu are **R**eset and **Q**uit. They signal the end of the current search operation. **R**eset removes all previous search-related ranges so that you can specify a different search location, condition, and Output range (if applicable). **Q**uit restores 1-2-3 to READY mode.

Searching for Specific Records

If you want to search for one or several records that meet certain criteria, you need to make two selections from the Data Query menu or Query Settings dialog box: **I**nput and **C**riteria. Then you select **F**ind from the Data Query menu.

Defining the Input Range

The /**D**ata **Q**uery **I**nput command defines the range of records you want to search. You must include the field names row in the Input range. (In contrast, remember that you do not include the field names in a sort operation.) If field names occupy more than one row, specify only the bottom row to start the Input range. Do not use a blank row or a dashed line to separate the field names from the database records.

Defining the Criteria Range

To search for data that meets certain conditions, or criteria, you must set up a special range called a *criteria range*. First find an empty area of the worksheet for your criteria range. Then retype exactly or copy the field names to that location. Then you will tell 1-2-3 where the criteria range is. You can use numbers, labels, or formulas as criteria. A criteria range can be up to 32 columns wide and 2 or more rows long. The first row must contain the field names of the search criteria, such as STATE. The rows below the unique field names contain the actual criteria, such as OH.

Finding Records that Meet the Criteria

After you enter the input and criteria ranges, you have completed the minimum requirements for executing a **F**ind.

Exercise 5.1: Finding Records in a Database

To find records in a database that match the criteria—female employees in the sales department—follow these steps:

1. Copy the field names from A1..F1 to A18..F18.
2. Type **sales** in cell D19 and **F** in cell E19.
3. Select /**D**ata **Q**uery **I**nput.
4. Move to cell A1, press [.], and highlight the database (A1..F13). Press [↵Enter].
5. Select **C**riteria.
6. Move to cell A18, and press [.]. Highlight over to column F and down one row so that the range is A18..F19.
7. Select **F**ind. The first record matching the criteria is highlighted (see fig. 10.9).

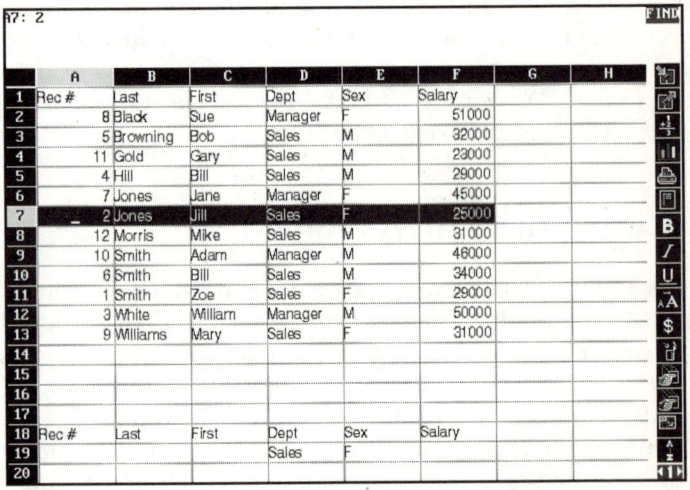

A7: 2 FIND

	A	B	C	D	E	F	G	H
1	Rec #	Last	First	Dept	Sex	Salary		
2	8	Black	Sue	Manager	F	51000		
3	5	Browning	Bob	Sales	M	32000		
4	11	Gold	Gary	Sales	M	23000		
5	4	Hill	Bill	Sales	M	29000		
6	7	Jones	Jane	Manager	F	45000		
7	2	Jones	Jill	Sales	F	25000		
8	12	Morris	Mike	Sales	M	31000		
9	10	Smith	Adam	Manager	M	46000		
10	6	Smith	Bill	Sales	M	34000		
11	1	Smith	Zoe	Sales	F	29000		
12	3	White	William	Manager	M	50000		
13	9	Williams	Mary	Sales	F	31000		
14								
15								
16								
17								
18	Rec #	Last	First	Dept	Sex	Salary		
19				Sales	F			
20								

Fig. 10.9 The criteria range at the bottom—with the criteria F and sales—determines what records are highlighted.

8. Press [↓] to find other matches. 1-2-3 will beep when there aren't any more matching records.
9. Press [Esc] to quit the **F**ind option.
10. Select **Q**uit to leave the menu.

To Search for Records

Listing All Specified Records

The /Data Query Find command has limited use, especially in a large database. The command must scroll through the entire file if you want to view each record that meets the specified criteria. As an alternative to the Find command, you can use the Extract command. This command copies to a blank area of the worksheet only those records that meet specified conditions. Before you issue the command, you must define the blank area of the worksheet as an Output range. You can view a list of all the extracted records or print the range of the newly extracted records.

Defining the Output Range

Choose a blank area in the worksheet as the Output range to receive records copied in an extract operation. In the first row of the Output range, copy the field names from the Input range.

You can create an open-ended Output range by entering only the field names row as the range. The Output range, in this case, can be any size, according to how many records meet the criteria. You also can set the exact size of the extract area so that no data located below the area is accidentally overwritten.

Exercise 5.2: Extracting Data

To define the Output range where 1-2-3 will copy records meeting the specified criteria, follow these steps:

1. To change the criteria, erase the old criteria from row 19 of the criteria range.
2. Type a new criteria; for this example type **Manager** in cell D19.
3. Copy the exact field names from A1..F1 of your database to the section of the worksheet where you want to locate the Output range. For example, **A22..F22**.
4. Select **/D**ata **Q**uery.
5. Select **O**utput from the menu or **O**utput range from the dialog box.
6. Highlight the range A22..F22, and press ⏎Enter.
7. Select **E**xtract and **Q**uit (see fig. 10.10).

243

Managing Data

Fig. 10.10
This figure shows the criteria range and the Output range with the extracted records, which match the criteria manager.

	A	B	C	D	E	F
9	10	Smith	Adam	Manager	M	46000
10	6	Smith	Bill	Sales	M	34000
11	1	Smith	Zoe	Sales	F	29000
12	3	White	William	Manager	M	50000
13	9	Williams	Mary	Sales	F	31000
14						
15						
16						
17						
18	Rec #	Last	First	Dept	Sex	Salary
19				Manager		
20						
21						
22	Rec #	Last	First	Dept	Sex	Salary
23	8	Black	Sue	Manager	F	51000
24	7	Jones	Jane	Manager	F	45000
25	10	Smith	Adam	Manager	M	46000
26	3	White	William	Manager	M	50000
27						
28						

Exercise 5.3: Using a More Complex Criteria

You can have 1-2-3 match several fields. Matches on numeric data can be in the form of formulas. The formula must tell 1-2-3 to look at the first cell containing a number in the field, so you give a reference cell in the formula. 1-2-3 will respond with a 0 or a 1 in the criteria range, depending on the contents of the reference cell. Follow these steps to extract Females in Sales who make more than $30,000:

1. Move to row 19 and delete any criteria.
2. In cell D19, type **Sales**.
3. In cell E19, type **F**.
4. In cell F19, type **+F2>30000**.
5. Select /**D**ata **Q**uery **E**xtract **Q**uit. The data is extracted (see fig. 10.11).

Performing Other Types of Searches

In addition to Find and Extract, you can use the **Unique** and **Delete** options of the **Data Query** menu to perform searches. By issuing the Unique command, you can produce (in the Output range) a copy of just the first occurrence of a duplicate record that meets the specified criteria in the Output range. The **Delete** command enables you to update the contents of your 1-2-3 database by deleting all records that meet the specified criteria. After entering the search conditions, you need to specify only the input and criteria ranges before you issue the **Delete** command.

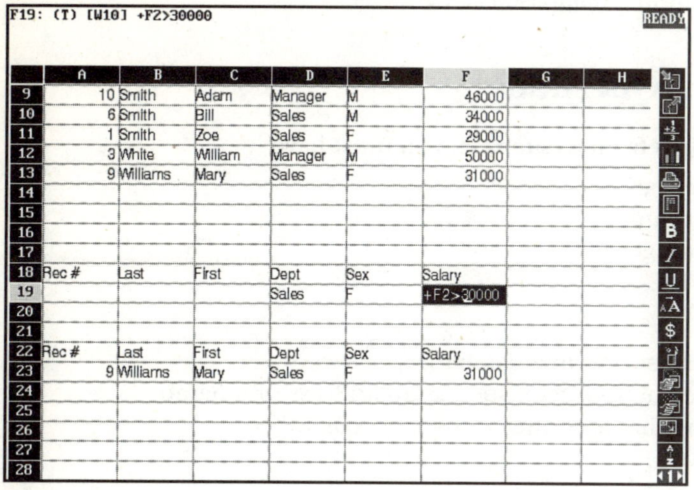

Fig. 10.11
In this figure, you can see the criteria range (the formula is formatted so that it is visible) and the Output range with the matching records.

Summary

Lotus 1-2-3 has powerful database capabilities such as sorting, finding, and extracting data. After becoming familiar with databases, you used 1-2-3 to create a database. Then you organized the database by sorting on a primary key and breaking ties in that field by identifying a secondary key. Finally, you found and extracted records based on one or more criteria.

Testing Your Knowledge

True/False Questions

1. A field is a collection of data organized so that you can list, sort, or search its contents.
2. Lotus 1-2-3's data retrieval techniques rely on finding data by field names.

Managing Data

3. You can create a counter field before you sort so that you can return the database to its original order.
4. A record is a collection of associated fields.
5. The smallest unit in a database is a field.

Multiple Choice Questions

1. To extract records from a database, you must have
    A. an Input range.
    B. an Output range.
    C. a criteria range.
    D. all the above.

2. A field
    A. is the smallest unit in a database.
    B. is one information item, such as an address or a name.
    C. has a name that identifies it, such as ADDRESS.
    D. all the above.

3. To sort a database, you must have
    A. a criteria range and an Output range.
    B. a data range and a primary key.
    C. a data range and a criteria range.
    D. a primary key and a criteria range.

4. To find records in the database, you must have
    A. a criteria range and an Output range.
    B. a data range and a primary key.
    C. a primary key and a criteria range.
    D. a criteria range and an Input range.

5. To break a tie in the primary key field, you must define
    A. a data range.
    B. a secondary key.
    C. a criteria range.
    D. a second primary key.

Fill-in-the-Blank Questions

1. A _____ is a collection of data organized so that you can list, sort, or search its contents.
2. The _____ command organizes the database in ascending or descending order based on one or two specified fields.
3. The _____ command offers different options for performing search operations and manipulating the found data.
4. The _____ range lets you specify the conditions for searching the database.
5. The _____ range enables you to specify the range where you want to locate the records extracted from the database.

Review: Short Projects

1. Creating and Sorting an Address Database

    Create an address book of your friends. Include all fields necessary to make this complete. Enter at least 10 records. Sort the database by name, save it, and print it.

2. Creating and Sorting a Library Database

    Create a library database of your videos or books. Include all fields necessary to make this complete. Enter at least 10 records. Sort the database by title, save it, and print it.

3. Creating and Sorting a Collection Database

    Create a tape, CD, or record collection database. Include all fields necessary to make this complete. Enter at least 10 records. Sort the database by artist, save it, and print it.

Review: Long Projects

1. Finding Records that Meet a Criteria

    Retrieve the checkbook register created in Chapter 3. Add a column that codes each check. For example, in the column next to the running total, enter **Code**. Add codes for each check, such as **H** for household, **A** for automobile expenses, and so forth. Create a criteria range, and have 1-2-3 find all checks matching the criteria. Create an Output range and, using the codes, extract checks based on the code criteria.

Managing Data

2. Creating, Sorting, and Searching for Records in a Database

    Create a database for a real estate company with the following fields: Area, Address, Price, Bedrms, Baths, Sq.Ft., Garage, and Extras. Use a code for the area field (such as A, B, C, or south, north, or east) that identifies the area. Enter the price, number of bedrooms, baths, square footage, and garage as numbers. Enter the address and any extras as text. You should have at least 20 records. Save and print the database.

    Sort the database primarily by Area in ascending order and secondarily by Price in descending order. Save and print the database.

    Extract records based on multiple criteria, such as a three-bedroom, two-bathroom house in a certain area, over a certain price. Print the Output range.

Understanding Macros

11

In addition to the capabilities available from the commands in 1-2-3's main menu, another feature makes 1-2-3 the most popular spreadsheet program available. Macros and the advanced macro commands enable you to automate and customize your applications and thus reduce tasks requiring multiple keystrokes to a two-keystroke or SmartIcon operation. Just press two keys, and 1-2-3 does the rest, whether you're formatting a range, creating a graph, or printing a worksheet. You also can control and customize worksheet applications by using 1-2-3's advanced macro commands. These built-in commands give you a greater range of control over your 1-2-3 applications.

Objectives

1. To Become Familiar with Macros
2. To Become Familiar with the Learn Feature
3. To Execute Macros
4. To Debug and Edit Macros
5. To Add Macros to SmartIcons
6. To Use the Macro Library Manager Add-In

11 Understanding Macros

Key Terms in This Chapter	
Macro	A series of stored keystrokes or commands that 1-2-3 carries out when you press two or more keys or click a user-defined SmartIcon.
Program	A list of instructions in a computer programming language, such as 1-2-3's advanced macro commands, which tells the computer what to do.
Advanced macro commands	1-2-3's programming language consisting of more than 50 built-in commands that are not accessible through the 1-2-3 menu system.
Tilde (~)	The symbol used in a macro to signify the **Enter** keystroke.
Key names	Representations of keyboard keys used in macros. Enclose key names in braces: for example, {EDIT}.
Documented macro or program	A macro or program that contains information explaining each step in the macro or program.
Learn feature	A feature that records keystrokes, enables you to copy keystrokes into a worksheet cell as a label, and automatically creates a macro.
Bug	An error in a macro or program.
Debugging	The process of identifying and fixing errors in a macro or program.

Objective 1: To Become Familiar with Macros

A macro, in its most basic form, is a collection of stored keystrokes that you can replay at any time. These keystrokes can be commands or simple text and numeric entries. Macros provide an alternative to typing data and commands from the keyboard. Macros, therefore, can save you time by automating frequently performed tasks. Figure 11.1 shows some macros.

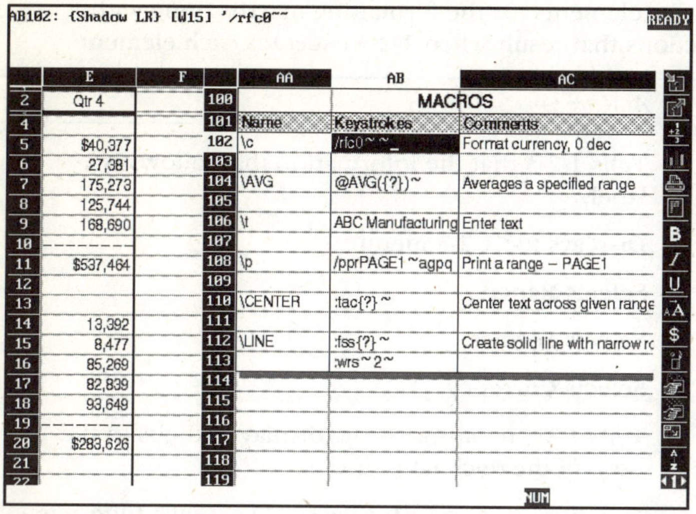

To Become Familiar with Macros

Fig. 11.1
This figure shows six simple keystroke macros in the window on the right. The window on the left displays worksheet data.

A simple macro, for example, can automate the sequence of seven keystrokes that format a cell in Currency format with 0 decimal places. You can execute the seven keystrokes in cell AB102 by pressing two keys: **Alt** and **C**.

You can name macros in two different ways. One way is to use the backslash key (\) and a single letter. Execute an **Alt+***letter* macro by holding down Alt and pressing the letter that identifies the macro. This method is the only one available for use with versions of 1-2-3 before Release 2.2. In Releases 2.2, 2.3, and 2.4, you can name macros using descriptive names of up to 15 characters long. Access these macros by pressing **Alt+F3** (Run). When the list of range names appears, highlight the name of the macro you want to use, and press **Enter**.

The Elements of Macros

1-2-3 macros follow a specific format, whether they are simple keystroke macros or macros that perform complex tasks. A macro is nothing more than a text cell. You create all macros by entering into a worksheet cell the keystrokes (or representations of those keystrokes) to store. Suppose that you want to create a simple macro that will format the current cell to appear in Currency format with no decimal places. The macro looks like this:

'/rfc0~~

Understanding Macros

Following are the macro elements for the formatting macro, along with descriptions of the actions that result when 1-2-3 executes each element:

Macro Element	Action
'	Tells 1-2-3 that the information that follows is a label.
/	Displays the 1-2-3 menu.
r	Selects **R**ange.
f	Selects **F**ormat.
c	Selects **C**urrency.
0	Tells 1-2-3 to suppress the display of digits to the right of the decimal point.
~~	Functions as two **Enter** keystrokes. (Each tilde acts as one **Enter** keystroke.)

You enter this macro into the worksheet in exactly the same way you would any other label. Type a label prefix followed by the characters in the label. The label prefix (displayed only in the control panel) informs 1-2-3 to treat what follows as a label. Every macro that starts with a nontext character (/, \, +, –, or a number) must begin with a label prefix. If you did not use a prefix, 1-2-3 would automatically interpret the next character (/) as a command to execute immediately instead of a label stored in the cell. Any of the three 1-2-3 label prefixes (', ", or ^) works equally well.

The next four characters in the macro represent the command used to create the desired format. After all, /rfc is simply shorthand for **R**ange **F**ormat **C**urrency. The 0 (zero) tells 1-2-3 that you want no digits displayed to the right of the decimal point. If you were entering this command from the keyboard, you would type the 0 in response to a prompt.

At the end of the macro are two characters called *tildes*. When used in a macro, a tilde (~) represents the **Enter** key. In this case, the two tildes signal 1-2-3 to press **Enter** twice: to accept the number of decimal places, and to select the current cell as the range to format.

Other elements used in macros include range names and cell addresses. Although you can use these two elements interchangeably, you should use range names instead of cell addresses whenever possible. If you move data included in specified ranges, or insert or delete rows and columns, the range names adjust automatically and the macro continues to refer to the correct cells and ranges. Cell references used in macros do not adjust to any changes made in the worksheet and you must change them manually.

Some macro examples in this chapter include the {?} command. The {?} is actually a type of advanced macro command. Use it to pause the macro so that you can type information, such as a file name, from the keyboard. The macro continues executing when you press **Enter**. A macro that sets column widths, for example, can include the {?} command to let you type the new column width when the macro pauses. Then you can press **Enter** to complete execution of the macro.

Note: Characters in macro commands are not case-sensitive. You can use capitalization wherever you want. For readability, however, this book uses lowercase letters in macros to indicate commands. Range names and key names are in uppercase letters.

Macro Key Names and Special Keys

1-2-3 uses symbols besides the tilde (~) to stand for other keystrokes. You can add to the formatting example key names and special keys that highlight a range as if you were using /**R**ange **F**ormat:

'/rfc0~.{END}{RIGHT}~

The added part of the macro anchors the range and highlights all occupied cells to the right in the current row. This revised macro is similar to the preceding one, except that the .{END}{RIGHT} portion causes the cell pointer to move. You can use this version of the macro to format an entire row instead of just one cell.

Once again, notice the apostrophe (') at the beginning of the macro (displayed in the control panel) and the tilde (~) at the end. Notice also the phrase .{END}{RIGHT} in the macro. The period (.) anchors the cell pointer. The {END} key name stands for the **End** key on the keyboard. The {RIGHT} key name represents the → key. This phrase has the same effect in the macro as these three keys would have if you pressed them in sequence from the keyboard. The cell pointer moves to the next boundary between blank and occupied cells in the row.

Use representations like these to signify key names and special keys on the keyboard. In every case, enclose the key name in braces. {UP}, for example, represents the ↑ key. {ESC} stands for the **Esc** (Escape) key, and {GRAPH} represents the **F10** function key.

11 Understanding Macros

Tables 11.1 through 11.4 provide lists of macro key names and special keys grouped according to their uses. They include function keys, direction keys, editing keys, and special keys.

Table 11.1 Macro Key Names for Function Keys

Function Key	Key Name	Action
F1 (Help)	{HELP}	Accesses 1-2-3's on-line help system
F2 (Edit)	{EDIT}	Edits the contents of the current cell
F3 (Name)	{NAME}	Displays a list of range names in the current worksheet
F4 (Abs)	{ABS}	Converts a relative reference to absolute, converts an absolute reference to relative, or predefines a range
F5 (GoTo)	{GOTO}	Jumps the cell pointer to the specified cell address or range name
F6 (Window)	{WINDOW}	Moves the cell pointer to the other side of a split screen or displays dialog boxes while a macro is running
F7 (Query)	{QUERY}	Repeats the most recent /Data Query operation
F8 (Table)	{TABLE}	Repeats the most recent table operation
F9 (Calc)	{CALC}	Recalculates the worksheet
F10 (Graph)	{GRAPH}	Redraws the current graph on-screen

To Become Familiar with Macros

Table 11.2 Macro Key Names for Direction Keys

Direction Key	Key Name	Action
↑	{UP} or {U}	Moves the cell pointer up one row
↓	{DOWN} or {D}	Moves the cell pointer down one row
←	{LEFT} or {L}	Moves the cell pointer left one column
→	{RIGHT}	Moves the cell pointer right one column
Shift+Tab or Ctrl+←	{BIGLEFT}	Moves the cell pointer left one screen
Tab or Ctrl+→	{BIGRIGHT}	Moves the cell pointer right one screen
PgUp	{PGUP}	Moves the cell pointer up one screen
PgDn	{PGDN}	Moves the cell pointer down one screen
Home	{HOME}	Moves the cell pointer to cell A1; if /Worksheet Titles is on, moves the cell pointer to the top left cell outside the titles area
End	{END}	Used with {UP}, {DOWN}, {LEFT}, or {RIGHT}; the cell pointer moves in the indicated direction to the next boundary between blank cells and cells that hold data. Also used with {HOME} to move the cell pointer to the lower right corner of the active area of the worksheet.

Understanding Macros

Table 11.3 Macro Key Names for Editing Keys

Editing Key	Key Name	Action
[Del]	{DELETE} or {DEL}	Used with {EDIT} to delete a single character from a cell entry; also deletes the contents of a cell when 1-2-3 is in READY mode
[Ins]	{INSERT} or {INS}	Toggles between insert and overtype modes when you are editing a cell
[Esc]	{ESCAPE} or {ESC}	Signifies the [Esc] key
[←Backspace]	{BACKSPACE} or {BS}	Signifies the [←Backspace] key
[Ctrl]+[Break]	{BREAK}	Clears the command and returns to READY mode

Table 11.4 Macro Key Names for Special Keys

Special Key	Key Name	Action
/ (menu)		Displays the command menu
[↵Enter]	~	Signifies the [↵Enter] key
~ (Tilde)	{~}	Causes a tilde to appear in the worksheet
{ (Open brace)	{{}	Causes an open brace to appear in the worksheet
} (Close brace)	{}}	Causes a closing brace to appear in the worksheet

To Become Familiar with Macros

Note: A few keys or key combinations do not have a key name to identify them. These include **Shift**, **Caps Lock**, **Num Lock**, **Scroll Lock**, **Print Screen**, **Alt+F1** (Compose), **Alt+F2** (Step), **Alt+F3** (Run), and **Alt+F4** (Undo). You cannot represent any of these keys or key combinations in macros.

To specify more than one use of a key name, you can include repetition factors inside the braces. You can, for example, use the following statements in macros:

Statement	Action
{PGUP 3}	Press [PgUp] three times
{L 4}	Press [←] four times
{RIGHT JUMP}	Press [→] the number of times indicated by the value in the cell named JUMP

Planning Macros

A simple keystroke macro can be thought of as a substitute for keyboard commands, so the best way to plan a macro is to step through the series of instructions one keystroke at a time. You should step through the instructions before you start creating the macro. Take notes about each step as you proceed with the commands on-screen; then translate the keystrokes that you have written into a macro that conforms to the guidelines discussed in this chapter.

Stepping through an operation at the keyboard is an easy way to build simple macros. The more experience you have with 1-2-3 commands, the more easily you will be able to "think through" the keystrokes you need to use in a macro.

For more complex macros, the best approach is to break them into smaller macros that execute in a series. Each small macro performs one simple operation, and the series of simple operations together performs the desired application.

This approach starts with the result of an application. What is the application supposed to do or produce? What form must the results take? If you start with the desired results and work backward, you are less likely to produce the wrong results.

Understanding Macros

Next, consider input. What data do you need? What data is available and in what form? How much work will it take to go from data to results?

Finally, look at the process. How do you analyze available data and, using 1-2-3, produce the desired results? How can you divide calculations into a series of tasks—each of which can have a simple macro?

This "divide-and-conquer" method breaks a complex task into smaller and simpler pieces. It is the key to successful development of macros and complex worksheets. Although this method entails some initial work, you will be able to detect and correct errors more easily because you can locate them in a smaller section of the macro.

Positioning Macros in the Worksheet

Usually, you should place macros outside the area occupied by data on your worksheet. This practice helps you avoid accidentally overwriting or erasing part of a macro as you create your model.

Macros should be positioned to the right of and below the main part of the worksheet (see fig. 11.2).

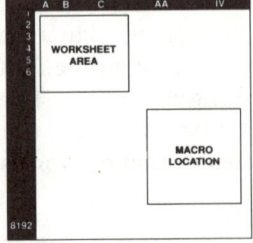

Fig. 11.2
Place macros outside the area occupied by data.

This positioning lessens the chance that you will accidentally include the macro's range in worksheet operations. With this placement, deleting rows or columns in the worksheet area will not affect the cells in the macro location. However, deleting rows and columns as well as moving data may accidentally cause a range name to lose its definition. When a range name loses its definition, it will no longer work properly in a macro. If you delete the row or column of the upper left or lower right corner of a range or move data into the upper left or lower right corner of a range, the range will lose its definition and no longer refer to a range address. Also, moving data in and out of a range can cause the range to change in the direction of the move.

Documenting Macros

Professional programmers usually write *documented* programs. This term means that the program contains comments that help explain each step in the program. Document your 1-2-3 macros by placing comments in the column to the right of the macro steps. Place the name of the macro to the left of the macro steps (see fig. 11.3).

Including comments in your macros will make them far easier to use. Comments are especially useful when you have created complex macros that are important to the worksheet's overall design. Suppose that you have created a complex macro but have not looked at it for a month. Then you decide that you want to change the macro. Without built-in comments, you may have a difficult time remembering what each step of the macro does.

Naming Macros

You must give a macro a name before you can execute it. You name a macro by using a backslash (\) followed by a single letter (Alt+*letter*). Alternatively, you can name a macro with a descriptive name, like a typical range name.

If you choose to use the single-letter naming convention, select a character that in some way helps describe the macro. You could, for example, use \c to name a macro that formats a range as currency.

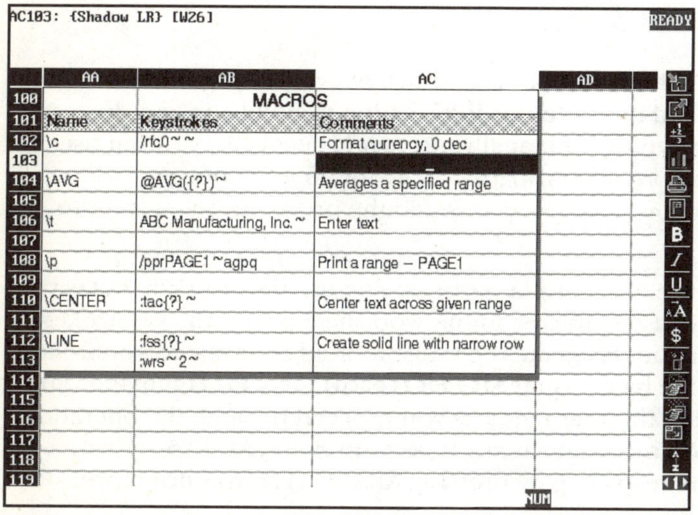

Fig. 11.3
Document your macros.

Exercise 1.1: Creating a Macro

To create a macro, follow these steps:

1. In cell W1, type '/wcs, and press ↵Enter.

    The apostrophe tells 1-2-3 that this is a label. Then the macro displays the menu and chooses Worksheet Column Set-Width.

2. Select /Range Name Create.
3. Type \ and the letter w, and press ↵Enter.

    The prompt Enter range: appears.

4. Press ↵Enter to select the range W1.
5. Move to cell X1, and document the macro by typing widens columns.
6. Move to cell V1, and type '\w. This creates the macro. You execute it in Exercise 3.1.

The advantage of using a single letter for a macro name is that you can activate the macro more quickly from the keyboard. A disadvantage is that a single-letter name doesn't offer as much flexibility in describing what the macro does. Therefore, remembering the name and purpose of a specific macro may be difficult.

Objective 2: To Become Familiar with the Learn Feature

In Release 2.2, 2.3 and 2.4, 1-2-3 can keep track of every keystroke and command you issue, and then use this information to build a macro. Instead of creating a macro by typing it manually into worksheet cells, you can use the Learn feature to record all keyboard activity for an indefinite period. The macro is built for you as you step through the procedures you want to include.

To use the Learn feature to record keystrokes, first use the /Worksheet Learn Range command to set aside an area in the worksheet where the keystrokes are to be stored. After you designate the range to hold your macro keystrokes, activate recording mode by pressing **Alt+F5** (Learn). All your commands and keystrokes are stored in the Learn area as you proceed through the operations you want. You can stop recording at any time by pressing **Alt+F5** (Learn) again. You can resume recording by pressing **Alt+F5** (Learn) once more.

Exercise 2.1: Using the Learn Feature

To use the Learn feature to record keystrokes for a macro, follow these steps:

1. Move to cell W3.
2. Select /Worksheet Learn Range.
3. Highlight down 20 rows, and press ⏎Enter.
4. Move the cell pointer to cell B1, and press Alt+F5 (Learn) to begin recording keystrokes.

   Notice the LEARN indicator at the bottom of the screen.
5. Type each of the 12 months and press → after each one to move to the next column.
6. Press Alt+F5 (Learn) to stop recording keystrokes.
7. Move to cell W3.
8. Select /Range Name Create.
9. Type the name **Months**, and press ⏎Enter twice.
10. Move to cell B1, and erase the 12 months.

Objective 3: To Execute Macros

Alt+*letter* macros named with a backslash and a single letter are the simplest to run. If necessary, move the cell pointer to the appropriate position before you execute the macro.

Exercise 3.1: Executing an Alt+Letter Macro

To execute an **Alt**+*letter* macro, follow these steps:

1. Move to cell A1.
2. Press and hold down the Alt key.
3. Press the letter in the macro name; for the one you created, press W.
4. Release both keys.

The menu should have processed the Worksheet Column Set-Width command, and be waiting for you to type a new width, and press Enter.

Understanding Macros

When you identify a macro with a longer descriptive name, it takes only a couple more keystrokes to execute the macro. You must first press **Alt+F3** (Run) to display a list of range names. Highlight the macro name, and press **Enter**. The list of names you see when you press **Alt+F3** (Run) will include range names as well as macro names.

Exercise 3.2: Executing a Macro with a Descriptive Name

To execute a macro with a descriptive name, follow these steps:

1. Move to cell A1.
2. Press [Alt]+[F3] (Run) or select the Macro Run SmartIcon.
3. Highlight the name of the macro you want to execute; for the one you created, highlight Months, and press [⏎Enter].

When you issue the command to execute a macro, the macro starts to run. If the macro contains no special instructions (such as a pause) and no bugs, the macro continues to run until it finishes. The macro executes each command much faster than if you tried the command manually. You can store many macro keystrokes or commands in a single cell. Some that are especially long, or that include special commands, must be split into two or more cells. When 1-2-3 starts executing a macro, the program begins with the first cell and continues until it executes all the keystrokes stored there. Next, 1-2-3 moves down one cell to continue execution. If the next cell is blank, the program stops. If that cell contains more macro commands, however, 1-2-3 continues reading down the column until it finds the first blank cell.

Objective 4: To Debug and Edit Macros

Few programs work perfectly the first time you run them. In nearly every case, errors cause programs to malfunction. Programmers call these problems *bugs*. *Debugging* is the process of eliminating bugs.

Like programs written in other programming languages, 1-2-3 macros usually need to be debugged before you can use them. 1-2-3 has a useful feature, STEP mode, that helps make debugging much simpler. When in STEP mode, 1-2-3 executes macros one step at a time. 1-2-3 literally pauses between keystrokes stored in the macro. Using this feature means that you can follow along step-by-step with the macro as it executes.

To Debug and Edit Macros

When you discover an error, you must get out of the macro and return 1-2-3 to READY mode by pressing **Ctrl+Break**. Then you can start editing the macro.

Common Errors in Macros

Like all computer programs, macros are literal creatures. They have no capacity to discern an error in the code. For example, you recognize immediately that {GOTI} is a misspelling of {GOTO}. However, a macro cannot make this distinction. The macro tries to interpret the misspelled word and, being unable to, delivers an error message. Here are four reminders to help you avoid some of the most common macro errors:

- Save your worksheet before you execute a macro.
- Verify all syntax and spelling in your macros.
- Include all required tildes (~) to represent **Enter** keystrokes in macros.
- Use range names in macros whenever possible to avoid problems with incorrect cell references. Cell references in macros are always absolute. They never change when you make modifications in the worksheet.

If a macro is not working correctly, you can use two 1-2-3 features to help you correct worksheet and macro errors. Use the **Alt+F4** (Undo) feature to "undo" damage to the worksheet created by the faulty execution of a macro. Also, use STEP mode to help pinpoint the location of an error in a macro.

Using STEP Mode To Debug Macros

You need to debug most programs before you use them. If you cannot locate an error in a macro, enter STEP mode and rerun the macro one step at a time. After each step, the macro pauses and waits for you to type any keystroke before continuing. Although you can use any key, you should use the space bar to step through a macro. As you step through the macro, each command appears in the control panel, and the macro code is displayed at the bottom left of the screen.

Exercise 4.1: Debugging a Macro with STEP Mode

To use STEP mode to debug a macro, follow these steps:

1. Press [Alt]+[F2] (Step) or select the Step Mode SmartIcon.

   The mode indicator STEP appears at the bottom of the screen.

2. Execute the macro by pressing [Alt] followed by the letter of the macro name. Alternatively, press [Alt]+[F3] to select the macro name, and press [↵Enter].

   The macro code and its associated address appear at the bottom of the screen as you run the macro in STEP mode.

3. Evaluate each step of the macro, pressing the [Spacebar] after you have checked each step.

   A message box displays an error message. In this example, the misspelled key name in cell AB103 caused the error (see fig. 11.4).

4. When you discover an error, press [Ctrl]+[Break] to return 1-2-3 to READY mode.

5. When 1-2-3 is in READY mode, edit the macro. You can edit the macro while the STEP indicator is displayed at the bottom of the screen.

6. To exit STEP mode, press [Alt]+[F2] (Step).

Editing Macros

After you identify an error in a macro, you can correct the error. Fixing an error in a macro is as simple as editing the cell that contains the erroneous code. You don't need to rewrite the entire cell contents. You need only to change the element in error. Although editing a complex macro can be much more challenging than editing a simple one, the concept is exactly the same.

Use the **F2** (Edit) key to correct the cell that contains the error.

Objective 5: To Add Macros to SmartIcons

You already have seen how SmartIcons speed up creating and modifying a worksheet. You also can add your own macros to a palette of SmartIcons. The last palette of SmartIcons is reserved entirely for you to add your own macros. After you add macros, you can copy them to the custom palette 1 if you desire.

To Add Macros to SmartIcons

11

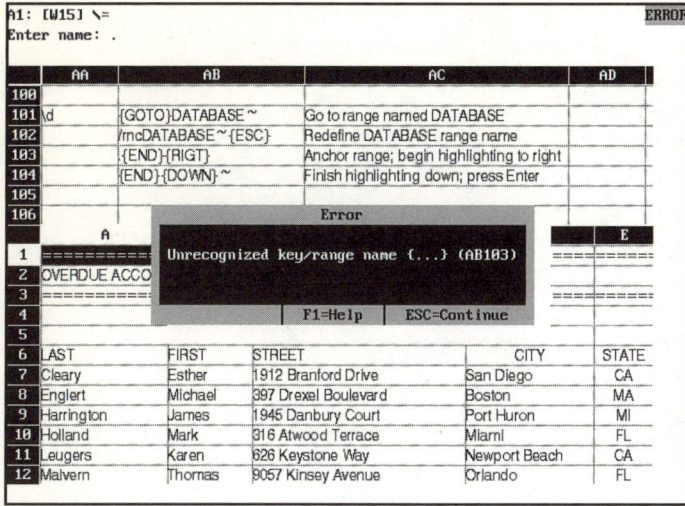

Fig. 11.4
The error message box.

Exercise 5.1: Adding Macros to SmartIcons

To add a macro to the last palette, follow these steps:

1. Move to the next-to-last SmartIcon palette.

    To cycle through the SmartIcon palettes and find the one you want, click the left- or right-arrow icons at the bottom of the palettes. These icons are located to the left and right of a number; this number tells you what palette of SmartIcons is displayed on-screen.

2. Click the Attach Macro SmartIcon.

    The User icon enables you to add a macro to an icon (see fig. 11.5). The User Icon Descriptions dialog box appears (see fig. 11.6).

3. Click the left and right parentheses located next to the icon you want to assign.

4. Select the Assign Macro to Icon command button at the bottom of the dialog box. The User-Defined Icon dialog box appears (see fig. 11.7).

5. Type a description of the new icon in the Icon **D**escription text box.

    When you select the icon by using the right mouse button or the keyboard, the description that you assign will appear on the third line of the control panel.

265

Understanding Macros

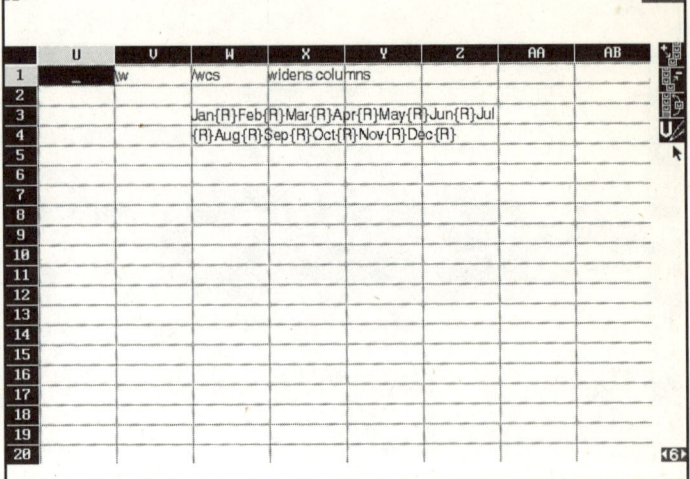

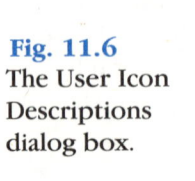

Fig. 11.5
The User icon.

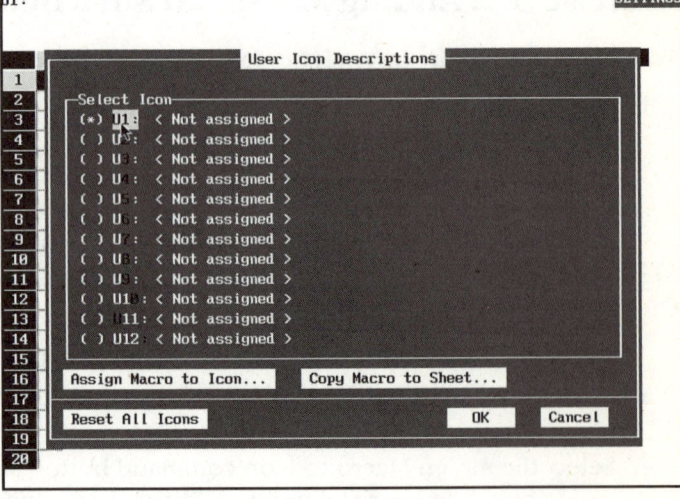

Fig. 11.6
The User Icon
Descriptions
dialog box.

6. If you want to retrieve a macro from the worksheet, type the macro name or cell reference in the Source range text box. Select the Get Macro from Sheet command button to bring the macro into the Macro Text box. The text box will accept up to 240 characters.

In this example, type **MONTHS** in the Source range text box, and select Get Macro from Sheet (see fig. 11.8).

266

To Add Macros to SmartIcons

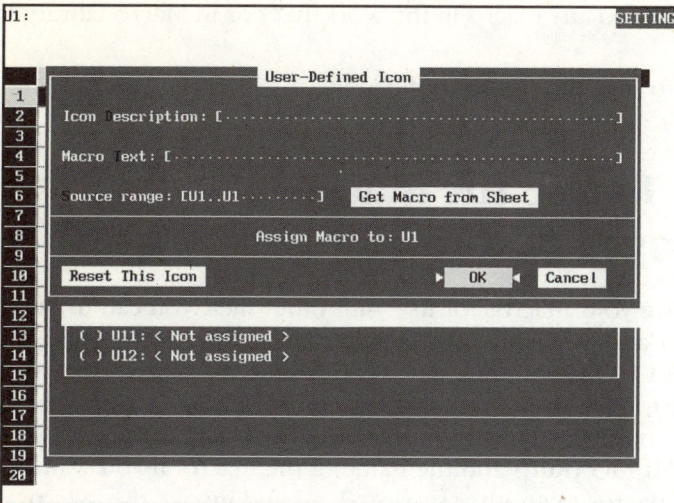

Fig. 11.7
The User-Defined Icon dialog box.

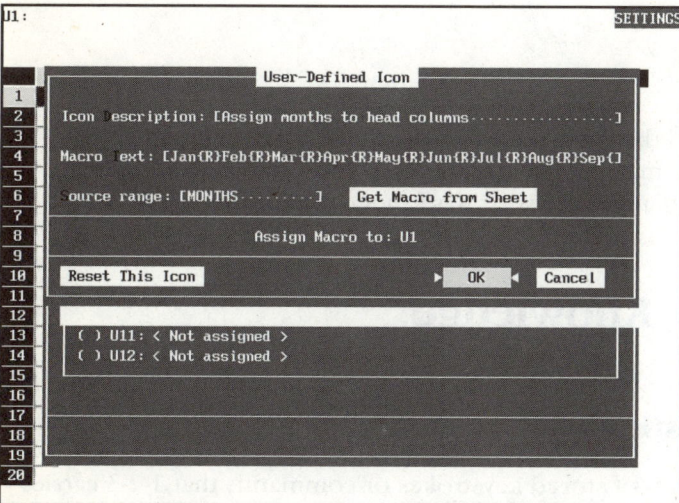

Fig. 11.8
Type **MONTHS** and select **G**et Macro from Sheet.

7. Type or edit the macro keystrokes in the Macro **T**ext box.

   Note: User-defined macros will not execute any advanced commands except {BRANCH}. They will execute all the macro key names and any characters including LICS (Lotus International Character Set). When a user-defined macro encounters an advanced macro command except {BRANCH}, it displays the error message Illegal command in

Understanding Macros

You can {BRANCH} to any macro in the worksheet or in Macro Library Manager.

8. Select OK twice to save the macro to the icon.

Objective 6: To Use the Macro Library Manager Add-In

If you would like to save your macros for use with other files, you can use the Macro Library Manager add-in. First, you attach and invoke the Macro Library Manager with the **Alt+F10** (Add-in) key. After you invoke the Macro Library Manager, choose **S**ave to save macros to a macro library. During the current session of 1-2-3, you can invoke a macro in the library with the **Alt+***letter* combination or with **Alt+F3** (Run) and the name of the macro. If you want to use a saved library of macros in another session, load and invoke the macro manager, choose **L**oad, and select the .MLB file that you saved earlier.

Summary

This chapter provided the basic information you need to begin creating your own simple keystroke macros. Macros are tools you can use to save time, reduce repetition, and automate your worksheet applications.

Testing Your Knowledge

True/False Questions

1. A macro is a series of stored keystrokes or commands that 1-2-3 carries out when you press two or more keys.
2. A bug is a feature that records keystrokes for you.
3. Many macros are named with the [Ctrl] key and a letter of the alphabet.
4. A macro is nothing more than a text cell.
5. The tilde (~) represents the [↵Enter] key in macros.

Testing Your Knowledge

Multiple Choice Questions

1. A macro can be named
   - A. \ and a letter.
   - B. any descriptive name.
   - C. `Ctrl` and any letter.
   - D. both A and B.

2. A macro can be run
   - A. by pressing `Alt` and a letter of the alphabet.
   - B. `Alt` + `F3` and choosing the name by pressing `↵Enter`.
   - C. by pressing `Ctrl` and a letter of the alphabet.
   - D. both A and B.

3. To use the Learn feature, you must set aside an area in the worksheet known as a (an)
   - A. learn range.
   - B. data range.
   - C. input range.
   - D. criteria range.

4. To debug your macros, 1-2-3 provides
   - A. the Learn feature.
   - B. STEP mode.
   - C. `Alt` +key combination.
   - D. the Run key.

5. In order to use macros in other files, 1-2-3 provides
   - A. the Learn feature.
   - B. STEP mode.
   - C. the Macro Library Manager Add-in.
   - D. the Run key.

Fill-in-the-Blank Questions

1. A _____ is an error in a macro or program.
2. A _____ in its most basic form is a collection of stored keystrokes that you can replay.
3. Macros should be _____, which means that the program contains comments that explain each step in the program.
4. You can use the _____ feature to record all keystrokes.
5. To find bugs in your macros, you can use _____ mode.

Understanding Macros

Review: Short Projects

1. Creating a Macro Manually

   Manually write a macro to erase a range. Name the macro \e. Try the macro, and debug it if necessary.

2. Creating a Macro Using Learn

   Use the Learn feature to write a macro that puts the days of the week across a range of cells. Name the macro Days. Try the macro, and debug it if necessary.

3. Creating a Macro Using Either the Learn Feature or Manually

   Write a macro which formats a range for comma 0 decimal places. Name it \c. Try the macro, and debug it if necessary.

Review: Long Projects

1. Creating a Complex Macro

   Retrieve one of the databases created in the short projects in Chapter 10. As you sort the database, write down the keystrokes on a piece of paper. Move to an empty part of the worksheet, and type in the keystrokes you recorded. Name the macro \s. Try the macro, and debug it if necessary.

2. Creating a Complex Macro

   Retrieve one of the databases created in the short projects in Chapter 10. As you print the database, write down the keystrokes on a piece of paper. Move to an empty part of the worksheet, and type in the keystrokes you recorded. (In a macro, before you define a range to be printed, you must always clear the old print range.) Name the macro \p. Try the macro, and debug it if necessary.

Enhancing and Printing Graphs in Wysiwyg in Releases 2.3 and 2.4

Wysiwyg offers its own set of graphing commands. However, the Wysiwyg :Graph commands are not for creating graphs—they are primarily for embellishing graphs you create in 1-2-3 and other graphics programs.

Adding Graphs to the Worksheet

Before you can include a 1-2-3 graph in a Wysiwyg-formatted report, you must add the graph to the worksheet with the :Graph Add command or the Add Graph SmartIcon. This command enables you to define the worksheet range where you want the graph to appear—and you actually see the graph in the worksheet.

Lotus 1-2-3 SmartStart

To add a graph into the worksheet, follow these steps:

1. Select :Graph Add.
2. Select one of the following options:

   Select Current to insert the current 1-2-3 graph (the same graph that appears when you press F10).

   Select Named to insert a 1-2-3 graph that you named with the /Graph Name Create command.

   Select PIC to insert a 1-2-3 graph created with the /Graph Save command. The file has the extension PIC.

   Select Metafile to insert a Metafile graphic. 1-2-3 Release 3 or an external graphics package created this file, and it has the extension CGM. Release 2.4 comes with 44 CGM files.

   Select Blank to insert an empty placeholder. Use this option if you have not yet created the graph but want to reserve space for it. You can also use this option to create your own graphic drawing.

   Choose the Current option only if the worksheet contains a single graph. If the worksheet has multiple graphs, 1-2-3 replaces the graph with the new current graph every time you create a new graph or use the command /Graph Name Use. When the worksheet contains more than one graph, you can save time by naming the graph before adding it.

3. If you chose Named, PIC, or Metafile, Wysiwyg prompts you for the name of the graph. Type the name or highlight one of the graphs listed. Press ↵Enter.
4. When the prompt appears, indicate the range to accept the graph. Press ↵Enter.
5. To exit the Wysiwyg menu, select Quit. The graph appears in the worksheet.

Note: Before you add a graph to the middle of a worksheet report, insert blank rows or columns where you want the graph to appear. Otherwise, the graph overlays worksheet data. The graph range should include only blank cells; be sure that you insert enough rows and columns to make the graph the size you want. Be careful when you insert rows or columns. Don't forget that a row is inserted from column A all the way to column IV. Also, if you have macros in your worksheet, inserting rows and columns can cause unexpected results.

Appendix A

Using SmartIcons in 2.4

To use the Add Graph icon to add the current graph to the worksheet, follow these steps:

1. Drag the mouse to highlight the range to receive the graph.
2. Select the Add Graph icon. The current graph appears in the range.

Making Changes to the Added Graph

You can make many changes to your added graph. You can replace, reposition, move, resize, or remove a graph.

Replacing a Graph

If you add the wrong graph or create a different graph that you want to insert into that same-sized range, you can replace the existing graph with another. You do not need to remove one graph before adding another in the same location.

To replace a graph, follow these steps:

1. Select **:Graph Settings Graph**.
2. Indicate the graph you want to replace by moving the cell pointer to one cell in the graph range, and pressing [⏎Enter]. If your cell pointer is not near the graph, press [F3] (Name), and select the graph name from a list.
3. Select the type of graphic (**C**urrent, **N**amed, **P**IC, **M**etafile, or **B**lank).
4. If you chose **N**amed, **P**IC, or **M**etafile, Wysiwyg prompts you for the name of the graph.
5. Type the name or move the cursor to one of the graphs listed. Press [⏎Enter].

Any enhancements (such as annotations) to the initial graph also appear in the new graph. If you don't want these enhancements in the new graph, use **:Graph R**emove to delete the initial graph. Insert the new graph with **:Graph A**dd.

273

Repositioning a Graph

After adding a graph, you may realize that the range isn't appropriate for your graph, or you may want it positioned in a different area of the worksheet. The :Graph menu offers several commands for changing your graph's position. You can move, resize, or remove the graph.

Moving a Graph

To move a graph from one worksheet location to another, use the :Graph Move command. This command retains the graph's original size and shape (number of rows and columns). The only change is the graph's position in the worksheet.

To move a graph in the worksheet, follow these steps:

1. Select :Graph Move.
2. Indicate the graph by moving the cell pointer to one cell in the graph range and pressing [Enter]. If your cell pointer is not near the graph, press [F3] (Name), select the graph name from a list, and press [Enter].
3. Type the name or move the cell pointer to the upper left corner of the target range, and press [Enter]. (You don't need to highlight the entire range.)

Resizing a Graph

After you add a graph, you may realize that the range you specified is either too large or too small for your graph. The :Graph Settings Range command enables you to resize an existing graph.

To change the size of a graph, follow these steps:

1. Select :Graph Settings Range.
2. Indicate the graph you want to resize. Move the cell pointer to one cell in the graph range, and press [Enter], or press [F3] and select the graph name from a list. 1-2-3 highlights the current graph range.
3. Type the new range, or move the cell pointer to highlight a larger or smaller area. If you want to specify a new range to be different from the existing one, press [Esc] or [Backspace]. Then move the cursor and specify the new range.
4. Press [Enter] after you have set the new range.

Appendix A

Removing a Graph

After you are finished with a graph, you may want to delete the graph from the worksheet.

To erase a graph from the worksheet report, follow these steps:

1. Select **:G**raph **R**emove.
2. Indicate the graph you want to remove. Move the cell pointer to one cell in the graph range, and press **Enter**, or press **F3** and select the graph name from the list.

Using the Graphics Editor

Wysiwyg includes a graphics editor that enables you to add and manipulate graphic objects. Using this graphics editor, you can add text, arrows, boxes, and other geometric shapes. After adding these objects, you can modify, rearrange, duplicate, and transform them.

To place a graph in the graphics editing window, follow these steps:

1. Select **:G**raph **E**dit.
2. Indicate the graph you want to change. Move the cell pointer to one cell in the graph range, and press **Enter**, or press **F3** and select the graph name from the list.

To use a mouse to place the graph in the graphics editing window, place the mouse pointer on the graphic, and then double-click the left mouse button. The graph is displayed in the graphics editing window.

Being in the graphics editing window is almost like being in a different world. You see only your graphic—not your worksheet. This feature lets you concentrate on the task at hand: enhancing your graphic. Furthermore, the editing menu permanently remains at the top of the screen; the **Esc** key or right mouse button does not clear the menu. The only way to exit from the graphics editor is to choose the **Quit** menu option or press **Ctrl+Break**.

Note: The Undo command does not work on options in the **:G**raph **E**dit menu.

Adding Objects

Wysiwyg lets you add the following types of objects to your graphic: text, lines, polygons, arrows, rectangles, and ellipses. You can also draw freehand. These

275

objects help you add text to explain your graphs. You can, for example, add a brief explanation of why a data point is unusually high or low.

Adding Text

You do not type text directly on the graph. Instead, you add the text in two steps. First, type the text at the Text: prompt at the top of the screen. Second, position the complete phrase where you like. The text phrase can be up to 240 characters long.

To add text to your graph, follow these steps:

1. From the :Graph Edit menu, select Add.
2. Select Text.
3. Type the text you want. To insert the contents of a cell, press \ followed by the cell's coordinates or range name.
4. Position the pointer where you want the text positioned. Either move the pointer with the arrow keys and press Enter, or move the pointer with the mouse and click the left mouse button.

    Note: The arrow keys move in such small increments that you will probably prefer to use the mouse if you have one.

Small, filled-in squares, called *selection indicators*, surround the text. These boxes mean that the object is selected and that you can perform another operation on it (such as move it, change its font, and so forth). To change the font, use the Edit Font command. To change the content of the text, use the Edit Text command.

The text you add can include formatting sequences (for example, bold, italic, outline, or fonts).

Adding Lines and Arrows

The processes of drawing lines and drawing arrows are the same. The only difference is the arrow's arrowhead at the second point of the line.

To draw a line or arrow, follow these steps:

1. From the :Graph Edit menu, select Add.
2. Select Line or Arrow.

Appendix A

3. When the screen prompts you to `Move to the first point:`, use the arrow keys to move the pointer to one end of the line.
4. Press the **space bar** to anchor this point or click the left mouse button.
5. When the screen prompts you to `Stretch to the next point:`, use the arrow keys to move the pointer to the other end of the line.
6. Press **⏎Enter** to complete the line, or use the mouse to move to the second point, and click the left mouse button twice to complete the line.

If you are adding an arrow, the arrowhead points from the end of the line (the second point you indicated). To switch the direction of the arrow, use the Edit Arrowheads option. To change the line width, use the Edit Width option.

You can connect several lines by pressing the **space bar** or by clicking the left mouse button for each line ending. When you finish drawing lines, click the left mouse button twice or press Enter.

When drawing horizontal, vertical, or diagonal lines, you notice that drawing straight lines is difficult; the lines look somewhat jagged. To prevent this jagged look, press and hold down **Shift** before you anchor the last point. The line segment automatically snaps to 45-degree angles, enabling you to draw perfectly straight lines.

As previously mentioned, you can enhance your graphs in many other ways. For example, you can add polygons, rectangles, and ellipses. You can enhance your work with freehand drawings. After you add objects to a graph, you can use the mouse to select, move, edit, and otherwise manipulate these objects. You can also change color, patterns, and sizes of graphic elements. Take time to explore these advanced features of the program.

Index

Symbols

\# (page-number character), 166
\#OR\# operator, 142
^ (exponentiation) mathematical operator, 59-60
|| nonprinting symbols, 162
… (ellipses), 275
* (multiplication) mathematical operator, 59-60
+ (addition/positive) mathematical operator, 59-60
- (subtraction/negative) mathematical operator, 59-60
/ (division) mathematical operator, 59-60
/ (slash) key, 27
: (colon), 178
< (less than) operator, 141
<= (less than or equal to) operator, 141
<> (not equal) operator), 141
= (equal to) operators, 141
> (greater than) operator, 141
>= (greater than or equal to) operator, 141
\ (backslash) key, 251
_ (underscore), 68
~ (tilde), 252
1-2-3
   exiting, 25-48
   starting
      from Access menu, 23-25
      from DOS, 23
1-2-3-Go! on-line tutorial, 45
3-D bar graphs, 215

A

absolute cell addressing, 108, 118-120
Access menu, 22
Add-in (Alt+F10) shortcut key, 268
Add-In command, 42
Add-ins, 8
addition (+) mathematical operator, 59-60
addresses, cells, *see* cell addressing

aligning
    labels, 52
    text, 55
alphanumeric keys, 22, 27-29
#AND# operator, 142
applying named-styles, 195
arguments, 126
arithmetic mean, 127-128
arrows, 275-277
assigning fonts to ranges, 182
automatic
    calculations, 10
    worksheet recalculation, 101-103
@AVG function, 127-128
axes, 210
    origin, 202, 211
    scaling, 214
    tick marks, 202, 211
    zero line, 202
    see also x-axis; y-axis

B

background (graphs), 217-218
backslash key (\), 251
bar graphs, 208
    3-D, 215
    color, 213
boldface, 189
borders
    cells, 152
    reports, printing, 158-160
boundaries, printing, 192
bugs, *see* debugging

C

calculations
    automatic, 10
    cells, 61-64
    recalculating, 10
categories axis, 202
    see also x-axis
cell addressing, 108, 252
    absolute addresses, 118-120
    macros, 252
    mixed addresses, 115
    relative addresses, 116-118
cell pointer, 8, 30
    moving, 13, 30-35
cell references, *see* cell addressing
cells, 8, 13
    calculating, 61-64
    copying
        between, 112
        contents, 111-122
        one to many, 112-113
    counting entries, 128-130
    editing, 64-65
    formats, copying, 122
    inserting data, 50-57
    moving with SmartIcons, 39-41
    printing
        boundaries, 192
        listing contents, 168-170
    ranges, 79-83
        deleting names, 83
        erasing, 80-81
        naming, 82
    shading, 186

Index

clearing print settings, 170
clicking, mouse, 34-36
colon (:), 178
color
    bar graphs, 213
    graphs, 215
columns
    contiguous, 92-93
    default, 12
    deleting, 100-101
    inserting, 99-101
    printing, excluding, 160-162
    reports, borders, 158-160
    totaling, 64
    transposing, 120
    width, 89-92
commands, 8
    Add-In, 42
    /Copy, 42, 108, 111-122
    /Data, 42
    /Data Distribution, 232
    /Data Matrix, 232
    /Data Parse, 232
    /Data Query, 232, 239-241
    /Data Query Delete, 240
    /Data Query Extract, 240
    /Data Query Find, 240
    /Data Query Input, 240-241
    /Data Query Output, 240
    /Data Query Quit, 240
    /Data Query Reset, 240
    /Data Query Unique, 240
    /Data Regression, 232
    /Data Sort, 232, 237
    /Data Table, 232
    Display, 44
    /File Retrieve, 36, 42, 72
    /File Save, 68
    /Fill, 231
    /Format, 44
    :Format, 179
    :Format Bold, 189
    :Format Font, 182
    :Format Font Library Retrieve, 185
    :Format Font Replace, 183-185
    :Format Lines, 190-191
    :Format Shade Dark, 186
    :Format Shade Light, 186
    :Format Underline, 188
    :Format Font Library Save, 185
    /Graph, 42, 44, 203
    :Graph Add, 271
    :Graph Edit, 275
    :Graph Move, 274
    /Graph Name Create, 218, 272
    /Graph Name Use, 272
    /Graph Options Color, 215
    :Graph Remove, 273, 275
    /Graph Save, 68, 218, 272
    :Graph Settings Graph, 273
    :Graph Settings Range, 274
    /Labels, 43
    /Move, 42, 108-109
    :Named-Style Define, 45, 194
    /Quit, 25, 42, 45
    /Print, 42, 44, 152
    :Print, 176
    :Print Configuration Orientation Landscape, 196
    /Print Encoded, 69
    :Print Go, 195
    :Print Preview, 196

Lotus 1-2-3 SmartStart

/Print Printer, 153
/Print Printer Clear, 170
/Print Printer Range, 71
:Print Range, 195
/Range, 42-43
/Range Erase, 52, 80
/Range Format, 80, 85, 87-88
/Range Format Date, 137
/Range Format Hidden, 162
/Range Input, 80
/Range Justify, 80
/Range Label, 80
/Range Labels Right, 52
/Range Name, 80, 82
/Range Name Delete, 83
/Range Protect, 80
/Range Search, 80
/Range Trans, 80, 120
/Range Unprotect, 80
/Range Value, 80, 120
selecting, 41-45
/Settings Image, 223
/Special, 44
:Special Copy, 193
/System, 42
/Text, 45
:Text Edit, 65
undoing, 65-67
/Worksheet, 42, 44
/Worksheet Column, 84
/Worksheet Column Column-Range, 91
/Worksheet Column Hide, 161
/Worksheet Column Set-Width, 235, 261
/Worksheet Delete, 84, 100
/Worksheet Erase, 84-85

/Worksheet Global, 84
/Worksheet Global Format, 85, 87
/Worksheet Global Recalculation, 102
/Worksheet Global Zero, 97
/Worksheet Global Zero No, 99
/Worksheet Insert, 84, 99
/Worksheet Learn, 84
/Worksheet Learn Range, 260
/Worksheet Page, 84, 162
:Worksheet Row Set-Height, 186
/Worksheet Status, 84
/Worksheet Titles, 84, 97
/Worksheet Titles Clear, 97
/Worksheet Window, 84, 93
/Worksheet Window Clear, 94
/Worksheet Window Sync, 96
/Worksheet Window Unsync, 96
compressing printing, 197-198
conditional tests, 141-143
contiguous columns, 92-93
control panel, 22, 37
converting
    date to serial number, 138-141
    formulas to values, 120-121
copying
    between cells, 112
    between ranges, 114
    cells, 111-122
    columns, transposing, 120
    formats, 122, 193
    formulas
        absolute addressing, 118-120
        relative addressing, 116-118
    one to many, 112-113

Index

ranges
  unequal, 114-115
  with keyboard, 109-110
  with mouse, 108-109
rows, transposing, 120
@COUNT function, 127-130
counting cell entries, 128-130
creating
  databases, 233-235
  graphs, 203-206
    specifying ranges, 211-213
  macros, 257-260
criteria range, 241-245
current date and time, 137-138
cursor, 30

D

data
  extracting, 243
    from databases, 239-241
  inserting, 50-57
    in databases, 234-235
data labels (graphs), 202
Data menu, 231-232
databases, 15, 230-231
  creating, 233-235
  data
    extracting, 239-241
    inserting, 234-235
  fields, 231
  output, 233-234
  output range, 243
  positioning, 234
  records, 231
    listing, 243
    locating, 239-245
    sorting, 235-238
  search criteria, 241-245
@DATE function, 138-141
date and time
  converting date to serial numbers, 138-141
  current, 137-138
  functions, 137-139
deactivating Undo feature, 66
debugging macros, 262-264
Default Printer Settings dialog box, 166
Default Settings dialog box, 66
defaults
  columns, 12
  layout, changing, 166
  printing, 152
defining ranges for graphs, 211-213
defining styles, 194-195
deleting
  columns, 100-101
  graphs, 275
  range names, 83
  rows, 100-101
dialog boxes
  Default Printer Settings, 166
  Default Settings, 66
  Global Settings, 91, 98
  Graph Legends & Titles, 217
  Graph Settings, 203, 206, 214
  Print Settings, 152, 155-157
  Query Settings, 239
  Sort Settings, 235
  User Icon Descriptions, 265
  User-Defined Icon, 265

dingbats, 184
direction keys, 8, 29, 255
displaying
    color, graphs, 215
    grid lines, 192
    menus with mouse, 178
    Wysiwyg menu, 178
division (/) mathematical operator, 59-60
documenting macros, 259
DOS, starting 1-2-3, 23
drawing
    arrows, 276-277
    lines, 276-277
drivers, mouse, loading, 33-34

E

Edit key (F2), 64
editing
    cells, 64-65
    graphs, 273-275
    macros, 262-264
    text, 65
    with Edit key, 64
editing keys, macro key names, 256
electronic spreadsheet, 8
ellipses (…), 275
entering functions, 126
entries, tables, 145
equal to (=) operator, 141
erasing
    cells, ranges, 80-81
    worksheets, 85
    Wysiwyg from memory, 179
errors
    in formulas, 60-61
    in macros, 263

excluding in printing
    columns, 160-162
    ranges, 162
    rows, 162
executing macros, 261-262
exiting
    1-2-3, 25-48
    Wysiwyg menu, 272-277
exponentiation (^) mathematical operator, 59-60
extracting data, 239-243

F

fields, 231
/File command, 42
/File Retrieve command, 36, 72
/File Save command, 68
files
    naming, 67-69
    retrieving, 72-73
    saving, 69-71
    text, printing to, 156
Fill command, 231
financial functions, 133-136
font sets, 182, 185
fonts, 176
    assigning to ranges, 182
    dingbats, 184
    libraries, 185
    point size, 176, 181
    soft fonts, 176, 181
    worksheets, 183-185
    Wysiwyg, 181-185
    see also typeface
footers, 152, 165-166
    cell contents, 164
    printing, 163-164

Index

/Format command, 44, 80
formats
    copying, 122, 193
    named-styles, 193-194
formatting
    graphs, 213-218
        in Wysiwyg, 271-277
        printing, 223-224
    macros, 252-253
    ranges, 87-88
    spreadsheets, 88-89
    with SmartIcons, 87
    worksheets, 85-99
    Wysiwyg, 179
formatting options, 86-87
formulas, 8, 10, 13-15
    converting to values, 120-121
    copying
        absolute addressing, 118-120
        relative addressing, 116-118
    errors, 60-61
    inserting, 58-61
    mathematical operators, 59-60
    range names, 82
    values, 57
frames (graphs), 202
freezing titles on-screen, 96-97
function keys, 22, 29-30, 254
functions, 8, 13-15, 126
    arguments, 126
    date and time, 137-139
    entering, 126
    financial, 133-136
    inserting, 61
    logical, 140-143
    special functions, 143-147
    statistical, 126-132
    syntax, 126

future values, 135-136
@FV function, 135-136

G

Global Settings dialog box, 91, 98
/Graph command, 42, 44
:Graph Add command, 271, 273
:Graph Edit command, 275
Graph Legends & Titles dialog box, 217
Graph menu, 204
:Graph Move command, 274
/Graph Name Create command, 272
/Graph Name Use command, 272
:Graph Remove command, 273, 275
/Graph Save command, 68, 272
Graph Settings dialog box, 203, 206, 214
:Graph Settings Graph command, 273
:Graph Settings Range command, 274
graphics
    Metafile, inserting, 272
    monitors, 203
    printers, 203
graphics editor
    in Wysiwyg, 275-277
    inserting objects, 275-276
graphs, 14, 202
    arrows, 276-277
    axes, 210
        tick marks, 202
        x-axis, 202
        y-axis, 202
        zero line, 202
    background, 217-218
    bar graphs, 208, 215

color, 213-215
creating, 203-206
data labels, 202
defining ranges, 211-213
deleting, 275
editing, 273-275
formatting, 213-218, 271-277
frames, 202
grid lines, 217
HLCO graphs, 209
inserting in worksheets, 272-273
legends, 202, 215-216
line graphs, 207
lines, 276-277
mixed graphs, 210
moving, 274
naming, 218
pie graphs, 209
printing, 220-225
replacing, 273
repositioning, 274
resizing, 274
saving, 218-219
stacked-bar graph, 208
text, 215, 276
titles, 216-217
types, 212
viewing, 203
XY graphs, 207
greater than (>) operator, 141
greater than or equal to (>=)
 operator, 141
grid lines, 192-193
   displaying, 192
   graphs, 217

H

hardware
   printers, 224
   requirements, viewing graphs, 203
headers, 152, 164-166
   cell contents, 164
   page numbers, 163
   printing, 163-164
Help Index, 45
help system, 45
HLCO graphs, 209
@HLOOKUP function, 145-147

I

icon palette, 22
icons, 39-41
@IF function, 141-143
inserting
   arrows, 276-277
   columns, 99-101
   data, 50-57, 234-235
   formulas, 58-61
   functions, 61
   graphics, 272
   graphs in worksheets, 272-273
   labels, 51-55
   lines, 276-277
   macros in SmartIcons, 264-268
   numbers, 56-57
   objects, 275-276
   rows, 99-101
   text, 276

J–K

key names in macros
   for direction keys, 255
   for editing keys, 256
   for function keys, 254
   for special keys, 256
keyboard, 26-33
   / (slash) key, 27, 261
   alphanumeric keys, 22, 27-29
   copying ranges, 109-110
   direction keys, 8, 29
   function keys, 22, 29-30
   moving
      cell pointer, 30-32
      ranges, 109-110
   numeric keys, 22, 29
   special keys, 27-29

L

labels
   aligning, 52
   inserting, 51-55
   prefixes, 51
/Labels command, 43
landscape orientation, 196
layout defaults, 166
Learn feature, 260-261
legend (graphs), 202, 215-216
less than (<) operator, 141
less than or equal to (<=) operator, 141
libraries (fonts), 185
line graphs, 207
lines, 275-277

listing
   cell contents, printing, 168-170
   records, 243
loading mouse drivers, 33-34
loan payments, 134-135
locating records in databases, 239-245
logical functions, 140-143

M

Macro Library Manager add-in, 268
macros, 16, 250-260
   cell addresses, 252
   creating, 257-260
   debugging, 262-264
   documenting, 259
   editing, 262-264
   errors, 263
   executing, 261-262
   formatting, 252-253
   inserting in SmartIcons, 264-268
   key names
      direction keys, 255
      editing keys, 256
      function keys, 254
      special keys, 256
   naming, 259
   positioning in worksheets, 258
   range names, 252, 263
   retrieving, 266
   saving, 268
   tracking, 260-261
   user-defined, 267
manual worksheet recalculation, 101-103

margins
    changing prior to printing, 166-168
    settings, 168
mathematical operators, 59-60
@MAX function, 127, 130-132
MENU mode indicator, 178
menus
    Data, 231-232
    displaying with mouse, 178
    Graph, 204
    PrintGraph, 221-222
    selecting, 44
    Wysiwyg, 44-45, 178
Metafile graphics, 272
@MIN function, 127, 130-132
mixed graphs, 210
mixed addressing, 115
monitors, graphics, 203
mouse, 8
    clicking, 34-36
    copying ranges, 108-109
    displaying menus, 178
    loading driver, 33-34
    moving ranges, 108-109
    pointing, 34
    selecting menus, 44
Move command, 42
moving
    cell pointer, 13, 30-35
    cells, 39-41
    columns, transposing, 120
    graphs, 274
    ranges, 110
        with keyboard, 109-110
        with mouse, 108-109
    rows, transposing, 120
    undoing, 110

multiplication (*) mathematical operator, 59-60

N

/Named-Style command, 45
named styles, 193-195
naming
    files, 67-69
    graphs, 218
    macros, 259
    ranges, 82
negative (-) mathematical operator, 59-60
nonprinting symbol (||), 162
#NOT# operator, 142
not equal (<>) operator, 141
@NOW function, 137-138
numbers, inserting, 56-57
numeric keypad, 22, 29

O

objects, inserting, 275-276
on-line tutorial, 45
operators
    #AND#, 142
    #NOT#, 142
    #OR#, 142
    < (less than), 141
    <= (less than or equal to), 141
    <> (not equal), 141
    = (equal to), 141
    > (greater than), 141
    >= (greater than or equal to), 141
    mathematical
        addition/positive (+), 59-60
        division (/), 59-60

Index

exponentiation (^), 59-60
multiplication (*), 59-60
subtraction/negative (-), 59-60
order of precedence, 59
see also mathematical operators
options
   formatting, 86-87
   Graph menu, 204
   printing, 162-171
order of precedence, 59-60
orientation, 196
origin (axes), 202, 211
outlining, 190-191
output from databases, 233-234
output range in databases, 243
overlapping ranges, 122
overriding order of precedence, 60

P

page breaks, 162-163
page numbers in headers, 163
palettes, 8, 39
pie graphs, 209
pitch (characters per inch), 168
@PMT function, 134-135
POINT mode, 111
point size (fonts), 176, 181
pointing with mouse, 34
polygons, 275
positioning
   databases, 234
   macros in worksheets, 258
positive (+) mathematical operator, 59-60
prefixes, labels, 51
previewing printing, 196
/Print command, 42, 44

/Print Encoded command, 69
/Print Printer menu, 154
/Print Printer Range command, 71
print range, 157-158
Print Range SmartIcon, 155
Print Settings dialog box, 152, 155-157, 163
printers, 224
   fonts, 181
   graphics, 203
   pitch, 168
PrintGraph, 220-223
   menu, 221-222
   settings, 225
printing, 16
   cell contents, listing, 168-170
   cell boundaries, 192
   changing layout, 166
   columns, excluding, 160-162
   compressing, 197-198
   controlling, 224
   defaults, 152
   footers, 163-164
   from other programs, 171
   graphs, 220-225
      formatting, 223-224
      with PrintGraph, 222-223
   headers, 163-164
   landscape orientation, 196
   margins, changing, 166-168
   options, 162-171
   previewing, 196
   Print Range SmartIcon, 155
   ranges, excluding, 162
   reports
      border columns, 158-160
      multiple pages, 157-158
      single-page, 153-155

to printer, 153
Wysiwyg, 195-196
rows, excluding, 162
settings
    clearing, 170
    saving, 225
spreadsheets, 152-157
to text file, 156
worksheets, 71, 162-163
Wysiwyg, 195-198

Q–R

Query Settings dialog box, 239

Range Sum SmartIcon, 64
ranges, 79-83
    copying
        unequal, 114-115
        with keyboard, 109-110
        with mouse, 108-109
    copying between, 114
    defining for graphs, 211-213
    erasing, 80-81
    fonts, assigning, 182
    formatting, 87-88
    moving, 110
        with keyboard, 109-110
        with mouse, 108-109
    names, 82
        deleting, 83
        in formulas, 82
        in macros, 252, 263
    overlapping, 122
    printing, 157-158
        compressing, 197-198
        excluding, 162
    underlining, 188

Recalculate SmartIcon, 102
recalculating, 10, 101-103
records (databases), 231
    listing, 243
    locating, 239-245
    sorting, 235-238
rectangles, 275
relative cell addressing, 108, 116-118
removing shading, 188
replacing
    fonts, 183-185
    graphs, 273
reports, printing
    border columns, 158-160
    in Wysiwyg, 195-196
    multiple pages, 157-158
    single-page, 153-155
    to printer, 153
repositioning graphs, 274
resizing graphs, 274
retrieving
    files, 72-73
    macros, 266
rows
    deleting, 100-101
    height, 186-188
    inserting, 99-101
    printing, excluding, 162
    totaling, 64
    transposing, 120
Run (Alt+F3) shortcut key, 268

S

saving
    files, 69-71
    font sets, 185
    formatting, Wysiwyg, 179

Index

graphs, 218-219
    naming, 218
    settings, 218-219
macros, 268
options, printing, 170
settings, printing, 225
scaling axes, 214
screens, splitting, 93-94
search criteria, 241-245
selecting
    commands, 41-45
    menus, 44
    selection indicators, 276
setting margins, 168
settings
    graphs, saving, 218-219
    print settings, clearing, 170
    printing, saving, 225
shading, 185-188
shadows, 191
size, fonts, 176
slash (/) key, 27
SmartIcons, 8, 273
    cell-movement, 39-41
    Copy, 108
    formatting, 87
    macros, inserting, 264-268
    Move, 108
    palettes, 39-48
    Print Range, 155
    Range Sum, 64
    Recalculate, 102
    text, aligning, 55
    Wysiwyg, 179-181
soft fonts, 176, 181
solid shading, 186
Sort Settings dialog box, 235

sorting records in databases, 235-238
special functions, 143-147
special keys, 27-29, 256
splitting screens, 93-94
spreadsheets, *see* worksheets
stacked-bar graph, 208
starting 1-2-3
    from Access menu, 23-25
    from DOS, 23
statistical functions, 126-132
status line, 22, 38
@STD function, 127
STEP mode, 262-263
styles (named styles), 193-194
subdirectories, 73
subtraction (-) mathematical operator, 59-60
@SUM function, 61-64, 127
suppressing zeros, 97-99
syntax, 126

T

tables, 145
text
    aligning, 55
    editing, 65
    graphs, 215
    inserting, 276
    selection indicators, 276
text files, printing to, 156
three-dimensional graphs, *see* 3-D bar graphs
tick marks (axes), 202, 211
tilde (~), 252
time, *see* date and time

titles
    graphs, 216-217
    worksheets, freezing, 96-97
totaling columns/rows, 64
tracking macros, 260-261
transposing columns/rows, 120
tutorial, 45
typeface, 176
    see also fonts

U

underlining, 188
underscore (_), 68
Undo feature, 65-67
undoing
    commands, 65-67
    move operations, 110
User Icon Descriptions dialog box, 265
User-Defined Icon dialog box, 265
user-defined macros, 267

V

values, 57
    converting from formulas, 120-121
values axis, 202
    see also y-axis
@VAR function, 127
viewing
    graphs, hardware requirements, 203
    worksheets, 93-94
@VLOOKUP function, 145-147

W

What You See Is What You Get,
    see Wysiwyg
worksheet area, 22, 38
worksheet frame, 38
worksheet window, 12
worksheets, 8, 9-14
    calculating, 61-64
    deleting columns, 100-101
    erasing, 85
    fonts, 183-185
    formatting, 85-99
    formulas, 58-61
    functions, 61
    graphs
        deleting, 275
        editing, 273-275
        inserting, 272-273
        moving, 274
        replacing, 273
        repositioning, 274
        resizing, 274
    inserting
        columns, 99-101
        data, 50-57
        numbers, 56-57
    labels, 51-55
    macros
        positioning, 258
        retrieving, 266
    printing, 71, 152-157, 162-163
    recalculating, 101-103
    size, 11-12
    text, aligning, 55
    titles, 96-97
    viewing, 93-94
    zeros, suppressing, 97-99

Index

Wysiwyg, 8, 16, 176
   displaying menu, 178
   erasing from memory, 179
   fonts, 181-185
   formatting, 179
   graphics editor, 275-277
   graphs, formatting, 271-277
   menu, 44-45
   printing, 195-198
   SmartIcons, 179-181
   text editing, 65
   exiting, 272-277
WYSIWYG mode indicator, 178

X–Y–Z

x-axis, 202, 210
   see also axes; y-axis
XY graphs, 207

y-axis, 202, 210
   see also axes; x-axis

zero line (axes), 202
zeros, suppressing, 97-99

293

Count on Que for the Latest in DOS Information!

Using MS-DOS 6, Special Edition

Que Development Group
Version 6

$29.95 USA
1-56529-020-8, 1,000 pp., 7³/₈ x 9¹/₄

Easy DOS, 2nd Edition

Shelley O'Hara
Through Version 6

$16.95 USA
1-56529-095-x, 200 pp., 8 x 10

More DOS Titles from Que

I Hate DOS

Bryan Pfaffenberger
Version 6

$16.95 USA
1-56529-215-4, 384 pp., 7³/₈ x 9¹/₄

MS-DOS 6 QuickStart

Que Development Group
Version 6

$21.95 USA
1-56529-096-8, 420 pp., 7³/₈ x 9¹/₄

MS-DOS 6 Quick Reference

Que Development Group
Version 6

$9.95 USA
1-56529-137-9, 160 pp., 4³/₄ x 8

To Order, Call:(800) 428-5331 OR (317) 573-2500